Umbrellas are for Sissies

RANDALL J. BREWER

Copyright © 2026 by Randall J. Brewer
All rights reserved. No part of this book may be reproduced in any manner
whatsoever without written permission except in the case of brief quotations
embodied in critical articles and reviews.
First Printing, 2026

UMBRELLAS ARE FOR SISSIES

CONTENTS

INTRODUCTION — 1

1 **"STAND IN THE RAIN"** — 3

2 **"STABILITY UNDER PRESSURE"** — 12

3 **"DESIGNED FOR WARFARE"** — 21

4 **"STOP DODGING THE HARD THINGS"** — 30

5 **"CULTURAL RESISTENCE"** — 39

6 **"STRENGTH WITH COMPASSION"** — 48

7 **"SPIRITUAL TOUGHNESS"** — 58

8 **"STRENGTH THROUGH SUFFERING"** — 67

9 **"ANGER AND STRENGTH"** — 76

10 **"ENDURING FAITH"** — 85

11 **"MORAL COURAGE"** — 95

12 **"SPIRITUAL LEADERSHIP"** — 105

13 **"FINISH THE FIGHT"** — 114

14	"SPIRITUAL TRAINING"	123
15	"THE COMFORT TRAP"	132
16	"PROTECT WHAT MATTERS"	141
17	"HONEST CONVERSATIONS"	150
18	"LOVING WHEN IT'S DIFFICULT"	159
19	"MODELING TOUGHNESS"	168
20	"IRON SHARPENS IRON"	177
21	"OWNING YOUR MISTAKES"	186
22	"THE PATH OF FAITH"	195
23	"FREEDOM THROUGH DISCIPLINE"	204
24	"CONTINUOUS REFINEMENT"	213
25	"QUIET STRENGTH"	222
26	"SPIRITUAL AGGRESSION"	231
27	"INTEGRITY IN ISOLATION"	240
28	"GENERATIONAL IMPACT"	249
29	"EMOTIONAL ENDURANCE"	258
30	"THROW AWAY THE UMBRELLA"	267
	SUMMARY	276

INTRODUCTION

There is something about a storm that reveals a man. When the wind howls and the rain beats down, excuses wash away. Pretenses collapse. Comfort disappears. What remains is character. What remains is conviction. What remains is the truth about who you really are. For too long, men have been handed umbrellas. Umbrellas of excuse. Umbrellas of distraction. Umbrellas of comfort. Umbrellas of passivity disguised as "peace." We have been subtly taught to avoid pressure instead of embrace it. To seek ease instead of endurance. To protect our comfort instead of protect our calling. But here is the truth: The storm is not the problem. Your response to it is. Storms are inevitable. Pressure is promised. Resistance is part of the design. The question is not whether rain will fall. The question is whether you will stand.

Real strength is not built in comfort. It is forged in resistance. Steel is strengthened by fire. Muscles grow through strain. Faith deepens under pressure. And men are shaped in storms. In "Umbrellas Are For Sissies," Randall J. Brewer delivers a direct, unapologetic call to biblical manhood - the kind that does not shrink when life gets hard. This is not about ego. It is not about aggression. It is not about outdated stereotypes or cultural bravado. It is about spiritual backbone. Emotional steadiness. Moral courage. Relentless faith. It is about becoming the kind of man who does not panic when the winds rise. The kind of man whose family feels safe when everything else feels unstable. The kind of man who does not curse the rain but grows in it.

Because storms are not sent to destroy you. They are sent to develop you. The pressure you feel is not punishment. It is preparation. The resistance you face is not an accident. It is assignment. Every storm carries within it the potential to produce depth, discipline, discernment, and dominion - if you respond correctly. The rain will fall either way. You can hide beneath an umbrella of excuses and remain unchanged. Or you can stand in the storm and become something stronger. This book is a challenge. A challenge to reject passivity. A challenge to abandon comfort as your compass. A challenge to trade excuses for endurance. A challenge to build a life that does not collapse under pressure.

Biblical manhood is not loud. It does not need to shout to prove its strength. It is steady, rooted deep like a tree planted by living water, unmoved by shifting winds of culture or emotion. In a generation that confuses noise with strength and impulse with courage, this kind of man is desperately needed. If you are tired of running from resistance… if you are ready to grow through adversity instead of avoiding it… if you want to become the kind of man who stands firm when others fold - then close the umbrella. Step into the rain. Let the pressure refine you. Let the storm strengthen you. And let God use every drop to build in you a faith that does not flinch and a backbone that does not bend.

| 1 |

"STAND IN THE RAIN"

There are no umbrellas in the Kingdom of God. No devices to shield you from discomfort. No spiritual raincoats to keep you dry while others are being formed in the storm. The Kingdom is not built around convenience or climate control - it is built around character. God does not exempt His sons from pressure; He uses it. The wind that feels like resistance is often the very force shaping your resolve. The rain that soaks you is revealing what you truly trust. In the world, comfort is marketed as success. In the Kingdom, endurance is the pathway to strength. Transformation rarely happens under blue skies. It happens when prayers feel stretched, when obedience costs something, when faith must stand without visible proof. Storms strip away illusion. They expose weakness, but they also awaken courage. You discover who you are when you have nothing left to hide behind. So stand in the rain. Let it refine you. Because the man God is forming in the storm could never be shaped in the sunshine alone.

We live in a culture that worships comfort. Convenience is king, ease is the goal, and anything that feels difficult is labeled unnecessary. If it's hard, we avoid it. If it's painful, we medicate it. If it stretches us, we sidestep it. We've been discipled by drive-thrus, instant downloads, and pain-free promises into believing that the blessed life is the comfortable life. But comfort has become a counterfeit crown. It soothes us while slowly shrinking us. It promises peace yet produces passivity. A life built on ease may feel safe, but it rarely becomes strong. The Kingdom tells a different story. In God's economy, growth often comes wrapped in resistance, and purpose is forged in pressure. Storms are not interruptions to destiny; they are instruments of development. The blessed life is the life that says yes to refinement, yes to surrender, yes to the process. Because in the Kingdom, there are no umbrellas - only men who learn to stand in the rain and discover they were built for it.

Comfort promises safety, but it quietly produces softness. It trains us to retreat instead of advance, to preserve instead of pursue. Comfort builds padded lives but fragile spirits. It conditions men to seek ease over endurance and security over significance. The tragedy is what feels safe today often becomes the very thing that weakens us tomorrow. A life engineered around convenience slowly erodes courage. When everything is climate-controlled, nothing in us learns to withstand the storm. Yet both history and Scripture tell a different story. Greatness is never born in ease; it is forged in heat, in tension, in adversity. Warriors are formed in battle, not in comfort. The men who shaped nations and advanced the Kingdom did so through trials that stretched them beyond their limits. Adversity does not destroy a man - it reveals him. And when a man stops running from the rain and chooses to stand in it, that is where strength is formed, character is refined, and true greatness begins.

The cultural myth of comfort has discipled many into passivity. It has quietly preached that ease is the reward and convenience is the goal. It has trained strong men to prefer safety over sacrifice and entertainment over endurance. But easy lives rarely produce strong spirits. Muscles grow under resistance, not relaxation. Character is not formed in climate-controlled rooms but in moments that stretch conviction and test resolve. A life built around comfort may feel pleasant, but it will never feel powerful. God never designed men to be shaped by softness. He designed them to be strengthened through strain.

Faith grows under pressure, not in perpetual ease. Just as iron is forged in fire and muscles respond to weight, the soul expands when it is required to endure. Resistance reveals depth. Pressure exposes purpose. When we embrace the discipline of challenge, we rediscover what we were built for: strength of spirit, steadiness of character, and a faith that stands when the winds rise.

God does not develop men in spas. He develops men in storms. Comfort may soothe you, but it will never strengthen you. The wind is what shapes the tree - forcing its roots to dig deeper and its trunk to grow stronger. The waves test the vessel - revealing whether it was crafted for decoration or for destiny. And the battlefield reveals the warrior - not when the path is clear, but when the pressure is real. The very opposition you wish away is often the instrument God is using to forge endurance, discipline, and unshakable faith within you. You do not discover your strength when everything cooperates - you discover it when everything resists. When doors close, when critics speak, when resources are scarce, and when the outcome is uncertain - that is when hidden courage rises. Storms expose weakness, but they also awaken power. A man who stands firm when the winds howl and the waves crash learns something sacred: he was built for more than comfort - he was built for conquest.

The wind that pushes against you is the same force that strengthens your spiritual muscles. God does not send pressure to crush you but to carve you. The resistance you face is shaping your character, sharpening your discernment, and anchoring your faith in ways comfort never could. Sunshine may reveal your potential, but storms reveal your foundation. If it shakes you, it shows you where to stand stronger. If it stretches you, it proves there is more in you than you realized. The pressure you feel is not proof of God's absence but evidence of His investment. He does not waste resistance on what He plans to abandon. He trusts you with difficulty because He sees durability in you. Resilience is not built in calm seasons but forged in adversity. When heaven allows weight, it is because heaven has placed worth within you. The storm is not a sign that you are off course - it is confirmation that you are being prepared for greater capacity. Stand firm. What presses you today is producing strength for tomorrow.

Rain reveals what sunshine hides. Under bright skies, weaknesses can be concealed, and everything appears stable when life is calm and predictable. Success can mask insecurity. Comfort can disguise complacency. But when the clouds gather and the winds rise, foundations are tested. Storms expose cracks that were invisible in fair weather. They uncover shallow roots that never learned to go deep. Pressure has a way of stripping away illusion and revealing the true condition of the heart. Storms are not sent to destroy you, but to define you. They reveal what you are really made of - whether your strength is anchored in pride or humility, in convenience or conviction. When adversity comes, excuses wash away and authenticity rises to the surface. What remains after the rain is truth. If your foundation is solid, the storm will only prove it. If it is weak, the storm becomes an invitation to rebuild stronger than before. Rain reveals what sunshine hides, and in that revelation is the opportunity for growth.

Sunshine celebrates you. It highlights your victories, showcases your strengths, and draws applause from the crowd. Under clear skies, confidence feels effortless and progress seems obvious. In the warmth of comfort, everyone appears strong. Smiles are easy. Faith sounds bold. Promises flow freely. But sunshine does not test depth; it only reveals surface. It affirms what is visible, not what is rooted. Celebration is beautiful, but it does not measure endurance. Rain evaluates you. Storms do not care about appearances; they probe foundations. When winds rise and pressure intensifies, only what is anchored remains standing. Adversity separates the superficial from the steadfast. It exposes shallow roots and rewards deep ones. In the storm, excuses wash away and character is uncovered. What you have built in private is revealed in public. The rain does not come to destroy you - it comes to define you. And those who remain anchored do not merely survive the storm; they stand stronger because of it.

Rain has a way of stripping life down to what really matters. When the sky darkens and the winds begin to shake what once felt secure, your priorities are exposed. Storms reveal what you cling to when comfort disappears - whether it's status, stability, approval, or control. Sunshine allows distractions to flourish, but rain drives you to shelter. In those moments, you discover what you truly trust. If your confidence is rooted in circumstances, the shaking will rattle your soul. But if your confidence is anchored in covenant - God's unchanging promise - then even in the downpour, you remain steady. Rain forces a decision. It presses you to confront what actually holds you together when everything else feels like it's falling apart. Do you cling to temporary platforms, or do you stand on eternal truth? Storms do not create weakness; they reveal foundations. They uncover whether your peace is tied to outcomes or to obedience, whether your strength flows from pride or from surrender.

The kingdom does not offer umbrellas because umbrellas would prevent exposure. And exposure is necessary for growth. God does not design a life of insulation; He designs a life of transformation. Rain is not sent to destroy you but to reveal you. Pressure exposes cracks in character, but it also reveals courage, resilience, and faith that comfort could never produce. If you avoid the rain, you avoid the refining. The very discomfort you pray away is often the tool heaven is using to shape you. Growth requires contact. Maturity requires friction. Strength requires resistance. If you dodge the storm, you delay the strengthening. Storms stretch your capacity, deepen your dependence, and strip away illusions of self-sufficiency. Exposure humbles you, and humility prepares you. The kingdom understands that what stands in sunshine alone cannot endure the shaking. So the rain falls not to drown you, but to develop you. Stand in it. Let it teach you. Because what survives the storm emerges refined, rooted, and ready.

Many pray for promotion but resist pressure. They ask God for authority yet avoid adversity. We want the platform without the process, the spotlight without the stretching, the crown without the crushing. But heaven does not promote potential - it promotes proven character. Authority is forged in hidden battles no one applauds. It is built in the quiet decisions to stay faithful when quitting would be easier, to stand firm when compromise would be convenient, and to trust God when the outcome is unclear. The weight of leadership cannot rest on a man who has not first been strengthened by resistance. Long before anyone sees the public victory, there were unseen nights of prayer, silent wars in the mind, and lonely moments of obedience. God develops depth before He grants influence. He strengthens the shoulders before He adds the mantle. If you are under pressure, do not resent it - embrace it. The very adversity you wish away may be the tool shaping you for the authority you are asking for.

God develops men through storms because storms strip away illusion. When the winds rise and the rain falls, the masks come off. False confidence cannot survive sustained pressure. Storms expose what sunshine hides. They reveal whether your foundation is sand or stone. In the storm, what once looked like strength is exposed as fragility, and what once felt secure is shaken. That shaking is not destruction - it is refinement. Storms drive you to dependence. When your plans collapse, you begin to pray differently. Dependence on God is the beginning of true strength. A man who depends on himself is only as strong as his circumstances. A man who depends on God is anchored to something eternal. Storms teach you to trust, to surrender, and to stand - not in arrogance, but in assurance. And when the storm passes, you are no longer the same man. You are steadier, humbler, deeper. Not because you avoided the storm, but because God met you in it and built strength that sunshine never could.

Toughness in the kingdom does not begin with raised voices, clenched fists, or carefully crafted images of invincibility. It begins with surrender. It begins the moment a man lays down the exhausting burden of pretending he is self-made and self-sustained. The world teaches men to project strength, to dominate the room, to master every outcome. But the kingdom teaches that true strength is born when a man bows his knee. When he anchors his heart in the sovereignty of God, he steps into a deeper, unshakable toughness. Real kingdom toughness is forged when a man stops pretending he can control the weather and starts trusting the One who commands it. Storms will come but the mature man does not panic at thunder. He stands firm not because he controls the skies, but because he knows Who does. Surrender is the quiet confidence that comes from knowing that obedience is greater than ego and trust is stronger than pride. When a man yields to God's authority, he becomes immovable.

Surrender is strength under control and trust under pressure. When a man surrenders to God, he is not waving a white flag to defeat - he is placing his life into the hands of a faithful Father. Surrender is the decision to stand in the rain without resentment, to endure the wind without complaint, and to remain steady when the storm refuses to pass. It is the confidence that says, "This discomfort is not destroying me; it is developing me." The world calls that foolishness. Heaven calls it faith. True surrender sounds like this: "Lord, use this to build me." Use the criticism to refine me. Use the delay to deepen me. Use the hardship to strengthen my character." Instead of asking for escape, you ask for endurance. Instead of demanding relief, you request resilience. Surrender transforms storms into classrooms and pain into preparation. The man who gives over his struggle to God does not shrink in adversity - he grows through it. And when the rain finally stops, he stands taller, stronger, and more anchored than before.

True toughness is not the man who feels nothing, bends for no one, and hides behind emotional walls. That is not strength - it is self-protection. Real toughness is a soft heart with a strong backbone. It is the courage to remain compassionate in a cruel world, to stay tender toward God while being unmovable in your convictions. A hard heart breaks under pressure because it cannot bend. But a yielded heart can absorb impact without losing its shape. The kind of strength God builds in a man is forged, not fabricated. It is shaped in storms, refined in fire, and tested in moments where compromise would be easier than obedience. True toughness is the ability to remain yielded to God while standing firm against pressure. It is quiet confidence under attack, steady faith in uncertainty, and unwavering character when no one is watching. This strength cannot be faked, because it is formed in the hidden places of surrender. And when it is forged by God, it carries both power and purity.

There are no umbrellas in the kingdom because God is not trying to keep you dry - He is trying to make you durable. Comfort may preserve you for a moment, but it will never prepare you for destiny. The Father does not waste storms; He uses them. While the world scrambles for cover, heaven often calls you forward. Rain strengthens roots. Wind deepens foundations. Pressure reveals what is planted within. God is not protecting you from every storm; He is preparing you to walk through them. Umbrellas may keep you dry, but they also keep you dependent. God is raising up men who do not panic when the skies darken, who do not retreat when thunder rolls, who do not measure His faithfulness by the forecast. Durability is born in weather you did not ask for but refused to run from. The kingdom produces men who can stand in the rain with steady hearts, unshaken faith, and strengthened resolve because they understand that storms do not signal abandonment; they signal advancement.

Step out from under the shelter of comfort and into the place where growth actually happens. Let the rain fall on your plans. Let the wind challenge your balance. Let the pressure press against your faith. Comfort may feel safe, but it never builds character. Storms do. The rain exposes weak foundations, the wind tests what you're really anchored to, and the pressure reveals whether your convictions are shallow or secure. God does not waste storms; He uses them to strip away fear, pride, and dependence on ease. What feels like opposition is often divine construction. On the other side of the storm stands a man stronger, deeper, and more anchored than before. The storm carves depth into his soul and roots his confidence in something eternal. The wind may bend him, but it will not break him. The pressure may stretch him, but it will not shatter him. Because when a man walks through the storm with God, he does not just survive it - he is transformed by it.

In the kingdom, what feels like opposition is often divine construction. Wind strengthens roots. Rain deepens resolve. God does not waste weather; He uses it. The storm you prayed against may be the very process that answers your prayer. Character is not formed in comfort but carved in resistance. When the sky turns dark, heaven is not angry - it is active. The kingdom does not shield men from rain; it shapes men through it. And the men who refuse umbrellas become the men who cannot be moved. They do not run from pressure; they grow under it. They understand that toughness begins with surrender and that stability is born in surrender to God's refining work. While others look for cover, they stand in faith. While others complain about the downpour, they let it cleanse, stretch, and strengthen them. Storm-tested men are not easily shaken because they have learned that if God is sovereign over the storm, then the storm is working for them - not against them.

| 2 |

"STABILITY UNDER PRESSURE"

When it rains, most people look for cover. They scramble for comfort, search for shortcuts, and pray for the storm to pass as quickly as it came. But in the kingdom of God, rain is a revelation. It exposes foundations. It tests what is beneath the surface. It shows whether a man is rooted in convenience or conviction, in emotion or endurance, in hype or holiness. The downpour is not sent to destroy you, but to demonstrate what holds you steady when the winds rise and visibility fades. When pressure falls from the sky like a storm, the call of a man is simple: stand with anchored resolve. Stand when others panic. Stand when the crowd runs for shelter. A man grounded in truth does not dissolve under pressure; he deepens. He does not collapse when circumstances shift; he becomes immovable. Because rain may soak the surface, but it cannot uproot a life planted in eternal soil. And when the clouds finally part, the man who stood will not just have survived the storm - he will have been strengthened by it.

Stability under pressure is not loud. It does not announce itself or demand attention. Most of the time, it is almost invisible to the casual observer. But it is powerful. It is the quiet strength of a tree whose roots run deep beneath the surface. Storms may strip away leaves and shake every branch. But it does not uproot it. Why? Because long before the storm arrived, the roots were already established. In the same way, the man who stands in the rain has already decided who he is before the storm ever begins. His convictions were formed in the calm. His character was built in the unseen places. When adversity hits, unstable men react; stable men remain. Stability under pressure means your values do not shift with the wind and your integrity does not leak when the rain falls. The storm does not create the man - it reveals him. And the man who can stand in the rain without losing himself is a man who has already rooted his life deep in truth, discipline, and unwavering resolve.

There is a difference between emotional steadiness and emotional shutdown. Emotional shutdown is when a man hardens himself to avoid pain. He becomes cold, distant, unresponsive. But emotional steadiness is different. It is feeling the weight of the storm without being controlled by it. It is acknowledging fear without bowing to it. A shut-down man builds walls; a steady man builds strength. Shutdown numbs the heart. Steadiness anchors it. One is driven by fear of being hurt; the other is governed by the decision to stand firm no matter what comes. Emotional steadiness allows a man to experience pressure without losing clarity, and to face uncertainty without abandoning conviction. He does not silence his emotions; he disciplines them. He does not pretend the rain is not falling; he plants his feet in it. True masculine strength is not the absence of emotion - it is mastery over it. It is the quiet resolve to remain present, engaged, and faithful when everything inside him wants to retreat.

Shutdown builds walls that look like protection but function like prisons. A man who shuts down may appear strong on the outside, but inside he is retreating, bracing, withdrawing, insulating himself from the very growth that pressure is meant to produce. A steady man does not deny the rain - he endures it. He does not pretend the storm is pleasant - he simply refuses to be moved by it. Steadiness chooses discipline over denial. It chooses courage over comfort. It understands that pressure does not destroy character - it reveals it. When a man remains steady, he becomes like a rooted tree planted by streams of water, unshaken by wind and unafraid of heat. His strength is not loud, but it is unbreakable. He does not explode, and he does not evaporate. He stands. And in standing, he grows stronger. In enduring, he deepens. In feeling the weight and refusing to collapse, he becomes the kind of man others can lean on when their own storms begin to rage.

Pressure has a way of exposing what comfort conceals. In calm weather, everyone appears strong. In sunshine, everyone looks confident. But when the clouds gather and the thunder rolls, true character surfaces. Pressure squeezes the heart the way a vice squeezes steel, forcing to the surface whatever has been hidden beneath ease and applause. If anger is inside, anger comes out. If fear is inside, fear spills over. But if conviction is inside, conviction stands firm. When the storm hits, you discover whether your strength was built on inspiration or on foundation. That is why pressure is not your enemy - it is your revealer. It shows you what still needs refining and what has already been forged. A man who has cultivated discipline in private will display steadiness in public. A man who has rooted himself in truth will not be uprooted by thunder. Storms separate performance from principle. They strip away image and expose integrity. And when conviction lives deep within, pressure does not break you - it proves you.

Storms are necessary because they separate what is imagined from what is internalized. In calm seasons, faith is easy to speak about. Convictions sound strong when nothing challenges them. But when the winds rise and the rain beats against the house, the true strength of the structure is revealed. Storms reveal your foundation. They expose whether your faith is built on preference or on principle. Pressure does not invent cracks - it simply uncovers the ones that were already there. If your trust in God has only been theoretical, the storm will make that obvious. But if your roots run deep, the storm will also make that obvious. Trials show whether your worship continues when the blessings pause, whether your obedience stands when convenience disappears. Storms refine, strengthen, and anchor the man who leans into God rather than away from Him. The same rain that erodes shallow soil strengthens deep roots. And when the storm passes, what remains standing proves what was built to last.

Consider Job. He did not shut down emotionally when devastation struck his life. He tore his robe. He wept. He sat in ashes. He asked hard questions that echoed into heaven. Job did not pretend the pain was not real, and he did not mask his anguish with empty religious clichés. He grieved deeply, wrestled honestly, and spoke openly about his confusion. Yet in all of it, he refused to curse God. His worship was not rooted in comfort - it was rooted in conviction. His world collapsed around him, but his integrity did not collapse within him. That is the mark of a man who stands. Job stood not because he felt strong, but because he feared God. He stood not because he had answers, but because he had foundation. Pain shook him, but it did not sever him. When everything visible was stripped away, what remained was character. And when the storm exposes what is inside, may it find in us what it found in Job - reverence that does not break, faith that does not fold, and integrity that does not bow.

Consider David when he stood before Goliath. The rain of intimidation poured down on Israel's army as this towering warrior thundered threats across the valley. Seasoned soldiers shrank back under the pressure of one giant voice. Fear echoed louder than faith in their ranks. But David stood. Not because he was blind to the size of the giant, nor because he underestimated the danger, but because he understood something greater. He saw not merely a Philistine champion, but a defiance against the covenant of the living God. While others measured the height of the enemy, David measured the faithfulness of his God. Pressure has a way of revealing what is rooted within a man. In the same storm that exposed fear in trained warriors, it exposed faith in a shepherd boy. And that is the lesson: when pressure comes, it will expose whether you are governed by fear or grounded in faith. The giant did not create courage in David - he revealed it.

Think of Daniel who continued to pray when the decree was signed. The threat of the lions' den was not symbolic - it was real, immediate, and brutal. The order had the king's seal and the consequences were certain. Others would have folded quietly, saying, "God understands," or "I'll pray in my heart." But Daniel did not shift his posture to match the pressure. He opened his window as he always had. He knelt as he always had. He prayed as he always had. His consistency under threat revealed a character settled before the storm arrived. The rain fell. The night grew dark. Yet Daniel remained unmoved not because he trusted in his own courage, but because he trusted in his God. The lions were real, but so was his faith. When the stone was rolled away at dawn, it was clear that what stood in private had also stood in public. A steady man does not wait for danger to decide who he is. He decides long before the decree is signed. And when the world demands compromise, he simply continues to kneel.

Even Peter, who once folded under pressure, became a man who could stand. On the night of fear and firelight, he denied Christ not once, but three times. The voice that had boldly declared loyalty grew quiet when confronted by a servant girl. Pressure exposed what was still fragile within him. But failure was not the end of his story. The same man who trembled in a courtyard would later stand in the streets of Jerusalem and proclaim Christ with fearless conviction. After the resurrection and the refining work of grace, Peter faced persecution with boldness. The storm that once shook him became the very place he found resolve. Pressure no longer dictated his response - purpose did. He had been broken, restored, and strengthened. The rain still fell, but now he stood firm in it. His life declares a powerful truth: the place where you once failed does not have to define you. When surrendered to God, it can become the very ground where you stand strongest.

A man who stands firm is not flexing his strength for applause; he is fastening his soul to something unshakable. Like David before Goliath, he had already settled in the quiet fields who his God was and who he was because of Him. Crisis did not create his identity - it revealed it. When the winds rise and voices tremble, anchored men do not scramble for labels or approval. They draw from what has already been forged in prayer, obedience, and hidden faithfulness. Identity established before the battle is stability preserved during it. Anchored men refuse to let chaos dictate their character, because when storms rage around them, their identity, integrity, and faith remain firmly rooted in unshakable truth. They do not mirror fear; they model faith. They do not absorb the frenzy; they release peace. And in a world that folds under pressure, the man who stands steady becomes a refuge for others - a living reminder that storms may shake the surface, but they cannot uproot a soul that is anchored deep in God.

Emotional steadiness does not mean you never bend. It means you never break your foundation. A tree that refuses to bend in the storm is the one that snaps, but the tree with deep roots may sway violently and still stand when the winds pass. In the same way, a strong man of God is not a man without emotion - he is a man anchored beneath his emotion. You feel the pressure, you acknowledge the weight, but your identity is not built on the weather; it is built on the Rock. There will be seasons when the rain feels relentless, yet emotional steadiness is the quiet decision to remain planted. You may feel the full weight of the rain, but you do not surrender your ground. You stay prayerful when panic tempts you. You stay present when retreat seems easier. You stay faithful when feelings fluctuate. Because steadiness is not the absence of feeling - it is the mastery of it. And the man who learns to bend without breaking becomes the man who cannot be moved.

A man who stands in the rain knows that what feels like resistance is often refinement. Just as steel is tempered by fire and shaped by heat, a man's character is forged in adversity. Ease may comfort him, but it never completes him. The storm exposes weakness, but it also reveals strength he did not know he possessed. When the winds push and the rain falls hard, he does not curse the sky - he braces his feet. He understands that the very pressure pressing against him is strengthening the core within him. Every storm endured builds internal infrastructure. Every battle survived fortifies resolve. Muscles grow through strain, and so does maturity. Rain is not the enemy - it is the trainer. It teaches endurance, patience, and discipline. It strips away pride and exposes foundation. A man who refuses to run from the downpour discovers that adversity does not destroy him - it develops him. And when the skies finally clear, he does not just stand dry - he stands stronger, steadier, and more certain of who he is.

When leaders stand, families feel safe because steadiness creates shelter. A calm voice in chaos, a firm decision in uncertainty, a composed presence in crisis become anchors in a storm. When fathers stand, children learn courage not from lectures but from observation. They watch how he handles pressure, how he absorbs stress without exploding, how he refuses to retreat when things get hard. His stability becomes their security. His consistency becomes their compass. In moments of tension, they are not just seeing a man manage problems; they are witnessing what strength under control looks like. And that image imprints on their hearts. When pastors stand, congregations gain confidence because visible conviction produces collective courage. Sheep draw strength from a shepherd who does not panic at wolves or scatter in storms. Stability under pressure is contagious. It spreads quietly but powerfully, shaping atmospheres and elevating expectations. Strength multiplies when it is visible.

Standing in the storm is never an accident - it is the fruit of preparation. A tree does not wait for hurricane winds to begin growing roots; it buries itself deep long before the sky turns dark. In the same way, roots are grown in hidden places where no applause is heard and no recognition is given. Prayer builds roots. Discipline builds roots.

Integrity builds roots. The man who kneels when no one is watching will stand when everyone is looking. The habits formed in quiet mornings, the convictions guarded in private battles, and the choices made behind closed doors become the unseen foundation that keeps you upright when the pressure hits. Private obedience prepares you for public pressure. When the winds rise and others bend, the rooted man remains steady not because the storm is weak, but because his foundation is deep. He has already fought smaller battles in secret. He has already said no when compromise whispered. He has already chosen faithfulness over convenience.

There will always be voices that tell you to fold, to blend in, to retreat. The world rewards convenience, not conviction. It applauds compromise if it keeps things comfortable. But a man of the kingdom understands that truth is not adjusted to fit culture; culture must bow to truth. He does not measure his stance by applause or opposition. He measures it by alignment with God. When pressure mounts, he does not dissolve into the crowd. He remembers who he is and whose he is. Kingdom men are not reeds swayed by every wind of opinion, emotion, or trend. They are pillars that hold their ground. A reed bends with the breeze but a pillar is planted deep. Conviction anchors them. Prayer strengthens them. Integrity steadies them. They may bend in humility, but they do not bow in compromise. When others retreat to preserve comfort, they advance to preserve truth. And long after the winds have died down and the noise has faded, it is the pillars that remain standing - steady, unshaken, and faithful.

When it rains, stand. Do not run for cover at the first sign of discomfort. Do not bow when the wind begins to howl. Stand in your faith when doubt tries to whisper louder than truth. Stand in your calling when distraction tries to pull you into lesser assignments. Stand in your character when compromise offers you an easier road. Rain tests foundations. Wind tests roots. Pressure tests resolve. And what is rooted deeply in conviction will not be uprooted by circumstance. Let the storm reveal strength, not weakness. Let the pressure expose integrity, not insecurity. Anyone can look solid on a sunny day, but it is in the downpour that true substance is uncovered. When adversity presses against you, let it prove that your faith is real, your calling is settled, and your character is anchored. Do not shrink back when challenged. Do not fold when confronted. Stand steady. Stand anchored because when the rain stops - and it always does - the man who remained standing will be the one others look to for shelter.

In the end, the rain does not last forever. Storms may rage with fury, winds may howl with accusation, and dark clouds may seem to stretch endlessly across the horizon, but no storm has permanent permission. The pressure that pounds against a man's life is temporary, even when it feels relentless. Trials pass. Seasons shift. Clouds break. But the testimony of a man who refused to bow, refused to run, and refused to quit—that becomes legacy, the quiet sermon preached long after the thunder has gone silent. And when the clouds finally clear, the one still standing will realize that the wind that tried to bend him had strengthened his roots. The rain that threatened to erode him washed away weakness. The darkness that surrounded him sharpened his discernment and deepened his faith. So when the sun breaks through again, the man who stood will not look the same as when the storm began. He will be steadier. Stronger. Wiser. Not because the storm was kind but because he remained immovable.

| 3 |

"DESIGNED FOR WARFARE"

A man was never designed for retreat - he was designed for warfare. From the beginning, masculinity carried assignment, authority, and responsibility. When God formed man from the dust and breathed life into him, He did not place him in the garden to be passive, but to cultivate and to guard. A man was built with shoulders broad enough to carry vision, hands strong enough to build what matters, and a heart courageous enough to confront what threatens what he loves. He was not formed for comfort zones but for conflict zones. He was built for battle, not blankets. Comfort may soothe for a moment, but resistance is what forges strength. The world needs men who will stand in conviction. Every challenge is an invitation to rise. When pressure comes, it reveals design. When opposition surfaces, it exposes purpose. The man who resists compromise, resists fear, and resists passivity becomes unmovable in a shaking culture. He does not run from the storm; he plants his feet in it.

In the Garden - before failure, before shame, before thorns and sweat - Adam was entrusted with responsibility. He was placed in Eden "to work it and to guard it." That word "guard" is not passive. It carries the weight of watchfulness, protection, vigilance, and defense. Even in a perfect environment before there was a serpent to confront, there was ground to cultivate and boundaries to defend. This reveals something powerful about masculine design: a man was not created merely to exist in beauty, but to steward it and stand watch over it. Responsibility was woven into his identity long before rebellion ever entered the story. Warfare, then, was part of the architecture. Adam's struggle did not create his assignment; it revealed what he had neglected. Even in paradise, there was a call to alertness. That means the instinct to protect, to build, and to guard what is sacred is not a flaw in a man - it is a fingerprint of his design. Long before life felt like a battlefield, you were engineered to stand your ground.

Masculinity is intentional. From the beginning, God designed man with purpose etched into his bones and fire placed within his spirit. Strength in his frame was never meant for intimidation but for protection. Resolve in his spirit was not given for stubborn pride but for steadfast leadership. Courage in his calling was not an optional trait but a sacred assignment. The male soul was wired to stand between danger and what is precious, to rise when others retreat, and to anchor the atmosphere when storms threaten what God has entrusted to his care. Biblical masculinity is about responsibility, conviction, and sacrificial love. He was built to protect and to build. To protect what is vulnerable. To build what is broken. To guard truth in a culture of compromise and to cultivate strength in the next generation. A man of God understands that his strength is stewardship, his authority is accountability, and his calling is consecrated. Masculinity, rightly surrendered to God, becomes a force for good.

A man who only guards, corrects, and controls without ever cultivating, nurturing, or developing will eventually suffocate the very things he was called to steward. A man may dream, create, and invest his heart into what he loves but if he refuses to stand watch, confront threats, and draw boundaries, what he builds will be easily plundered. God never designed man to be passive, nor did He design him to be tyrannical. He was created to protect what is sacred and to cultivate what is significant. But when a man walks in divine design, he becomes both shield and architect. He guards what God entrusts to him while cultivating what God plants through him - vision, leadership, growth, legacy. His strength is not reckless; it is righteous. His authority is not selfish; it is stewardship. In this balance, he reflects the heart of God Himself - defender of covenant and builder of kingdoms. When a man embraces both roles, he leaves behind something that can withstand both time and storm.

Culture has worked tirelessly to soften what heaven strengthened. It offers blankets where God offers battlefields. What God forged through adversity, culture attempts to anesthetize with ease. It sells comfort as success and passivity as peace, but a life built on comfort will crumble when confronted with conflict. Heaven never designed you to be sedated by ease; it designed you to be sharpened by resistance. While the world whispers, "Relax," the Spirit commands, "Rise." Rise above apathy. Rise above fear. Rise above the low expectations that try to domesticate divine strength. Courage is not aggression without control; it is strength submitted to purpose. God calls men to stand watch, to build with conviction, and to confront darkness without flinching. The battlefield is not a place of chaos - it is the proving ground of calling. And the man who answers heaven's call will discover that what culture labeled as too intense is actually the fire required to fulfill his assignment.

Passive masculinity is very dangerous. A passive man leaves gaps in walls that others depend upon. Strength was never given to men for decoration; it was given for defense, direction, and development. Passivity may look like peace, but it breeds vulnerability. It creates spiritual drafts in homes, moral cracks in foundations, and leadership voids in cities and nations. What a man refuses to confront today will often confront those he loves tomorrow. God did not design men to drift; He designed them to stand. To watch. To guard. To build. When a man steps back from responsibility, the weight he avoids shifts onto weaker shoulders. Children grow without guidance. Wives carry burdens they were never meant to bear alone. A passive man may avoid conflict, but he cannot avoid consequence. The call is not to aggression without wisdom, but to courage with conviction. Stand in the gap. When a man embraces his role, what was exposed becomes protected and what was fragile becomes fortified.

The greatest threat to manhood is not opposition; it is apathy. A visible enemy awakens something primal and powerful inside a man. Resistance forces him to build strength he didn't know he possessed. When a man knows he is in a fight, he sharpens his focus and steadies his resolve. But apathy is far more subtle. It doesn't confront - it lulls. It whispers, "Rest a little longer." And while a warrior prepares for battle, a passive man slowly drifts from purpose without ever realizing he's surrendered ground. Blankets don't look dangerous, but they can suffocate destiny. A man who avoids hardship may feel safe, but safety without purpose becomes a slow fade into insignificance. Strength is not forged in climate-controlled living; it is formed in resistance, responsibility, and righteous burden. If opposition sharpens iron, comfort dulls it. The call of God was never designed to be fulfilled from a recliner - it was meant to be carried into the storm. Throw off the blankets. Rise again because you were built for more.

Muscles that are never strained will never strengthen, and a spirit that is never challenged will never mature. When convenience becomes king, conviction slowly becomes small compromises that feel harmless but hollow out a man's resolve. A man's calling requires early mornings, hard decisions, uncomfortable obedience, and the courage to stand when sitting would be simpler. A man who constantly chooses what feels good over what builds greatness will wake up one day strong in excuses but weak in impact. A warrior's assignment cannot be fulfilled by a spectator's lifestyle. You cannot carry a sword in one hand while clutching a cushion in the other. Purpose is forged in resistance, not recliners. If you are called to guard, to build, to lead, then you must reject the soft drift of passive living. Comfort may feel safe, but it will never make you significant. Step out of the stands. Embrace the strain. The battlefield of your calling is not won by those who seek ease - it is claimed by those who endure.

The battlefield may not always echo with the clash of swords or the thunder of shields. Sometimes it is silent. Sometimes it is fought on your knees at midnight when no one sees the tears you cry or hears the prayers you whisper. These are not small skirmishes; they are decisive moments. The enemy of your soul often fights through distraction, discouragement, and quiet compromise. But every unseen decision to stand firm is a victory that shakes the spiritual realm. Warfare is often invisible, but it is always real. The greatest battles are fought within the heart, where character is forged and conviction is tested. A man who wins in private will stand strong in public. A man who guards his thoughts, his words, and his commitments is not weak - he is armed. Heaven takes notice of the quiet victories that earth overlooks. When you choose integrity over gain, covenant over convenience, and obedience over applause, you are advancing the kingdom. The battlefield may be hidden, but the triumph is eternal.

The enemy does fear a comfortable man. He does not tremble at a man numbed by ease, softened by convenience, or distracted by pleasure. Comfort breeds passivity, and passivity poses no threat to darkness. But a consecrated man has drawn a line in the sand. He has surrendered his will to God, crucified his flesh, and disciplined his appetites. He understands that he was not created merely to consume blessings, but to contend for territory. The enemy fears the man who understands he was designed for warfare, the man who knows that spiritual battles require spiritual backbone. He fears the man who rejects ease, embraces discipline, and stands boldly in the authority God gave him. A man with spiritual backbone does not crumble in adversity because he knows who he serves and why he stands. He recognizes that the weapons of his warfare are not carnal but mighty through God. And when a man stands grounded in truth, clothed in righteousness, armed with faith - darkness must retreat.

God never promised men a life of security blankets - He promised them armor. Blankets are for comfort; armor is for conflict. Blankets insulate you from discomfort; armor prepares you for impact. When God clothes a man in armor, He is revealing purpose. Armor implies friction. It implies resistance. It implies that forces will oppose you, challenge you, and test your resolve. The very fact that God provides armor means He expects you to stand, to advance, and to endure when pressure mounts. Every blow that strikes the armor reminds you that you were built to withstand what tries to break lesser men. You are not called to shrink back into softness, but to rise with conviction, fasten your resolve, and step into the fight with faith. If armor rests on your shoulders, it is because heaven has measured your strength, trusted your character, and appointed you to stand where others cannot. And if something comes against you, it is only confirming what God already declared - you are strong enough to fight.

There is a holy aggression that must be rediscovered in this generation. It is the spirit that says, "As for me and my house, we will serve the Lord," and means it. It is the refusal to allow compromise to erode conviction, passivity to replace purpose, or cultural pressure to silence truth. It stands guard over marriages, children, purity, calling, and truth with a steady resolve that will not yield an inch of ground that belongs to God. This righteous intensity does not seek control - it establishes order. It crushes fear, apathy, lust, doubt, and every lie that dares to exalt itself above the knowledge of God. It is the courage to pray when others are silent, to lead when others shrink back, to speak when truth is unpopular, and to endure when the battle stretches long. There is a difference between being harsh and being holy. The former is rooted in flesh; the latter is rooted in fire. Ehen a man rediscovers this holy aggression, he becomes dangerous to darkness - not because he is violent, but because he is unwavering.

Holy aggression is the steady flame in a man's spirit that refuses to let culture disciple his children or fear dictate his obedience. When compromise becomes fashionable and conviction becomes costly, holy aggression digs its heels in and declares that truth is not for sale. It is the courage to lead your home in prayer when others stay silent, to guard your marriage when others drift, and to build altars to God in a world that bows to idols. Holy aggression is the backbone that remains straight when pressure tries to bend it. It stands firm in the boardroom, in the locker room, and in the living room. It does not fold under mockery or flinch under resistance. It chooses obedience over approval and faithfulness over popularity. This kind of resolve is not born in comfort - it is forged in private surrender and daily discipline. And when a man carries that fire, his home feels it, his children see it, and heaven honors it. It is the righteous intensity that says, "We will not drift. We will not bow. We will serve the Lord."

This aggression is driven by the burden to see God honored. It kneels before it ever stands. It is the kind of fire that calls on the name of the Lord until heaven answers. It is consumed with obedience. It seeks to establish worship in the home, integrity in the marketplace, and holiness in the secret place. This is not self-promotion; this is consecration. It is a man living in such a way that serving God becomes a daily reality. This aggression builds legacy, not applause. It raises sons who know how to bow their knees before they ever lift their voices, and daughters who understand that their worth was settled at the cross and cannot be negotiated by culture. It produces fathers who defend righteousness, mothers who nurture strength with tenderness, and leaders who are unafraid to stand when compromise is convenient. It forms communities where truth has a guardian and righteousness has a defender. This is holy intensity may not draw crowds, but it builds generations.

When men lay down their weapons for blankets, generations pay the price. A man who chooses ease over engagement may not see the damage immediately, but over time the absence of courage and spiritual conviction leaves a vacuum. And vacuums are always filled by something. When men refuse to stand guard in prayer, integrity, and conviction, culture gladly takes their place. But when men rise to their calling, entire bloodlines are strengthened. A man anchored in faith, disciplined in character, and bold in obedience becomes a spiritual thermostat, not a thermometer. He doesn't reflect the climate; he shifts it. His prayers change atmospheres. His example sets standards. His repentance breaks cycles. His courage builds confidence in his children and stability in his home. One man aligned with God can alter the trajectory of a family, ignite revival in a church, and influence the moral tone of a community. When a man wakes up to who he was created to be, generations wake up with him.

You were not created to drift with culture or to float wherever comfort pulls you. You were created to drive back darkness - to step into spaces where fear, confusion, and passivity have settled and bring the authority of heaven with you. God did not design you to hide in the shadows of other men's convictions; He designed you to hold ground when others retreat. When storms rise and voices grow loud, something deep within you stands taller. There is something in you that was forged for resistance. It was shaped in trials, strengthened in setbacks, and sharpened in seasons when quitting would have been easier. You feel it when compromise tries to whisper and something inside you says, "No." You sense it when darkness presses in and your spirit rises up instead of shrinking back. You were built to contend, to guard what is sacred, to push back what threatens your home, your faith, and your future. You are not an accident of survival - you are a weapon of light. Stand firm. Drive back the darkness.

God is not looking for men who burn bright for a moment and fade, but for men who build steady fires that outlast the storm. Disciplined strength bows in prayer before it ever stands in public. It trains the mind, guards the heart, and orders its steps with intention. It understands that power without restraint is destruction, but power under submission is dominion. This kind of strength is forged in the quiet places long before it is revealed in the battlefield moments. A man who knows his assignment fight battles that matter. He does not waste energy on petty wars or cultural noise. He saves his strength for what shapes eternity - his family, his faith, his calling. He stands when compromise is easy. He speaks when silence would be safer. He loves when pride would prefer distance. And when the real battles come, he is ready - not because he is reckless, but because he is prepared. Disciplined strength builds legacy, anchors homes, and leaves behind a testimony that heaven recognizes.

Throw off those security blankets. Pick up your assignment. Tighten your armor. There is a mantle with your name on it, a responsibility heaven entrusted to your shoulders before you ever drew breath. The enemy would love nothing more than to rock you to sleep with comfort and convince you that passivity is peace. But comfort has never advanced the kingdom, and ease has never raised up strong sons. You were built for battle. There is a warrior's grace on your life that awakens when you decide to stand. You were designed for warfare. This is the fight to guard your home, to cover your family in prayer, to hold the line when culture shifts and conviction is tested. Heaven is not waiting for perfect men; it is waiting for willing ones. When you rise, something shifts. When you take your place, darkness loses ground. When you tighten your armor and step forward in obedience, you align yourself with purpose that echoes into generations. Heaven is waiting not to do it for you, but to move through you.

| 4 |

"STOP DODGING THE HARD THINGS"

There comes a defining moment in every man's life when he must choose if he will stand and face what is hard, or will he turn and run from it? Difficulty has a way of exposing what comfort conceals. Pressure reveals character. Responsibility may feel heavy in the moment, but it is not designed to crush you; it is designed to shape you. The weight you feel is often the very thing forging your backbone. When a man embraces what is required of him - he steps into the arena where strength is formed. Avoidance breeds weakness. You cannot grow into strength while running from pressure. Muscles are formed under resistance, and so is character. God uses deadlines to teach discipline, conflict to refine courage, and responsibility to awaken leadership. The very burden you want removed may be the tool God is using to build you into a warrior. So stand your ground. Let the pressure press you forward instead of pushing you back. The weight is not there to break you - it is there to build you.

Avoidance is not strength. Silence is not maturity. Hiding behind busyness, distraction, humor, or anger does not make a man powerful - it makes him predictable. It becomes a pattern. Everyone learns where he will retreat, how he will deflect, when he will disappear emotionally. He may look steady on the surface, but inside he is shrinking from responsibility, from growth, from the refining fire that forges character. What he avoids today will eventually rule him tomorrow. Strength is revealed in confrontation, not concealment. It shows up when a man leans into the tension instead of running from it. It is forged when he stands his ground with humility and conviction. Real power is not loud; it is anchored. It does not explode in anger or evaporate in silence - it engages. A mature man does not dodge the hard things; he steps into them knowing that pressure produces depth. Confrontation is not about conflict for its own sake; it is about courage for the sake of growth. And that is where true strength is born.

Many men have mastered the art of deflection. They change the subject when conviction shows up. They blame others when correction knocks at the door. They withdraw when conflict demands courage. But avoidance never solves what it sidesteps. It only delays the inevitable reckoning. Every time a man dodges accountability, he forfeits growth. Every time he shifts blame, he surrenders strength. Deflection may protect the ego in the moment, but it weakens the character over time. What we refuse to confront will eventually confront us with greater force, greater cost, and fewer options. Manhood is not proven by how skillfully you escape hard conversations, but by how boldly you step into them. Growth begins where defensiveness ends. If you want to rise as the man God designed you to be, stop dodging the mirror. Embrace conviction. Welcome correction. Stand firm in conflict. Because the breakthrough you seek is often hidden inside the confrontation you've been trying to avoid.

Responsibility means stepping toward what intimidates you instead of shrinking back from it. It is choosing courage over comfort and conviction over convenience. It means owning your mistakes without excuse, without shifting blame, without rewriting the story to protect your pride. It means having the strength to say, "I was wrong," and meaning it. That kind of ownership builds integrity. It shapes character in the quiet places where no applause is heard. Responsibility is where excuses die and growth begins. It also means taking action where you once made promises. It is following through when the emotion fades and the work becomes difficult. Responsibility is not glamorous and it rarely gets celebrated. But it is powerful. It builds trust. It strengthens relationships. It turns intentions into results and potential into legacy. When a man embraces responsibility, he stops waiting for change and becomes the change. And in that decision, ordinary people become dependable, and dependable people become leaders.

Tough conversations build strong men. It's easy to stay quiet, to nod politely, and to avoid the tension but growth never happens in the shadows of avoidance. When you speak truth in love, even with trembling hands and a pounding heart, you are exercising spiritual courage. God often uses uncomfortable dialogue to stretch your faith, sharpen your discernment, and anchor you deeper in conviction. The conversations you avoid are often the very conversations God is using to mature you. Silence may feel safer in the moment, but it slowly weakens resolve and clouds clarity. Courage, however, produces character. When you address conflict with humility and grace, you grow in strength and integrity. You learn to stand firm without becoming harsh, to love without becoming passive, and to lead without shrinking back. Strong men are built by obedience in hard moments. Stand with conviction and watch how God uses your courage to shape you into a man of substance and spiritual steel.

A man who refuses hard conversations will slowly forfeit his authority. When correction is withheld, confusion multiplies. Leadership demands clarity, not comfort. Fathers must correct with steady hands and steady hearts. Husbands must communicate truthfully, not defensively. Brothers must confront in love, not gossip in secret. Pastors must challenge, not merely console. Authority is sustained by courage and courage speaks when silence would be easier. You cannot lead what you are afraid to address. The issues you avoid today will eventually rule you tomorrow. A man's spirit weakens when he continually sidesteps what must be said. But when he chooses truth over tension, strength returns to his voice and order returns to his sphere. Hard conversations are acts of stewardship. They protect marriages, guard children, sharpen friendships, and purify churches. A godly man understands that clarity is kindness, and that real love is willing to speak the truth no matter how hard it may be.

Hard conversations are about development. A man does not raise his voice to prove his strength; he steadies his voice to prove his character. Growth rarely happens in silence, and transformation rarely comes without tension. When truth is wrapped in humility and spoken in love, it becomes a chisel in the hands of wisdom, shaping rough edges into strength and turning blind spots into breakthroughs. Real leadership is not about overpowering someone else's will; it is about helping shape someone else's future. The strongest men are not the loudest; they are the most honest. They do not hide behind pride, avoidance, or intimidation. Instead, they lean into uncomfortable moments with courage and compassion. They understand that love tells the truth even when it trembles. Honesty builds trust and humility builds bridges. And when a man learns to speak truth without ego and listen without defensiveness, he becomes a force for transformation in his home, his workplace, and his legacy.

A man who welcomes accountability understands that growth does not happen in isolation and that blind spots cannot be corrected in the dark. When a man invites accountability into his life, he declares war on mediocrity. He steps into the refining fire because he values transformation more than comfort. He knows that correction is the steady hand of sharpening steel, shaping him into something stronger, steadier, and more dependable. Accountability humbles arrogance, exposes excuses, and demands ownership. It calls a man higher when he would rather stay hidden. It teaches him that true strength is not the absence of correction, but the willingness to receive it. Discipline becomes the training ground where character is forged and commitment is proven. A man who embraces accountability understands that greatness is built on honest evaluation and consistent refinement. In choosing accountability, he chooses excellence over ego and growth over comfort.

Many men resist accountability because it feels like exposure and exposure feels like weakness. It threatens the image, the reputation, the illusion of strength. Accountability does not exist to shame you; it exists to sharpen you. When something is brought into the light, it may sting at first, but light is your healer. What is buried grows roots in darkness, but what is exposed has the opportunity to be corrected, strengthened, and restored. The very thing you are trying to conceal may be the very thing God wants to transform. Responsibility requires transparency. You cannot grow beyond what you refuse to confront. Real strength is having the courage to admit you have flaws and the discipline to address them. When you open your life to wise counsel, you create space for growth. When you accept responsibility, you reclaim authority over your future. The light may reveal cracks, but it also reveals the path forward. Exposure is the beginning of healing, maturity, and lasting strength.

Discipline reminds your appetites, impulses, and emotions that they are servants - not masters. Your flesh may crave comfort, shortcuts, and applause, but discipline steps in and says, "You do not rule my destiny." Every time you choose integrity when compromise is easier, you are reclaiming authority over your own life. Discipline aligns your daily habits with your divine calling and teaches your body to bow to your spirit. When you show up on time, follow through on commitments, keep your word, and submit to correction, you are strengthening spiritual muscles that will carry you through storms. Faithfulness in small things builds fortitude for great battles. The man who governs himself is not easily shaken by pressure, criticism, or delay. Long before victory is visible, discipline has already secured it in the unseen places of character. Storms don't create strength - they reveal it. And disciplined obedience, practiced daily, ensures that when the winds rise and the rain falls, you will still be standing.

Growth lives on the other side of discomfort. The very resistance you feel is often the indicator that you are standing at the edge of expansion. Muscles do not grow without strain. Character does not deepen without pressure. Faith does not mature without testing. Every avoided challenge becomes a ceiling over your life - an invisible boundary you built with fear, hesitation, or convenience. But every faced challenge becomes a doorway. When you lean into what stretches you instead of shrinking back from it, you step into new capacity, new confidence, and new calling. The pain you endure today may be shaping the strength you rely on tomorrow. What seems like a setback may be preparing you for a greater assignment. Pressure refines focus. Resistance builds endurance. Trials develop resilience that comfort could never produce. The weight you carry now is training you to carry influence, responsibility, and victory later. Don't curse the discomfort - use it. The ceiling only exists if you refuse to rise up.

God does not call men to comfort; He calls them to courage. Comfort wraps itself around your ambition and whispers, "This is enough." But you were not created for enough. You were created for impact. Comfort lulls you to sleep in the very hour you are needed most. It convinces you that silence is safer than conviction, that ease is better than endurance, and that retreat is wiser than resistance. Yet every page of scripture reveals that when God calls a man, He calls him out of hiding, out of mediocrity, out of the familiar, and into the fire where courage is forged. Courage wakes you up. It stirs your spirit and reminds you that responsibility is not a burden but a badge of honor. Responsibility shakes you out of passivity and pushes you into purpose. It demands that you stand when it would be easier to sit, speak when it would be easier to be silent, and lead when it would be easier to follow. A man awakened by courage understands that he was designed to build, protect, provide, and advance the Kingdom of God.

Dodging hard things may feel safe in the moment, but it quietly erodes a man's strength. Comfort may soothe the flesh, but it starves the spirit. A man who continually sidesteps difficulty trains himself to retreat rather than rise. Over time, his confidence thins, his convictions soften, and his legacy weakens under the weight of what could have been. Excuses become his language, blame becomes his shield, and potential becomes a memory instead of a reality. But when a man chooses to face hard things, something powerful is forged within him. Resistance builds resilience. Pressure produces depth. The challenges he once feared become the very tools that fortify his character. He learns discipline instead of delay and responsibility instead of rationalization. Each battle faced strengthens not only his resolve but also the generations watching him. The path of courage builds legacy, honor, and impact. Hard things are not obstacles to manhood - they are the training ground for it.

Responsibility requires you to finish what you start. It calls you back to the unfinished project, the unkept promise, the hard conversation you hoped would disappear with time. It compels you to apologize when you failed rather than defend your pride. Responsibility is steady, consistent, and often inconvenient. It is choosing discipline over delay, ownership over excuses, and integrity over image. A man is not defined by how loudly he declares his intentions, but by how faithfully he completes them. To stand when you would rather sit. To speak when you would rather stay silent. These are the quiet, daily battles that shape a man's destiny. Every time you rise instead of retreat, every time you own your mistake instead of hiding it, you fortify your character. The quiet battles you win in private become the visible legacy that honors God long after you are gone. Because destiny is not formed in grand moments alone; it is forged in the ordinary decisions to do what is right, even when it is hard.

If you avoid discipline in private, you will lack power in public. What a man refuses to confront behind closed doors will eventually confront him in the open. Private habits shape public authority. It is there, in the quiet decisions to pray when tired, to study when distracted, to resist when tempted, and to act with integrity when compromise would be easier, that true strength is formed. Character is forged where no one is watching. The man who conquers himself can lead others with integrity because leadership begins with self-government. If a man cannot command his appetites, control his temper, guard his thoughts, and honor his commitments in private, he will struggle to guide others in public. But when he masters his impulses and aligns his heart with truth - he carries a quiet authority that cannot be manufactured. Influence flows naturally from integrity. Power that is built in secret becomes credibility that stands in the light. And the man who rules his own spirit is the man others can trust to lead theirs.

There is no shortcut around discomfort. Every calling worth answering will lead you through a place that stretches you, tests you, and strips away your excuses. The cross was not comfortable, and obedience rarely is. It asks you to lay down pride, surrender control, forgive when it hurts, give when it costs, and stand firm when it would be easier to walk away. We often pray for growth, strength, and impact but we resist the very pressure that produces them. If you avoid the struggle, you forfeit the shaping. If you run from the weight, you miss the strengthening. The seed must go into the ground before it rises. The old must die before the new can live. When you choose obedience in the uncomfortable place, you step into the workshop of God where character is forged and destiny is clarified. The pain has purpose. The stretching has meaning. Don't look for an easier path - look for the faithful one. Because beyond the cross is resurrection, and beyond obedience is power.

Stop dodging the hard things. The very resistance you feel is your training ground. Every uncomfortable conversation, every disciplined decision, every step taken when you would rather retreat is building something stronger inside you. Growth always demands stretching. It always costs comfort. And it always requires courage. The weight you keep walking around may be the very tool God is using to strengthen your faith, sharpen your character, and expand your endurance. What feels heavy today is preparing you to carry greater responsibility tomorrow. The pressure you are under is not proof that you are breaking; it may be proof that you are being enlarged. Muscles grow under tension. Character grows under testing. Faith grows when it is exercised. If you keep stepping toward the weight instead of away from it, you will discover something powerful: what once felt impossible becomes manageable, and what once intimidated you becomes the very platform God uses to elevate you.

Step up. Own your failures without excuses, without blame-shifting, without hiding behind pride. A man of strength does not pretend he is flawless; he confronts his flaws and lets them forge him. Embrace correction as sharpening, not shaming. Receive counsel as refinement, not rejection. Carry your responsibility with honor, knowing that every weight you lift builds more character inside you. When a man stops dodging the hard things, when he leans into the tension instead of running from it, he becomes dependable in chaos, disciplined in temptation, and dangerous to the forces that try to weaken him. Responsibility shapes your posture, steadies your words, and anchors your decisions. The man who embraces responsibility sees the need and steps forward. He doesn't collapse under pressure - he grows stronger because of it. And in a world searching for stability, clarity, and courage, the responsible man stands firm - unmoved, unshaken, and unafraid to carry what others drop.

| 5 |

"CULTURAL RESISTENCE"

We are living in a generation that celebrates softness in spirit and confusion in identity. Culture shifts with the wind redefining strength, reshaping truth, and rewriting what it means to be a man. What was once honored is now mocked. What was once firm is now labeled toxic. Conviction is called arrogance. Courage is called aggression. Leadership is called control. Yet in the middle of all this noise, God has not revised His design. While culture bends under pressure and popular opinion, the character of God remains unmoved, unshaken, and unedited. A godly man is not shaped by trends but by truth. He does not apologize for conviction, nor does he surrender clarity for approval. He stands anchored in what God has spoken, not what culture applauds. When the world grows uncertain, he grows more grounded. When identity becomes blurred, he becomes more defined. The standard of God stands eternal and the man who builds his life on that standard will not be shaken.

The world has constructed an emasculation narrative that suggests masculinity itself is dangerous. It subtly pressures men to apologize for being decisive, protective, and bold. But biblical masculinity was never rooted in domination; it was anchored in responsibility. God did not design men to shrink back in uncertainty but to stand firm in truth, to guard what is sacred, and to build what is broken. The enemy does not fear passive men; he fears awakened ones. He fears men who understand that courage and compassion are not opposites, that boldness and humility can walk hand in hand. A godly man does not apologize for being decisive - he ensures his decisions honor God. He does not retreat from protecting - he does so with integrity. He does not silence his convictions - he tempers them with grace. The world may attempt to redefine manhood, but heaven has already declared its design. And when a man embraces that divine blueprint, he becomes not a threat to society - but a foundation for it.

This narrative is not new. Throughout the Bible, whenever God raised up strong men, opposition rose to neutralize them. When deliverance was growing in Egypt, Pharaoh ordered the Hebrew sons to be killed because he feared what they would become. When courage began to stir in Israel's camp, Goliath stepped forward to taunt and intimidate, hoping to paralyze warriors before they ever drew a sword. The enemy has always recognized what many men forget - strength threatens darkness. Opposition is often confirmation that something powerful is being formed. What darkness fears most is not a perfect man - it is a surrendered man strengthened by God. When you stand firm in faith you expose the limits of the enemy's power. Just as Pharaoh could not stop Moses and Goliath could not silence David, no force can ultimately neutralize a man who draws his strength from the Lord. Strength anchored in God does not just survive opposition - it overcomes it.

Throughout Scripture, strong men were never raised up to dominate; they were raised up to protect, provide, and preserve. When a man withdraws from his God-given role, a vacuum forms. Homes lose covering. Children lose modeling. Communities lose stability. The silence of a shrinking man echoes louder than the voice of an opposing culture. Weakness in leadership does not create peace - it creates vulnerability. The enemy understands that if he can neutralize men, he can destabilize generations. When men step back from spiritual responsibility, prayer diminishes, conviction softens, and direction becomes unclear. But when a man stands firm in humility and strength, everything around him strengthens. His courage fortifies his home. His faith steadies his family. His integrity anchors his community. God never called men to shrink in shame, but to rise in servant-hearted authority. When men reclaim their spiritual ground the vacuum closes, order is restored, and light pushes back the darkness.

Biblical masculinity has always been about responsibility - about carrying weight without complaining, standing guard without applause, and leading with a servant's heart. True masculinity is strength under submission to God. It is the disciplined decision to bow your knee to heaven so you can stand tall on earth. When a man submits his will to the Lord, his strength becomes sacred, his leadership becomes safe, and his presence becomes a refuge rather than a threat. Power in the hands of a surrendered man is governed by purity. Courage in the life of a godly man is clothed in humility. He knows that the louder his platform, the deeper his prayer life must be. Biblical masculinity is not about proving you are strong - it is about proving you are faithful. When a man allows God to refine his heart, his power builds instead of breaks, his courage heals instead of harms, and his life becomes a testimony that true strength is found not in self-exaltation, but in holy submission.

Cultural masculinity draws its identity from what can be seen, counted, and envied. It is loud but often hollow - strong in appearance yet fragile in foundation. But biblical masculinity kneels for instruction. It understands that true strength is first forged in surrender. While culture teaches men to build platforms, God teaches men to build altars. One seeks validation from people; the other seeks transformation from the presence of God. Culture defines manhood by what a man can accumulate, dominate, and display. God defines manhood by what a man will obey, protect, and lay down. Biblical masculinity is not weak - it is disciplined. It is not passive - it is purposeful. It is not driven by ego - it is anchored in obedience, integrity, sacrifice, and love. The greatest men in the Kingdom are not those who flex the hardest, but those who kneel the lowest. For when a man bows before God, he rises with authority. When he submits to truth, he stands in power. And when he loves sacrificially, he reflects the very heart of Christ.

The world whispers, "Follow your feelings," as if emotion were a compass that never fails. But feelings shift like sand beneath our feet - strong one moment, silent the next. God calls us higher, saying, "Follow Me." When we lay down our will, we step into His purpose. When we release control, we receive clarity. The narrow road may resist our flesh, but it strengthens our spirit. The world redefines truth, bending it to preference and popular opinion. But God declares, "I am the Truth." Truth is not a trend to be rewritten; it is a Person to be followed. When we anchor our lives in Him, we are no longer tossed by cultural currents or emotional tides. To follow Christ is to choose conviction over convenience, obedience over applause, and eternal reward over temporary comfort. It is a daily decision to trust His Word above our feelings and His wisdom above our understanding. The world offers self-centered freedom; God offers soul-saving freedom. One path feeds the flesh. The other transforms the heart.

A soft culture resists absolutes because absolutes demand accountability. It prefers gray areas over guardrails because gray feels safer than surrender. When everything is negotiable, conviction fades, identity blurs, and purpose weakens. A culture allergic to moral clarity may call it compassion, but compassion divorced from truth becomes confusion. Without fixed anchors, hearts wander, standards erode, and souls slowly conform to whatever feels easiest in the moment. But a strong God establishes boundaries not to restrict us, but to redeem us. His commands are not cages; they are guardrails placed along dangerous cliffs. He defines right and wrong because He sees what we cannot. He draws lines because love protects, corrects, and directs. Divine boundaries are evidence of divine care. His truth is not harsh - it is holy. And in a world that bends with every cultural wind, His unchanging standards are not oppressive; they are the very foundation that keeps us strong, steady, and secure.

In every generation, there is a subtle but steady pressure to blend in, to soften convictions, to adjust truth just enough to avoid tension. Rarely does compromise begin with open rebellion; more often, it whispers in moments of convenience. It suggests that one small concession won't matter, that silence is safer than courage, that fitting in is wiser than standing firm. Cultural resistance rarely storms the gates of faith; it simply asks us to open the door a crack. Yet God has never called His people to quiet compromise. He calls us to conviction rooted in love and truth anchored in courage. One small concession may seem harmless, but every step away from conviction makes the next step easier. The strength of a believer is not measured by volume but by faithfulness. In a culture that rewards flexibility of belief, heaven honors steadfastness of heart. Stand firm - not in arrogance, but in assurance. For when you refuse to bow in the small things, you preserve the power to stand in the great ones.

Truth does not bend to the spirit of the age. It is not revised by public opinion or softened by cultural pressure. What heaven declared holy in ancient days has not expired with time, nor has it been edited to suit modern tastes. God is not governed by trends, and His standards are not updated by polls. He is the same yesterday, today, and forever. When He called something righteous in generations past, it remains righteous now. When He named something sin in ancient times, it has not somehow transformed into virtue because society grew comfortable with it. In a world constantly shifting its definitions, God's unchanging Word becomes our security. We do not have to wonder where the lines are drawn or fear that the moral compass has been recalibrated overnight. His boundaries are expressions of love, not limitation. His commands are guardrails, not cages. The culture may drift, but the character of God does not. For those who build their lives on His eternal standard, there is strength, clarity, and peace.

Men of God must learn that conviction without cost is merely opinion. Anyone can stand tall when the crowd is cheering. But true spiritual backbone is revealed when faithfulness demands sacrifice. There comes a moment when standing firm may cost reputation, relationships, comfort, or opportunity. A man anchored in Christ does not shift with public opinion; he stands because truth is not negotiable, even when the price tag is high. Kingdom courage is proven when it is opposed. It is forged in resistance, refined in criticism, and strengthened in isolation. When obedience places you in the minority, when integrity makes you misunderstood, when righteousness invites resistance - that is when your roots go deep. The applause of men fades quickly, but the approval of God echoes into eternity. Stand firm not because it is popular, but because it is right. Stand firm not because it is safe, but because it is sacred. A man of God does not measure courage by comfort; he measures it by faithfulness.

Conviction is not cruelty - it is clarity. It is the steady, settled confidence that God's Word is higher than cultural waves and louder than popular applause. Men of conviction are not harsh; they are anchored. They are not driven by anger but by alignment. Conviction is the calm resolve that truth does not bend to trends, and righteousness is not rewritten by preference. When the crowd shifts, conviction stands. When opinions multiply, conviction simplifies. It asks one question above all others: What has God said? To live by conviction is to choose eternal approval over temporary acceptance. It is understanding that applause fades, but accountability remains. The fear of rejection may pressure us to soften the edges of truth, but conviction reminds us that faithfulness matters more than popularity. It keeps our backbone strong and our conscience clear. In the end, it is better to be misunderstood by people than misaligned with God. Conviction does not make us cruel - it makes us courageous.

The culture may call you outdated for believing scripture. It may label you rigid for holding to truth. But the applause of the moment has never been the measure of a man of God. Trends shift. Opinions evolve. Headlines change. Yet the Word of God stands unmoved by the winds of preference and pressure. When you anchor your life to scripture, you are standing on what is eternal. The world may celebrate flexibility, but heaven honors faithfulness. Noah looked foolish building an ark under a clear sky. Daniel seemed extreme when he would not bow. Yet history vindicated their obedience. What culture mocked, God exalted. Faithfulness has never been fashionable, but it has always been powerful. It may cost you popularity, promotions, or even relationships. It may isolate you in rooms where compromise is common and conviction is rare. But remember this: standing alone with God is stronger than standing with the crowd without Him. Stay steady. The tide will turn, but the Word will remain.

Strong men are shaped by holiness. A man of God becomes strong because his heart bows. Holiness is forged in the hidden place, where no crowd is watching. A strong man understands that his calling did not originate on a screen - it was written before the foundation of the world. He does not chase relevance; he pursues righteousness. His identity is rooted in Christ, not culture. When the winds of opinion shift and the voices of the age grow louder, the anchored man does not drift. His confidence is not built on affirmation but on adoption. He knows who he is because he knows whose he is. The world may redefine manhood with every generation, but Christ remains the same yesterday, today, and forever. A strong man stands firm not because he is stubborn, but because he is surrendered. He is led not by trends but by truth, not by impulse but by instruction, not by popularity but by purpose. And when his life is measured, it will not be by followers but by faithfulness.

Resistance is not the loudness of your voice but the firmness of your foundation. When the world pressures you to bend, true resistance is the quiet, unshaken decision to stay rooted in God's truth. It is refusing to let culture redefine what heaven has already declared. It is choosing conviction over convenience, obedience over applause. Resistance is sustained by righteousness. It is a heart so anchored in Christ that it cannot be moved by trending opinions or shifting values. It means standing like Daniel when everyone else kneels - calm, resolved, and unwavering. While others conform to survive, you remain faithful to live. Holy resistance is not rebellion against people; it is loyalty to God. It is the courage to stand alone if necessary, knowing you are never truly alone. When you align yourself with heaven, you may stand out on earth - but your stance becomes a testimony. And in that steadfast posture, God reveals that those who refuse to bow are the very ones He chooses to raise.

We do not fight culture with clenched fists; we confront it with consecrated lives. The weapons of the Kingdom have always been righteousness, obedience, and unwavering devotion to truth. Faithfulness is our resistance. It is choosing integrity when compromise would be easier. It is holding to scripture when trends shift like sand. It is standing firm without becoming harsh, being bold without becoming bitter. A steady life anchored in Christ speaks louder than a thousand arguments. We do not answer confusion with cruelty, but with clarity rooted in love. We model a higher way, a holier standard, a better spirit. When darkness spreads, we shine. When deception multiplies, we illuminate truth. Our calling is not to win debates but to reflect Christ so clearly that truth becomes undeniable. The culture may drift, but the faithful remain. And when we choose conviction over compromise and grace over aggression, we become living proof that there is still a narrow road and it still leads to life.

A soft culture may shift like sand, reshaping itself with every new opinion and every passing trend, but our God is a Rock. He is not moved by headlines, polls, or cultural pressure. His strength does not waver when storms rage, and His authority does not bend when voices grow loud. When a man anchors his life to that Rock, he does not drift with the tide of popular thought. He stands firm because he is secured to something eternal. God's Word does not age, and His design for manhood does not expire. Long before culture defined masculinity by comfort, applause, or emotion without responsibility, God defined it by courage, integrity, sacrifice, and holy strength. True manhood is not discovered in trends; it is revealed in truth. It is forged in obedience, shaped by the Word, and strengthened by surrender to Christ. When everything around us feels unstable, the call remains clear: build your life on the Rock. For when the sand shifts - and it always will - the man grounded in God will still be standing.

When the winds of compromise blow, plant your feet on the unshakable Word of God. Speak truth with authority born from time in prayer and obedience. Love boldly in a world that confuses love with approval. Let your love be anchored in righteousness and wrapped in grace. Lead courageously in your home, your church, and your community. A soft culture may celebrate passivity, but you were not designed for silence or surrender. You were called to reflect the strength of a holy God in the way you live, speak, and serve. Let your life preach when your words are few. Let your integrity speak in private what your mouth declares in public. Let your conviction be steady, your courage visible, and your faith active. Biblical manhood is steadfast. It is not reckless - it is restrained and submitted to Christ. So rise with quiet strength. Stand with unwavering faith. And let your life be undeniable proof that conviction still lives, courage still rises, and godly manhood still stands.

| 6 |

"STRENGTH WITH COMPASSION"

A tough man is not a hard man. Hardness may look strong, but it is brittle. It snaps under pressure and shatters in relationships. Strength, however, is durable. It bends without breaking. It absorbs impact without losing integrity. Hardness shuts people out, building walls of pride and isolation; strength stands firm while keeping the door open. A godly man is anchored, not abrasive. He is steady, not sharp. When storms come, he does not collapse. He stands his ground with conviction, yet his heart remains teachable, merciful, and open to correction. In a culture that confuses aggression with masculinity and passivity with kindness, God is still shaping men with tough skin and tender hearts. These are men who can withstand pressure without losing compassion, who can confront sin without forfeiting love, and who can lead boldly without becoming domineering. Their strength is revealed in the steadfast faithfulness with which they stand, serve, and remain true when no one is watching.

Hardness develops when wounds go untreated. When pain is buried instead of brought before God, it hardens the heart, sharpens the tongue, and shortens the temper. A hard man reacts because he is still bleeding beneath the surface. But strength develops when wounds are surrendered to God. When a man lays his hurt at the altar instead of carrying it into every conversation, God turns his pain into perspective. A strong man has allowed the Great Physician to touch the places he once tried to hide. A hard man builds walls to protect himself; a strong man builds foundations to support others. One is driven by unresolved pain. The other is anchored in eternal purpose. When a man knows who he is in Christ, he can stand steady without becoming cold. A true man of God can lead with strength and authority while keeping his heart tender enough to show compassion. In a world full of warriors pretending to be unbreakable, God is still raising up men to be strong and humble enough to stay tender.

The making of a tough man requires pressure. Steel is not shaped in comfort, and neither is character. No soldier becomes battle-ready without resistance. Pressure reveals what is real. It exposes the cracks, the insecurities, the places where strength has not yet been built. Trials do not create weakness; they uncover it so it can be confronted, corrected, and refined. Every hardship is a forge. Every setback is a strengthening. What resists you is often what prepares you. Yet true toughness is not hardness of heart. Tough skin is formed in adversity, but a tender heart is formed in surrender. A man becomes strong by facing resistance, but he becomes wise by bowing before God. The strongest men are those who can endure pressure without losing compassion, who can stand firm without becoming cold. They carry scars but not bitterness. They fight battles but remain gentle with people. That is the mark of a finished man - resilient in conflict, refined in character, and surrendered in spirit.

Too many men live pendulum lives swinging from one unhealthy extreme to another. Some harden themselves until nothing moves them. They confuse emotional shutdown with strength and mistake silence for self-control. They build walls instead of wisdom, becoming calloused in the name of discipline. Others drift to the opposite edge, allowing every feeling to dictate their direction. They elevate emotional expression as proof of maturity yet forget that feelings make poor leaders when left unchecked. Scripture shows us that biblical masculinity is not emotional absence nor emotional excess - it is emotional authority under God. Anchored emotion is the mark of a mature man. He feels deeply, but he stands firmly, governed by truth rather than tossed by impulse. A godly man does not deny emotion; he disciplines it. He stands firm in conviction while remaining tender in compassion. This is biblical masculinity - strength with sensitivity, power under control, and a heart fully submitted to God.

The model for true manhood is found in Christ. Jesus did not conform to the extremes of hardness or passivity; He revealed a strength rooted in obedience and a tenderness anchored in truth. He spoke with authority that silenced storms and confronted corruption, yet His heart was moved by the broken, the blind, and the bound. He flipped tables in righteous authority, refusing to tolerate what dishonored His Father, and He wept at a grave in holy sorrow, entering fully into human pain. In Him, we see that godly power is never cruel, and holy compassion never compromises. In Christ, courage walked hand in hand with mercy. His hands were strong enough to carry a cross and gentle enough to bless children. He rebuked hypocrisy without hesitation and restored the fallen with unwavering grace. This is the pattern for every man who seeks to reflect Him: anchored conviction without arrogance, deep emotion without instability, bold leadership without brutality.

Scripture reveals Christ as both the conquering Lion and the sacrificial Lamb. The Lion speaks of holy authority, of courage that does not flinch, conviction that does not bend, and victory that does not apologize. He stands firm in truth, guards what God has entrusted to him, and confronts darkness without fear. Yet the Lamb kneels in humility. He chooses surrender over self-promotion, sacrifice over selfishness, and mercy over revenge. In Christ we see power under control and strength wrapped in compassion. A godly man must carry both images in his spirit. If he embraces the Lion without the Lamb, he becomes harsh, domineering, and intoxicated with control. If he embraces the Lamb without the Lion, he becomes passive, fragile, and afraid to stand. But when both dwell within him, masculinity becomes bold yet broken before God, strong yet tender with people, authoritative yet submitted to heaven. Remove one, and the image is distorted. Keep both, and a man reflects Christ.

A man driven only by lion energy can become harsh, forceful, and domineering. Yet a man who lives only with lamb energy can drift into passivity, confusing gentleness with weakness and silence with peace. God designed man to reflect divine balance for this is the mark of mature masculinity. The lion gives him courage to stand when others bow, to confront darkness without flinching, to defend truth without apology. The lamb gives him tenderness to kneel when others posture, to restore when others condemn, to carry burdens instead of casting stones. A godly man roars at injustice, but he kneels in compassion. He confronts sin yet restores the sinner. He defends truth with bold conviction yet loves deeply with open hands. He is firm without being cruel, tender without being timid. When lion and lamb live together under the lordship of Christ, a man becomes dangerous to darkness and safe for people. That is not weakness. That is the mark of a masculine man who is totally submitted to God.

Tough skin is not the absence of feeling; it is the presence of a solid foundation. When criticism comes, it does not cripple you because your identity is not anchored in applause but in assignment. When rejection stings, it does not redefine you because God already named you before people ever judged you. You remember that your calling was given by heaven, not handed out by human approval. So you absorb the blow, but you don't drop the banner. Spiritual maturity teaches you how to take a hit without losing your holiness. You refuse to let bitterness rewrite your character or pain reshape your purpose. You choose forgiveness over fury, growth over grudges, and obedience over offense. Tough skin means you can stand in the storm without becoming the storm. It means you guard your heart without building walls around it. And when life tests you, you rise stronger not because it didn't hurt, but because you decided your calling is greater than your scars.

A tender heart means you feel the weight of injustice; you care when someone is hurting, and you pause long enough to truly listen. In a world that hardens itself to survive, you have refused to numb your soul. You have not silenced compassion to appear strong. Instead, you have allowed the Spirit of God to keep your heart sensitive to His voice and responsive to the needs of others. A tender heart keeps loving in a world that desperately needs it. It protects the vulnerable, speaks gently to the broken, and refuses to grow cold when love would be easier to abandon. But tenderness does not mean uncontrolled emotion; it means surrendered emotion. Your feelings are no longer your master - they are under the authority of the Spirit. You feel deeply, but you are not ruled by what you feel. You care passionately, but you are guided by truth. You grieve, yet you hope. You are moved, yet you remain steady. That is spiritual maturity: strength wrapped in compassion, conviction clothed in love.

Emotional control does not mean emotional absence. God did not design men to be stones with no feelings. A strong man feels deeply - he just refuses to let his feelings take the wheel. Christ Himself wept, yet He did not waver. He felt anguish in Gethsemane, yet He chose obedience over impulse. Emotional discipline is when a godly man pauses before he speaks, prays before he reacts, and considers the weight of his words before releasing them. A strong man is not emotionally silent; he is emotionally governed. He does not explode at every inconvenience nor implode under pressure because he has learned that self-control is a fruit of the Spirit. He governs his responses rather than being governed by them. When tension rises, he remains anchored. His stability becomes a refuge for his family and a testimony to the world. In a culture that confuses emotional chaos with authenticity, a disciplined man is calm, clear, and controlled. His emotions serve his calling; they do not sabotage it.

There is power in restraint. A man who walks with God understands that strength is not proven by noise, but by control. Jesus stood silent before His accusers not because He was weak, but because He was secure. Restraint is not passivity; it is authority under submission to the Spirit. It is the calm voice in the storm, the steady hand in the conflict, the anchored soul when others are drifting. Anyone can dominate a room with intimidation, but few can lead it with calm authority. A tough man does not need theatrics to prove his strength. His consistency speaks louder than his volume. He shows up. He follows through. He keeps his word. His presence brings peace, not pressure. He does not posture for attention; he carries conviction without chaos. In a culture addicted to outrage and performance, the restrained man stands out. He understands that true power is not in overpowering others - it is in mastering himself. And a man who has mastered himself is a man heaven can trust with influence.

Leading with strength and compassion requires discernment born in the presence of God. When a man anchors his convictions in compassion, he reflects the heart of Christ. He is firm in truth, yet gentle in spirit. His strength does not threaten; it protects. His standards do not suffocate; they steady. When a man leads this way, those around him feel both safe and strong. Safe because his mercy assures them they are valued beyond their failures. Strong because his strength calls them higher than their excuses. He does not bend truth to comfort feelings, nor does he weaponize truth to win arguments. He stands rooted in righteousness while extending grace with open hands. This is mature manhood - discipline without harshness, authority without arrogance, correction without cruelty. And in a culture that often swings between extremes, the man who carries both steel and mercy becomes a pillar in the world - steady, trustworthy, and reflective of the God who is both Lion and Lamb.

A man of God does not apologize for strength, but neither does he weaponize it. People need correction that builds character and comfort that builds confidence. Discipline without love hardens a heart; love without discipline weakens it. Strength that never softens becomes harsh; softness that never strengthens becomes unstable. God calls you to both. Your community needs courage and kindness living in the same man. It needs a voice that speaks truth without flinching and hands that serve without hesitation. Jesus was bold in the temple and gentle with the broken. He confronted sin and restored sinners. Real strength is not proven by domination but by disciplined love. When you stand tall in conviction and kneel low in compassion, you become a pillar your family can lean on and a refuge your community can trust. That is the picture of a man shaped by Christ - steel in his spine, warmth in his arms, and the heart of a shepherd leading with both authority and grace.

Tough skin allows you to carry responsibility without collapsing. A man called by God cannot afford to be shaken by every criticism, discouraged by every delay, or derailed by every disappointment. Strength is the ability to stand firm when pressure mounts and expectations rise. Responsibility is heavy, but God never assigns weight without also supplying backbone. Tough skin absorbs friction without losing focus. It endures misunderstanding without surrendering mission. It holds the line when storms come. But toughness alone is only half the equation. A tender heart ensures you carry people without crushing them. The same hands that hold responsibility must also hold people with care. A tender heart listens before it speaks, understands before it corrects, and restores before it replaces. When tough skin and a tender heart walk together, stability is born. People lean into leaders who are strong enough to withstand pressure and gentle enough to value souls.

A man forged by God stands firm where it matters most. He is anchored in conviction, rooted in Scripture, and is unwilling to compromise righteousness for approval. When pressure mounts and culture shifts, he does not sway with the wind. He resists evil without apology and guards his heart and his calling with courage. Yet his firmness is not harshness; it is holy stability. It is the quiet confidence of a man who knows who he serves and why he stands. But the same man who stands tall in truth knows how to bend low in service. He kneels to wash feet. He lowers his voice to lift the wounded. He receives the broken with gentleness and makes room for the struggling without surrendering his standards. He is unmovable in conviction yet approachable in spirit. He is strong enough to confront sin, tender enough to restore the sinner. In him, courage and compassion coexist. And because he has learned when to stand and when to bow, people feel both protected by his strength and safe within his presence.

A man who walks with God understands that true authority is not proven by how loudly he speaks, but by how deeply he loves. Jesus demonstrated this balance perfectly. He was firm with truth, yet tender with the broken; unwavering in righteousness yet overflowing with mercy. When a leader can correct without humiliating and challenge without shaming, he reflects the heart of a Father who disciplines to develop, not to destroy. Compassion gives strength a conscience and power a purpose. People may obey out of intimidation, but they follow out of respect. When strength is fused with compassion, it creates a safe place for growth. It calls people higher without crushing them under the weight of their mistakes. And in that atmosphere, loyalty is born. Hearts open. Trust deepens. Influence expands. The strongest men are those who can carry authority and kindness in the same hand, and by doing so, they lead in a way that reflects both the justice and the mercy of God.

The making of a tough man is not the death of his emotions but the discipline of them. God never asked a man to suppress what He Himself designed. Anger, grief, passion, desire, and zeal are not weaknesses to be buried; they are forces to be governed. A weak man is ruled by his feelings. A hardened man is numb to them. But a godly man makes them submit to his authority. When your anger bows to righteousness, when your sorrow kneels in prayer, when your passion burns for purity, and when your love is anchored in truth - your emotions become servants of your calling instead of saboteurs of your character. A sanctified heart feels deeply but responds wisely. It loves fiercely but stands firmly. The tough man in Christ is not emotionally absent - he is spiritually anchored. His tears are not weakness; they are worship. His passion is not chaos; it is consecrated. And his strength is not measured by how little he feels, but by how faithfully he submits every feeling to the Lordship of Christ.

Pray for thick skin and a soft heart. Ask God to build in you a holy resilience that does not crumble under criticism, pressure, or adversity. A man of God must be steady in storms and tender in sacred spaces. He must be unshaken by opposition yet deeply moved by the needs of others. True strength is not found in shutting down emotion; it is found in submitting emotion to the Spirit. When your skin is thick, you are not easily offended. When your heart is soft, you are not easily hardened. That is spiritual maturity - courage anchored in conviction and compassion rooted in Christ. The world has enough cold, distant, harsh men who confuse aggression with authority. What it desperately needs are men who are strong enough to stand firm and humble enough to kneel low. Strength without tenderness becomes tyranny; tenderness without strength becomes instability. But when God forges both in the same man, He creates a leader who protects without crushing and corrects without condemning.

Be the man who can endure hardship without losing his humanity. A godly man learns to stand in the fire without smelling like smoke. He carries conviction without cruelty, truth without arrogance, authority without oppression. His backbone is steel, but his spirit is surrendered. He does not confuse aggression with leadership or silence with strength. He knows that real power is restrained power that is submitted to God, governed by love, and guided by wisdom. Be the man whose presence feels steady and safe. When you walk into a room, let anxiety decrease and courage increase. Let your words build, not bruise. Tough skin. Tender heart. That is the making of a godly, dangerous, dependable man. Dangerous to darkness because he refuses compromise. Dependable to people because he refuses to quit. He is firm in battle and gentle at home. He carries the weight, absorbs the shock, and still chooses kindness. That is strength under control. That is masculinity redeemed.

| 7 |

"SPIRITUAL TOUGHNESS"

Discipline is not abuse; it is alignment with the heart of God. It positions your character for promotion, your integrity for influence, and your calling for fulfillment. What feels like restriction and denial is often divine design. In a world that resists boundaries and resents correction, the kingdom teaches us that pruning produces fruit, and refinement reveals gold. God disciplines to shape you into someone who can carry glory without collapsing under it. In a culture that confuses restraint with repression, heaven calls it strength. Self-control is not weakness; it is spiritual authority over your own flesh. It is the power to say no when temptation screams yes. It is the courage to govern your appetites so your appetites do not govern you. The man who rules his spirit is stronger than one who conquers a city, because true dominion begins within. When you submit your impulses to the Spirit of God, you are not losing freedom - you are gaining mastery. And mastery under Christ is bold, disciplined, Spirit-led authority.

The apostle Paul told Timothy that God has not given us a spirit of fear, but of power, love, and a sound mind. That sound mind is disciplined thinking under the authority of Christ. A man who cannot govern his thoughts will never govern his life, because behavior always follows belief. When a man allows fear, lust, anger, or insecurity to roam unchecked, those thoughts eventually shape his words, decisions, and destiny. But when he disciplines his thinking, he strengthens the foundation of his character. Discipline begins in the mind long before it appears in action. A strong life is built on strong thought patterns rooted in scripture, anchored in identity, and aligned with purpose. Before a man ever leads a family, builds a business, or stands firm in adversity, he must first learn to command his inner world. The battle for manhood is won or lost between the ears. Govern your thoughts with truth, and your life will follow in order. Guard your mind with discipline, and your steps will walk in power, love, and unwavering clarity.

Self-discipline is spiritual toughness. It is the forged steel of the soul that stands firm when emotions surge and impulses demand to be obeyed. It is the quiet mastery of self under the authority of the Spirit. It is the daily crucifixion of the flesh and the steady alignment of the heart with God's will. Toughness in the Spirit is consistent. It does not boast; it builds. It does not flare up; it endures. It is the steady cadence of a disciplined life that prays when it doesn't feel like praying, serves when it would rather be served, and stays planted when the winds of culture shift. Spiritual toughness is not about domination over others; it is dominion over self. It is the man who refuses to bend to every impulse, who quietly decides again and again to do what is right even when it is hard, unnoticed, and unrewarded. That kind of discipline becomes strength. That kind of strength becomes character. And that character becomes a testimony that heaven recognizes, even if the world never applauds.

When Paul wrote in 1 Corinthians that he "disciplines his body and brings it into subjection," he was proclaiming self-mastery. The apostle understood that unchecked appetites can dethrone purpose. He reminds us that the body is a gift from God, but it was never meant to sit on the throne of our lives. Discipline is bringing your physical appetites under the authority of a renewed spirit so that you can run your race with endurance and finish strong. The body makes a wonderful servant but a terrible master. When it serves, it becomes an instrument of righteousness - hands that bless, eyes that see with compassion, a mouth that speaks truth, strength that labors faithfully. But when it rules, it demands comfort over calling, pleasure over purpose, and ease over obedience. Self-mastery is choosing eternal reward over temporary relief. Through the power of the Spirit, we learn to govern ourselves so that nothing governs us but Christ. That is not bondage - that is freedom.

Discipline is self-preparation. An athlete doesn't enter the gym to injure his body, but to increase its capacity. He embraces repetition, resistance, and routine because he understands that growth lives on the other side of strain. In the same way, spiritual discipline is about training your spirit to respond with strength, wisdom, and obedience. Prayer builds endurance in your faith. Fasting strengthens your dependence on God. Study sharpens your discernment. When you submit to spiritual discipline, your character expands to carry weight you once could not bear. Just as muscles grow under resistance, integrity grows under pressure, patience grows under delay, and humility grows under correction. Discipline shapes you into someone trustworthy. It prepares you for greater assignments. The stretching may be uncomfortable, but it is never pointless. Through discipline, God increases your strength so that when opportunity arrives, your character is strong enough to sustain it.

A man without discipline drifts into bondage. When appetite is left unchecked, it begins to rule the heart like a quiet tyrant. The appetite for comfort whispers, "Take it easy." The appetite for pleasure insists, "Feel good now." None of these desires are evil in themselves but when they sit on the throne instead of character, they enslave the very man they were meant to serve. A man led by impulse will always be pulled by the strongest craving in the room. And cravings make cruel masters. Discipline is the guardrail of destiny. It is the internal governor that tells appetite where it may go and where it must stop.

Strength is not proven by how loudly a man roars, but by how firmly he can say no to himself. What you refuse to master will eventually master you. If you do not rule your desires, they will rule your decisions. But when a man submits his appetites to God, harnesses them with conviction, and tempers them with self-control, he becomes focused, faithful, and free.

Mastering appetites is one of the clearest signs of maturity. Hunger is natural. Desire is human. God created us with longings - for food, for affection, for achievement, for intimacy - but He never intended those longings to rule us. Self-control is the quiet authority of a life surrendered to God. When you choose when and how a desire is fulfilled, you demonstrate that your spirit is leading your flesh - not the other way around. That is dominion not over others but over yourself. True dominion begins within. Before you can lead a family, influence a culture, or build a legacy, you must govern your own appetites. A man who cannot say no to himself cannot say yes with power to God. Mastery over appetite produces clarity, strength, and integrity. It forges patience in a hurried world and conviction in a compromised one. When you control your desires instead of being controlled by them, you reflect the image of a disciplined King. That is maturity. That is authority. And that is the quiet strength that sets a man apart.

The fruit of the Spirit listed in Galatians ends with self-control for a reason. It is the safeguard of every other virtue. Self-control is the spiritual backbone that keeps every other fruit aligned with God's will. It is what keeps love holy, joy steady, peace guarded, patience enduring, kindness sincere, goodness pure, faithfulness consistent, and gentleness strong. Without self-control, even good intentions can drift into excess. But when the Spirit governs our appetites, emotions, words, and reactions, our character becomes trustworthy and our witness becomes credible. Self-control is the daily decision to let the Spirit lead rather than the flesh rule. In a culture that excuses excess, self-control stands as evidence that Christ truly reigns within.

It keeps passion focused, conviction balanced, and calling disciplined. When the Spirit produces self-control in a man of God, every other virtue flourishes safely. For where there is self-control, there is maturity, and where there is maturity, there is lasting impact.

Strong men understand that feelings are real, but they are not reliable leaders. A man who is ruled by his moods will build nothing that lasts, because moods change with the wind. But a man who is ruled by purpose will stand steady in every season. He does not rise each morning consulting his emotions; he rises consulting his assignment. Feelings fluctuate - calling does not. Discipline becomes the anchor that holds him firm when the tides of frustration, fatigue, or discouragement try to pull him off course. He understands that leadership, fatherhood, service, and obedience are not mood-based responsibilities - they are covenant commitments. When storms come, he does not drift with the waves; he lowers his anchor deeper into truth. He prays when he doesn't feel like it. He works when he's tired and weary. He loves when it's inconvenient. Why? Because he knows greatness is not built on inspiration, but on consistency. And the man who masters his spirit will never be mastered by his emotions.

Morning routines matter because they are holy ground. Before the noise of the world rises, before demands press in, before distractions compete for attention, a man has an opportunity to choose who will lead his day: his flesh or his spirit. When a man rises early to pray, to read the Word, to prepare his heart, he is not simply managing time; he is mastering himself. He is stepping into alignment with God before stepping into responsibility. Victory at noon is often decided at dawn. When a man gets up while others sleep and seeks the face of God, he is declaring war on passivity. He is rejecting laziness, silencing compromise, and strengthening conviction before temptation ever knocks. The discipline of the morning builds the backbone of the day. It sharpens discernment, fortifies courage, and steadies resolve. A man who conquers the early hours carries authority into every other hour. And when the sun climbs high, he does not react to the day - he leads it.

There is something sacred about the first moments of the morning. Before the noise of the world begins its relentless pull there is a window of divine opportunity. Prayer before pressure steadies the soul. When a man kneels before he stands, he does not face the day alone; he rises armed with perspective, anchored in truth, and strengthened by the Spirit. The early hours are formative. What you feed your spirit at dawn will shape how you fight your battles at noon. The disciplined morning builds a fortified mind. It teaches you to rule your thoughts before circumstances attempt to rule you. Intention replaces impulse. Conviction overpowers distraction. In a world addicted to urgency, the man who chooses stillness first becomes unshakeable later. When you meet God before you meet the world, your confidence is not fragile and your peace is not accidental. It is built. Brick by brick. Prayer by prayer. Verse by verse. And by the time pressure comes knocking, it does not find panic - it finds a prepared heart.

The strong man understands that destiny is not discovered by accident but developed through intention. While others drift through days led by impulse, he orders his steps with prayer, clarity, and resolve. He rises with vision, not vagueness. He guards his time because he values his calling, knowing that every hour wasted is a seed never planted. To him, time is sacred ground. He plans because he believes God has something specific for him to build, protect, and complete. Discipline is stewardship of the life God entrusted to him. It is the quiet refusal to be ruled by moods, distractions, or comfort. A disciplined man treats his body, his mind, his family, and his faith as responsibilities, not options. He knows that calling without structure collapses, but calling with discipline creates legacy. So he lives measured, focused, and faithful because he understands that one day he will answer for how he managed the strength, time, and purpose placed in his hands.

Self-control shows up most clearly in a man's speech. A disciplined man does not feel the need to broadcast every thought, defend every slight, or win every argument. He understands that words carry weight, and once released, they cannot be retrieved. In a culture that rewards loud opinions and instant reactions, the godly man practices restraint. He knows that silence can be strategic, that gentleness can be powerful, and that timing can determine whether words heal or harm. Power restrained is greater than power displayed. Anyone can speak quickly; few can speak wisely. The disciplined man understands that true authority is not proven by volume but by control. He governs his tongue because he has first learned to govern his heart. When he does speak, his words carry clarity, conviction, and calm strength. He builds rather than breaks. He leads rather than lashes out. His speech becomes evidence of his maturity, proof that his spirit is submitted to God and his strength is under control.

Anyone can ignite a spark of passion for a moment, but it takes character to tend the flame day after day. God is not merely looking for men who can shout on the mountain - He is looking for men who will walk steadily through the valley. A burst of zeal may draw applause, but steady obedience draws heaven's approval. The race of faith is not won by those who sprint for a season, but by those who endure with unwavering devotion. Intensity impresses people for a moment. Consistency builds a legacy over decades. It is the daily prayer, the repeated discipline, the quiet integrity, the unseen sacrifice that shapes a life of impact. Great marriages are built consistently. Strong character is forged consistently. Spiritual authority is developed consistently. When you choose to show up every day you are laying bricks that will outlast your lifetime. Stay steady. Stay faithful. Stay obedient. Because in the kingdom of God, it is not the flash of the moment that changes generations - it is the faithfulness of a lifetime.

Spiritual growth is not forged in the fire of emotional spikes but in the quiet rhythm of daily surrender. Anyone can feel close to God in a powerful moment, but maturity is built when you bow your heart in simple obedience day after day. God is not looking for occasional intensity; He is forming steady devotion. It is in the ordinary mornings, the whispered prayers, and the consistent return to His Word that roots grow deep and faith becomes unshakable. Small acts repeated become strongholds of character. A single choice to forgive, to serve, to speak truth, or to kneel again in prayer may seem insignificant but multiplied over time, those choices build a life anchored in Christ. Daily surrender trains the heart to trust, the mind to renew, and the will to obey. What feels small today becomes strength tomorrow. What feels routine becomes resilience. Do not despise the quiet disciplines; they are the bricks of a legacy that will stand long after emotions fade.

When a man chooses discipline, he is choosing to guard what God has entrusted to him. Discipline protects your marriage by teaching your eyes where to look and your heart where to rest. It protects your children by modeling consistency, patience, and strength under control. It protects your ministry by aligning your private life with your public calling. Integrity is preserved by boundaries. The fences you build around your life are declarations of value. You guard what you treasure. Boundaries are not prisons; they are preservation. A river without banks becomes a flood, but a river with structure brings life to everything it touches. Discipline gives direction to desire and strength to conviction. It keeps you steady when emotions rise and culture shifts. It is structure that sustains freedom, order that protects purpose, and restraint that releases power. When you embrace discipline, you are not limiting your life - you are securing it for generations to come.

A man who practices self-discipline does not bend with every emotion or react to every impulse because he has submitted his inner world to the leadership of the Spirit. In private he has wrestled his flesh, surrendered his pride, and crucified his impulses. What looks like restraint on the outside is actually freedom on the inside - freedom from being controlled by whatever he feels in the moment. He is steady in storms because he trained in calm seasons. When life was quiet, he built habits of prayer. When no one was watching, he strengthened his character. When there was no battle, he sharpened his sword. So when pressure comes, he does not panic. When winds rise, he does not drift. Self-discipline is the quiet forge where spiritual resilience is formed. It is the daily choosing of purpose over pleasure and calling over comfort. And in a world of instability, the disciplined man becomes grounded, trustworthy, and unwavering because the Spirit within him is stronger than the impulses around him.

Discipline is cultivation of the soul. God does not call men to discipline to diminish them, but to develop them. Discipline is submission to something higher than impulse, higher than emotion, higher than appetite. It is the daily decision to bow your will before purpose. When you master your appetites and choose consistency over intensity, you are training your spirit to lead your flesh, rather than letting your flesh lead your future. True strength is not loud, reckless, or uncontrolled. It is steady. It is governed. It is anchored. The world celebrates domination of others, but heaven honors dominion over self. The man who can conquer his temper and command his thoughts walks in a power that cannot be shaken. In that rising - quiet, disciplined, intentional - you prove that real authority begins within. And when you rule your own spirit, you become trustworthy with greater responsibility, because the strongest man is not the one who overpowers others, but the one who has learned to overcome himself.

| 8 |

"STRENGTH THROUGH SUFFERING"

Pain is one of life's greatest teachers. Though we often resist it and pray for its quick departure, pain carries a voice that comfort rarely possesses. When life is easy, the soul can drift into complacency, but pain interrupts our routines and awakens our awareness. It humbles our pride, strips away illusions, and forces us to confront the deeper realities of our hearts. In those difficult moments, God often uses pain as a classroom where faith is refined, character is strengthened, and dependence upon Him grows deeper. What comfort softly whispers, pain declares with unmistakable clarity. Through hardship we learn endurance, through loss we discover what truly matters, and through broken moments we encounter the healing presence of God. Pain reminds us that our strength is limited but God's grace is sufficient. When received with faith, even suffering becomes a teacher that leads us toward wisdom, humility, and a deeper walk with the One who can turn every trial into transformation.

Many of the deepest truths in life are not discovered in moments of comfort but in seasons of hardship. When life is easy, the soul often drifts into complacency. But when struggle comes, it awakens something deeper within us. Trials force us to slow down and to seek wisdom beyond our own understanding. In those difficult moments, God often speaks the loudest, shaping our character and refining our faith.

What comfort could never teach, adversity patiently reveals. Pain, though unwelcome, compels us to think, to reevaluate our priorities, and to grow in ways we never would have chosen on our own. In the classroom of life, pain teaches perseverance, humility, and dependence on God. While we may resist its lessons at first, those who endure hardship with faith discover that their struggle has produced strength and their trials have prepared them for a deeper purpose. In the end, what once seemed like suffering becomes a sacred tool in God's hands to shape a stronger and more faithful life.

Trials are not random disruptions in the believer's journey; they are instruments skillfully used by God to shape the soul. Just as gold must pass through fire to remove impurities, the human heart is refined through seasons of adversity. In moments of comfort we often coast, but in moments of struggle we awaken to deeper dependence on God. Pain has a way of stripping away illusions, exposing what truly matters, and drawing us closer to the One who sustains us. What may look like loss or destruction is often divine preparation taking place beneath the surface. God uses pressure to produce perseverance that builds strength of character and clarity of purpose. The very trials that feel like they are breaking us are often the same trials God uses to build us. In His hands, suffering becomes a shaping tool, forming courage, humility, and unshakable faith. When we trust Him in the fire, we discover that the heat was never meant to destroy us - it was meant to refine us for something greater.

In seasons of ease, it is easy for the heart to drift toward shallow ambitions and priorities that carry little eternal value. Yet when hardship arrives, it has a way of burning away what is unnecessary. Pain forces the soul to reevaluate what truly matters. In those difficult moments, the noise of the world grows quiet, and the deeper call of God becomes clearer. What once seemed important fades into the background, and purpose begins to stand out with greater clarity. Through hardship, God often sharpens our focus and redirects our steps toward eternal significance. Pain strips away the clutter that once clouded our vision and reveals the deeper reason we were created. It reminds us that life is not about comfort but about calling, not about convenience but about commitment. In the refining fire of struggle, character is strengthened, faith is deepened, and purpose is purified. When pain does its work, it leaves behind a life that is focused and more aligned with the purpose God has placed within us.

Many people discover their calling in the very place where they were once wounded. What once felt like devastation often becomes the birthplace of destiny. The wounds that once brought tears can become the very wells from which compassion flows. When a heart has known struggle, it learns to recognize the struggles of others. Through hardship, God awakens a deeper awareness, a stronger faith, and a calling that could never have been discovered in comfort alone. Pain, though difficult, often becomes the tool God uses to shape courage and ignite resolve within us. It pushes us into a life that carries eternal meaning. What once felt like loss can become the spark that fuels determination to help others rise, heal, and hope again. In the hands of God, nothing is wasted - not even the deepest wounds. The very places that once felt like endings can become the starting lines of a greater mission, where purpose is born, compassion is strengthened, and destiny begins to unfold.

Loss has a way of speaking truths that comfort and success often hide. When something dear is taken from us, the soul becomes quiet enough to hear the deeper lessons of life. In those sacred moments of sorrow, we begin to understand the true value of people, the fleeting nature of time, and the things that truly matter. Relationships become more precious, moments become more meaningful, and faith becomes more necessary than ever before. Loss removes the illusions that distract us and opens our eyes to the deeper purposes of God. The pain that accompanies loss often becomes the classroom where faith is strengthened and perspective is restored. Through sorrow we learn to lean more deeply upon God, to cherish the gifts He has placed in our lives, and to live with greater gratitude and intentionality. Though loss may wound the heart, it also refines the spirit, reminding us that while earthly things may pass away, the lessons God writes through our trials remain with us forever.

Loss has a way of bringing us to the end of ourselves. The confidence we once placed in our own strength, plans, and control suddenly feels fragile when grief or hardship enters the room. In those sacred and painful moments, we begin to see that human strength alone is not enough for the weight of life. God never wastes our sorrow; instead, He uses it to gently lead us into a deeper dependence on Him. What feels like weakness becomes the doorway to a stronger, more intimate walk with the Lord. When the heart is broken and the path forward seems uncertain, we discover that God's presence is not distant but nearer than ever. What begins as brokenness becomes an invitation to trust more deeply, pray more honestly, and lean more fully on the faithfulness of God. In His hands, even loss becomes a teacher, shaping our hearts to rely not on our own strength, but on the unshakable grace of the One who carries us through every storm.

Some of the strongest people in this world are not those who have lived without struggle, but those who have walked faithfully through the fires of suffering. Hardship has a way of revealing what truly lives inside a person. When storms rage and burdens grow heavy, faith becomes a lifeline. In those moments, endurance is formed, character is refined, and the soul learns to lean deeply upon God. The strength that emerges from suffering is steady, humble, and unshakable because it has been forged in the crucible of real trials. Those who endure hardship with faith carry a testimony that cannot be manufactured. Their scars become stories of God's sustaining grace. They have learned that pain can become a teacher, and that trials can become tools in the hands of a faithful God. What once threatened to break them becomes the very thing that builds them. Through suffering they discover a deeper resilience, a stronger trust, and a greater compassion for others who walk difficult paths.

When a person has walked through deep valleys, faced disappointment, or endured seasons of sorrow, something inside them changes. Their eyes become more sensitive to the silent struggles of others. Scripture reminds us that God "comforts us in all our troubles so that we can comfort those in any trouble with the comfort we ourselves receive from God." The very wounds that once caused tears can become instruments of healing in the hands of God. What once felt like a burden becomes a bridge that allows us to reach others with understanding rather than judgment. Those who have suffered carry a unique ability to shine light into dark places. Because they know what it feels like to be lost, discouraged, or overwhelmed, they can offer compassion that is genuine and sincere. Pain, when surrendered to God, enlarges the heart and deepens the well of mercy within us. It humbles the soul and teaches us how to walk gently with those who are hurting. In this way, our trials are never wasted.

When suffering is seen only as punishment or unfairness, the mind becomes trapped in frustration and bitterness. But God often uses the very things we wish to escape to shape the very character we need to grow. Just as gold is purified in the fire and steel is strengthened through pressure, the trials of life can refine faith, strengthen endurance, and produce wisdom that comfort never could. Pain, when placed in God's hands, becomes a sacred tool of transformation. Instead of crying out, "Why is this happening to me?" we begin to ask, "Lord, what are You forming in me through this?" In that moment, pain loses its power to poison the heart and instead becomes a classroom where God teaches perseverance, humility, and trust. What once felt like a setback becomes a setup for deeper faith and greater strength. Through the refining process, God is not shaping us into people who are stronger, wiser, and more prepared to fulfill the purpose He placed within us.

Hardship often feels like an unwanted interruption to the life we hoped to live, yet in God's hands it becomes a sacred classroom. The trials that stretch us are often the very moments that strengthen our faith, deepen our character, and refine our dependence on God. Scripture repeatedly shows that God forms His people through pressure - Joseph through betrayal, David through wilderness seasons, and Paul through persecution. What once looked like pain without purpose becomes evidence that God is shaping something stronger within us. When we learn to see hardship through the lens of purpose, suffering loses much of its power to discourage us. The struggle becomes part of the journey toward maturity, teaching patience, endurance, humility, and trust. Instead of asking, "Why is this happening?" we begin to ask, "What is God building in me through this?" In that moment, pain becomes bearable because it is no longer meaningless. It becomes a steppingstone rather than a stumbling block.

God often allows seasons of difficulty not as a sign of His absence, but as evidence of His workmanship in our lives. The trials we so quickly resist are often the very instruments God uses to shape our character and strengthen our faith. In those hard moments, He is developing us, teaching us to trust Him more deeply and to rely on His strength rather than our own. The virtues that define a strong and faithful life are rarely formed in comfort. Patience grows when waiting stretches longer than we hoped. Humility is learned when pride is stripped away. Perseverance is built when quitting seems easier than continuing. And faith becomes real when we must believe God even when circumstances feel uncertain. The furnace of adversity may feel intense, but it is in that refining fire that God forms men of depth, courage, and unshakable character. What feels like hardship today may be the very process God is using to prepare you for the strength, wisdom, and purpose He has destined for your life.

Scars tell a story. When the body is wounded, it does not simply surrender to the injury - it begins the remarkable process of healing.

What remains afterward is a scar, a visible reminder that pain once existed but restoration followed. In the same way, the spiritual scars we carry are not marks of defeat but evidence of God's healing work in our lives. The trials may have been painful, the battles difficult, and the seasons of hardship long, yet through it all God was quietly restoring, strengthening, and rebuilding what was once broken. Those spiritual scars become testimonies of grace. They remind us that what once wounded us no longer has the power to destroy us. Instead, God uses those very places to develop resilience, faith, and wisdom within us. Where there was once pain, there is now strength; where there was once struggle, there is now deeper trust in God. Your scars are not signs that life defeated you - they are proof that God healed you, carried you, and made you stronger than before.

When we surrender our pain to God, He begins a holy transformation within us. The wounds that once seemed only to bring sorrow become places where divine wisdom is formed. What once felt like loss becomes a classroom of grace where we learn patience, discernment, humility, and strength. Through His healing hand, the scars we carry are no longer reminders of defeat but testimonies of growth. In God's hands, pain becomes a teacher and suffering becomes a source of spiritual clarity. The very situations that once confused or hurt us now provide insight for the path ahead. God transforms our trials into instruction, allowing yesterday's pain to become today's wisdom. What once hurt us now helps us recognize danger, extend compassion to others, and walk more carefully in truth. In this way, pain becomes insight, and wounds become wisdom. Through God's redemptive power, even our hardest seasons can become the very tools He uses to shape us into wiser, stronger, and more faithful people.

Many of the wisest voices in history did not learn their lessons in comfort but in the classroom of suffering. Their words carry weight because they were forged in the fire of real life. They walked through valleys of heartbreak, faced opposition that tested their resolve, and endured trials that stripped away pride and illusion. Yet through those hard places, God shaped their character and deepened their understanding. Their experiences gave them authority, because they were not merely speaking theories - they were speaking truths they had survived. Those who have suffered and remained faithful often emerge with a clarity that cannot be taught in comfort. Their wounds become wells of insight, and their scars become testimonies of God's sustaining grace. What once seemed like a season meant to break them ultimately became a season that built them, proving that sometimes our greatest professor is the very pain we wished we could avoid.

Suffering is one of life's most powerful teachers, but only if we allow it to speak. Too often people try to escape hardship, numb it, or bury it, yet God often uses the very trials we wish to avoid to refine our character and strengthen our faith. When we bring our pain before the Lord instead of running from it, we discover that even our darkest moments can become sacred classrooms where the soul is shaped and faith is strengthened. Hardship can harden the heart or deepen the soul, and the difference is always found in our response. If we respond with bitterness, pain builds walls around us. But if we respond with faith, humility, and reflection, suffering becomes an instrument of transformation. What once felt like a burden becomes a blessing in disguise, because through it God is forming strength, wisdom, and spiritual maturity within us. When we refuse to waste our suffering, we allow God to turn our trials into testimonies and our wounds into wells of wisdom for others.

God never wastes pain in the life of a surrendered heart. What feels like loss, pressure, or confusion is often the very ground where God begins His deepest work. Just as gold is purified in fire, the believer is strengthened through seasons of hardship. What we endure with God becomes part of the testimony He is shaping in us - teaching patience, perseverance, and faith that cannot be shaken. Every hardship carries a lesson, and every valley holds the potential for transformation when we walk through it with the Lord. The pain we experience is never meaningless in His hands; it becomes the soil where wisdom grows and purpose takes root. In our darkest seasons, God is present, shaping, molding, and preparing us for what lies ahead. When we trust Him through suffering, what once felt like a breaking point often becomes a turning point, where our hearts are changed, our faith is deepened, and our lives begin to reflect His strength and grace more than ever before.

Pain may never feel pleasant, but it often becomes one of life's most powerful instructors. In the hands of God, what hurts us can also shape us. Scripture reminds us that trials test our faith and produce perseverance, and perseverance forms maturity. When we stop seeing pain only as an enemy and begin to recognize it as a teacher, our perspective changes. Hardships begin to carve strength into our character, deepen our dependence on God, and awaken a faith that comfort alone could never produce. What once felt like a burden can become the very tool heaven uses to refine our purpose. In the classroom of hardship, God often teaches the lessons that cannot be learned anywhere else. Pain humbles the heart, sharpens wisdom, and reveals what truly matters. Those who listen carefully during seasons of struggle often rise from them with a deeper understanding of grace, resilience, and calling. While the process may be difficult, the outcome can be life-changing.

| 9 |

"ANGER AND STRENGTH"

God placed powerful emotions inside men for a purpose. Among the strongest of these emotions is anger. Anger itself is not evil; it is a force placed within the human soul by a righteous Creator. Scripture even acknowledges this when it says, "Be angry, and do not sin." Anger is the internal alarm that sounds when injustice rises, when evil threatens what is good, or when something sacred is violated. It is the fire that awakens courage in a man's heart to protect, defend, and stand firm. Without it, men would remain passive in the face of darkness. But when it is surrendered to God, anger becomes a tool of righteousness - fuel that empowers a man to confront wrong, defend the weak, and pursue justice with conviction. God does not call men to extinguish their anger; He calls them to master it. Under the guidance of the Holy Spirit, anger is forged into disciplined strength. A godly man will allow God to shape it into a weapon for righteousness rather than a flame that consumes everything around him.

Many men have been taught that anger must be completely eliminated, as though the emotion itself were the problem. Sinful anger driven by pride, revenge, or uncontrolled emotion is the danger. But righteous anger is something entirely different. It is the God-given response of a heart that hates what is evil and refuses to tolerate injustice. When a man's anger is governed by wisdom and surrendered to God, it becomes a moral compass that alerts him when something sacred is being violated. Properly directed, righteous anger becomes a force for justice, courage, and protection. It is the fire that moves a man to defend the weak, confront evil, and stand firm when others shrink back. Jesus Himself displayed this kind of anger when He drove the money changers from the temple. Under the authority of the Holy Spirit, anger becomes a tool rather than a tyrant. Instead of destroying, it strengthens conviction, fuels courage, and empowers a man to rise up and fight for what is right.

Throughout Scripture we see anger used properly when it is governed by righteousness and aligned with God's purposes. When Jesus drove the money changers from the house of God, He was defending holiness, protecting worship, and confronting corruption. His response reminds us that anger, when surrendered to God, can become a force that stands against injustice and defends what is sacred. This teaches us an important spiritual principle: righteous anger is not about personal offense but about protecting God's honor and the well-being of others. When a man's heart is submitted to the Lord, even strong emotions can serve holy purposes. Instead of erupting in selfish rage, righteous anger becomes disciplined courage - the kind that speaks truth, confronts evil, and guards what matters most. When controlled by the Spirit, anger is no longer destructive fire; it becomes a refined flame that fuels conviction, justice, and bold obedience to God.

Anger can be a signal that something is wrong, that injustice has been done, or that a boundary has been crossed. But the problem arises when anger is left undisciplined and begins to rule the heart instead of being ruled by wisdom. Uncontrolled anger erupts in words that wound, decisions that fracture trust, and actions that leave behind a trail of regret. In a moment of fury, a man can destroy what it took years to build. The Bible compares a man without self-control to a city whose walls are broken down, a city open to attack and easily conquered. Walls represent strength, protection, and discipline. When anger controls a man, those protective walls collapse, leaving his character exposed and his influence weakened. But a wise man learns to master his spirit. He pauses before speaking, seeks understanding before reacting, and allows the peace of God to govern his heart. True strength is not found in explosive reactions but in controlled power.

Strength is a gift, but without discipline it becomes dangerous. A man may possess great ability, influence, and passion, yet if those forces are not governed by wisdom and self-control, they can tear down what they were meant to build. Scripture reminds us that "he that rules his spirit is better than he that taketh a city." True strength is not measured merely by what a man can conquer around him, but by what he can control within him. The strongest man is the one who can bridle his temper, guide his desires, and direct his power toward righteous purposes. Unrestrained power is predictable, impulsive, and easily manipulated. But a disciplined man becomes a formidable force for God's kingdom. When strength is harnessed by character and guided by the Spirit, it transforms from raw power into holy influence. Such a man does not merely react; he responds with wisdom, stands firm with patience, and uses his strength not to destroy but to protect, build, and lead.

Misused anger lashes out without restraint. It seeks to dominate rather than guide, intimidate rather than instruct, and punish rather than restore. When anger is driven by pride, wounded ego, or selfish desire, it becomes a destructive force that tears down what God intended to build. Words spoken in rage cut deeply, actions done in fury leave lasting scars, and relationships crumble under the weight of uncontrolled emotion. Scripture warns that "the anger of man does not produce the righteousness of God." When anger rules the heart, it blinds judgment and turns strength into a weapon that destroys lives instead of shaping them. Directed strength, however, is anger brought under the authority of wisdom and righteousness. It does not explode recklessly but stands firmly for what is right. This kind of strength seeks to protect the vulnerable, build what is broken, and correct what has gone astray. A mature man of God does not eliminate anger altogether - he disciplines it.

God did not design masculine strength to be reckless or destructive. He designed it to confront evil, protect the vulnerable, and stand firmly for what is right. True biblical manhood is not measured by how loudly a man shouts or how fiercely he lashes out, but by how wisely he directs the power God has placed within him. When anger is misdirected, it becomes a wildfire - burning through homes, wounding hearts, fracturing friendships, and damaging the testimony of the very faith a man claims to represent. The same fire that can destroy can also forge steel. A man filled with holy resolve learns to aim his strength at injustice, darkness, and the forces that seek to destroy what God has built. Instead of harming the innocent, he rises to defend them. Instead of tearing down relationships, he becomes a protector of peace and truth. In the hands of a man led by the Spirit, anger becomes a weapon against evil, a courage that stands firm for what is right, and a strength that reflects the heart of God.

The key is learning to channel that strength productively. Instead of exploding in rage, a wise man learns to convert that inner fire into action - discipline that shapes his habits, perseverance that pushes him through hardship, prayer that anchors his spirit, and courage that enables him to confront darkness without becoming part of it. When submitted to God, that powerful energy becomes a force for protection, leadership, and righteousness. The same intensity that could tear something down can also build something remarkable. A man who learns to govern his spirit becomes stronger than the man who simply unleashes his anger. He uses that fire to build families, strengthen communities, defend truth, and pursue the purposes God has placed in his heart. Instead of being ruled by emotion, he becomes a steward of strength. And when aggression is surrendered to the discipline of faith, it becomes a tool God uses to forge character, create impact, and leave a legacy.

Anger is not meant to erupt in reckless emotion or destructive behavior, but to awaken a man to what truly matters. When a man sees injustice, corruption, or evil threatening what God has entrusted to him, something within him should rise. That holy fire becomes fuel to protect his family, guard his integrity, and stand boldly for truth. In God's hands, anger is refined into courage, transforming raw emotion into disciplined resolve that refuses to bow to darkness. Righteous anger is not about losing control; it is about standing firm with conviction. It is the strength that compels a man to confront what is wrong and defend what is right, even when the cost is high. When guided by God's wisdom and restrained by His Spirit, anger strengthens a man's backbone, sharpens his sense of responsibility, and reminds him that silence in the face of evil is never the calling of a man of God. Properly submitted to the Lord, righteous anger becomes a catalyst for courage, integrity, and unwavering faith.

The Bible uses a powerful word to describe the balance between strength and humility: meekness. In our modern culture, meekness is often misunderstood as weakness, timidity, or a lack of courage. But biblical meekness is something far deeper and far stronger. It is the disciplined power of a heart submitted to God. A meek person is not powerless; rather, they possess the ability to act with force, authority, and conviction, yet choose to respond with wisdom, restraint, and righteousness. Jesus Himself described His own heart as "gentle and lowly," yet He carried the authority to calm storms, confront corruption, and carry the cross for the salvation of the world. True meekness does not diminish strength; it directs it toward God's purposes. Meekness teaches us when to stand firm and when to kneel, when to speak boldly and when to remain silent, when to fight and when to forgive. It is the calm confidence that comes from knowing our lives are surrendered to God's authority.

The meek are not weak; they are mastered by God rather than by impulse, pride, or anger. This is why Scripture declares that "the meek shall inherit the earth." Their strength is purposeful, steady, and guided by the hand of the Lord. In a world that celebrates loud power and uncontrolled ambition, meekness shines as the quiet strength of a life fully yielded to God. In ancient times the word "meek" was used to describe a powerful war horse that had been trained and disciplined for battle. The horse still possessed tremendous power, speed, and force, but it had learned to respond to the gentle touch of the rider. Its strength had not been diminished - it had been directed. In the same way, God does not remove the strength from a man's life when He calls him to meekness. Instead, He trains that strength, shaping it so that it moves at the command of His Spirit rather than the impulses of the flesh. This is the picture Jesus gives us when He says, "Blessed are the meek, for they shall inherit the earth."

Godly manhood is not measured by the amount of strength a man possesses, but by the way he governs it. Like a raging storm without direction, uncontrolled power harms more than it helps. But when a man submits his strength to the authority of God, discipline begins to shape his character. He learns patience, wisdom, and self-control. In that transformation, strength becomes a tool rather than a weapon. It becomes the quiet power that protects others, builds what is good, and stands firm when pressure rises. That is the picture of godly manhood - a man who has strength but has also mastered it. His power is not displayed through intimidation but through stability, humility, and consistency. People trust him because they know he will not misuse what he has been given. His words carry weight, his actions produce safety, and his presence brings confidence to those around him. This is the strength Christ forms in a man: strength that is governed by character, directed by wisdom, and surrendered to God.

God does not want to extinguish the fire within you - He wants to refine it. The passion, intensity, and strength that burn in your soul were placed there by Him for a purpose. Fire in its raw form can be destructive, but when it is controlled, it becomes powerful and useful. In the same way, God takes the reckless anger that once led to regret and shapes it into righteous courage that stands for truth. What once erupted in frustration can become a holy determination to defend what is right, protect what is sacred, and pursue what is good. Through the refining process, God transforms uncontrolled emotion into disciplined strength. Just as gold is purified in the furnace, the Lord allows pressure, challenges, and correction to shape the fire within you into something greater. He is teaching you how to harness your passion with wisdom, your strength with restraint, and your boldness with love. When the refining is complete, that same fire becomes a steady flame that lights the way for others to follow.

When a man surrenders his anger to God, something powerful begins to change within him. The fire that once drove reckless reactions becomes a disciplined strength directed by the Spirit. Instead of being controlled by emotion, he learns to stand steady in the moment. Where he once reacted impulsively, he now responds with wisdom. The same energy that once fueled frustration becomes courage, conviction, and clarity when it is placed into the hands of the One who refines the heart. Through this surrender, a man grows into a deeper strength. He learns patience without losing his boldness to stand for truth. He develops restraint without surrendering the courage to confront what is wrong. God teaches him that true power is not found in uncontrolled anger, but in Spirit-led authority. A man who walks this path becomes steady and strong - able to lead, protect, and speak truth with both firmness and grace. In God's hands, even a man's anger can be transformed into a force for righteousness.

This kind of man carries a strength that the world often fails to recognize. His power is not found in loud words, harsh reactions, or displays of dominance. Instead, it is rooted in the quiet confidence that comes from a life surrendered to God. While the world equates strength with noise, aggression, and control, the man shaped by God understands that true authority flows from character, discipline, and spiritual maturity. Like Jesus before His accusers, he does not need to shout to prove his strength, because he knows who he is and whose he is. When a man learns to master his spirit, he begins to walk in a power that cannot be shaken by circumstances or provoked by foolishness. This man's calm authority commands respect not because he demands it, but because it is evident in the way he lives. His words are measured, his actions are steady, and his presence brings stability where chaos once ruled. His strength becomes a testimony that real manhood is not proven by volume, but by victory over self.

True strength is not displayed in uncontrolled bursts of anger, but in the quiet authority of a man who has learned to govern his own spirit. It is revealed when a man feels the pressure, the frustration, and the temptation to lash out but instead chooses patience, wisdom, and restraint. That kind of control does not come from human effort alone; it is the fruit of a heart shaped by God. When a man masters his temper, he demonstrates a deeper victory than any outward conquest. He shows that his character is stronger than his impulses and that the Spirit of God governs his responses. Controlled strength reflects the character of Christ. In a world where anger is often celebrated and loud reactions are mistaken for power; the mature man stands apart. He proves that real masculinity is not about domination, but about disciplined authority. The strongest man in the room is often the one who has learned when to speak, when to stay silent, and how to remain steady when everyone else is losing control.

A man who learns to control his anger becomes a pillar of stability in a world often shaken by emotion and reaction. Strength is not proven by how loudly a man speaks or how fiercely he erupts, but by how firmly he governs his own spirit. When a man masters his temper, he creates an atmosphere of peace around him. His family senses security in his presence because they know his responses will be thoughtful rather than explosive. His home becomes a refuge rather than a battlefield, and his calm spirit anchors those who depend on him. Such a man carries quiet authority. His words are not dismissed as reckless reactions but respected as measured wisdom. Because he does not rule with intimidation, his leadership inspires confidence rather than fear. His children trust him, his wife leans on him, and those who follow his example learn that true strength is disciplined strength. By controlling his anger, a man reflects the character of Christ and becomes a stabilizing force in the world around him.

| 10 |

"ENDURING FAITH"

Faith is often imagined as something bright and triumphant - like a banner raised on a sunny day, waving proudly in calm skies. But the deepest, most enduring faith is not forged in comfort; it is formed in adversity. Enduring faith stands firm when prayers seem unanswered, when the path ahead is unclear, and when hope must be held with trembling hands. In those moments, faith becomes a quiet, determined trust that God remains present even in the storm. Such faith is not built on favorable conditions but on the unchanging character of God. When life shakes the foundations beneath our feet, enduring faith plants itself deeper in the promises of God. It refuses to surrender to fear or despair because it knows that storms do not last forever. The very winds meant to weaken us can instead strengthen our roots. And when the storm finally passes, the faith that endured it stands taller, steadier, and more radiant - proof that trust in God can withstand even the fiercest trials.

Many people believe easily when life is calm and blessings are obvious. Gratitude flows, confidence rises, and it is easy to declare that God is good when everything around us seems to confirm it. Yet faith that only lives in seasons of abundance has never been fully tested. The true measure of faith is not revealed when the sun is shining, but when the clouds gather and the path forward becomes unclear. The real test of faith comes when prayers seem to go unanswered and heaven feels silent. In those moments, faith must sink its roots deeper than what the eyes can see. It is there, in the stillness and uncertainty, that faith learns to trust not just in what God does, but in who He is. Silence does not mean absence, and delay does not mean denial. Sometimes God allows the quiet so our faith will grow stronger, steadier, and unshakable so that when the answer finally comes, we will know that our trust was never in the outcome, but in the faithfulness of the One who hears every prayer.

Unanswered prayers can challenge the heart in profound ways. We ask God for help, healing, direction, or deliverance, and sometimes the answer does not come when we expect it. The silence can feel heavy, and the waiting can test the deepest parts of our faith. Yet the silence of God is not the absence of God. Often it is an invitation to trust Him beyond what we can see. In those quiet seasons, God is still working beneath the surface shaping our character, strengthening our patience, and teaching us to lean on His wisdom rather than our own understanding. Faith that only survives when answers come quickly is fragile, but faith that endures through silence becomes unshakable. When heaven seems quiet, it is an opportunity to draw closer, to pray more sincerely, and to trust more deeply. What feels like delay to us is often preparation in His hands. So do not lose heart in the waiting. The God who hears every prayer is also the God who knows the perfect moment to respond.

Enduring faith trusts God both in the sunshine of visible blessings and in the hidden moments when nothing seems to be changing. It understands that God's work is not limited to what our eyes can see or what our hands can touch. Just as a seed is buried beneath the soil, unseen and silent while its roots stretch and its life begins to form, so God often works beneath the surface of our circumstances. Faith believes that what cannot yet be seen is still being prepared by the hand of God. Enduring faith stands firm in the storm, confident that God is cultivating something greater than the present moment reveals. While we wait, God is aligning circumstances, strengthening our character, and preparing the breakthrough that will eventually rise into view. The man who understands this does not lose heart during the hidden season, because he knows that God never abandons a promise once it has been planted. In time, what was once buried will rise and the quiet work of God will bloom into undeniable testimony.

Faith that pleases God is not dependent on what the eyes can see or what the hands can touch. Scripture declares that faith is "the substance of things hoped for, the evidence of things not seen." This means faith stands on something deeper than visible proof - it stands on the unchanging character of God. When answers are not yet visible, faith remembers who God is. He is faithful and true to His promises. Because His nature does not change, the believer can stand firm even when the path ahead is hidden. True faith learns to trust God's integrity more than the evidence of the moment. Even when the situation looks barren, faith knows that God is still at work behind the scenes, preparing what He has promised. The faithful heart rests in the assurance that God's reliability is greater than any temporary uncertainty. When faith is anchored in the character of God, it remains steady through every storm, confident that what is unseen today will one day be revealed by the hand of a faithful God.

Standing when heaven seems silent requires spiritual endurance. It is the quiet courage to keep believing when answers do not come quickly and when prayers seem to echo back without response. In these moments, faith is no longer supported by visible evidence but by a deep conviction that God is still present and still working behind the scenes. The silence of heaven does not mean the absence of God; often it is the classroom where patience is formed and trust is refined. Those who refuse to abandon their belief during these seasons demonstrate a loyalty to God that is not dependent on immediate understanding. Silence can test the limits of patience, but it also strengthens perseverance in ways that constant reassurance never could. When a believer continues to stand firm despite uncertainty, their faith grows deeper, stronger, and more resilient. The person who remains faithful in the silence develops a spiritual foundation that cannot easily be shaken by hardship or doubt.

Consider the farmer who plants a field. After the seeds are buried in the soil, the land appears quiet and unchanged. Days may pass without any visible sign that anything is happening. Yet beneath the surface, life is already at work. Roots are quietly stretching through the earth. Tiny shoots are forming where no eye can see. The farmer understands that growth does not begin when the plant breaks through the soil - it begins long before that moment, in the hidden places where God designed life to develop. Faith works in much the same way. There are seasons when prayers seem unanswered and progress appears invisible, but beneath the surface God is still working. Character is being formed, strength is being developed, and the foundations of something greater are quietly taking shape. What appears dormant may actually be developing. Just as the seed must first grow unseen before it can rise above the ground, so faith often grows strongest in the hidden seasons of waiting.

Enduring faith also learns to trust beyond emotion. Feelings rise and fall like the tide. One day we may feel confident and hopeful; another day we may feel uncertain or discouraged. Genuine faith is anchored in something far more stable than feelings - it is anchored in the unchanging character of God. When emotions fluctuate, faith remembers that God does not. His promises remain steady when our hearts feel restless, and His truth stands firm when our thoughts feel uncertain. Enduring faith learns to stand on the Word of God rather than the waves of emotion. This kind of faith does not deny feelings, but it refuses to be ruled by them. It chooses trust when emotions are quiet and when they are loud. It believes God in the sunshine and in the storm. When discouragement whispers that hope is fading, enduring faith answers with confidence that God is still at work. It presses forward not because everything feels certain, but because the One we trust is faithful.

Genuine faith is not built upon the shifting sands of emotion but upon the unchanging foundation of God's Word. Feelings rise and fall like the tides - strong one moment and uncertain the next - but the promises of God remain steady and immovable. When circumstances shake the heart and emotions become unreliable, faith reaches deeper. It anchors itself to the truth of what God has spoken. Faith remembers that God is faithful to His Word, even when our emotions struggle to keep up with that reality. In this way, faith is the choice to trust God when the heart feels uncertain, the choice to believe His promises when the mind is filled with questions. As we continue to stand upon what God has said, something powerful begins to happen - our emotions slowly come into alignment with our faith. What began as a deliberate act of trust becomes a confident assurance in the soul. And through that process, faith grows stronger, steadier, and more deeply rooted in the truth of God Himself.

There will be seasons in every man's life when the heart feels dry, when enthusiasm fades, and when the excitement of spiritual experience seems far away. Faith, however, was never meant to be sustained by emotion alone. Enduring faith is built on something deeper than feelings - it rests on trust in the unchanging character of God. In those quiet and difficult seasons, when prayers feel routine and spiritual fire seems dim, the mature man does not abandon the path. Instead, he continues walking forward, confident that God has not moved even when His presence feels less tangible. These seasons are not signs of failure; they are often the very places where faith grows strongest. Just as roots grow deeper in dry soil searching for water, the soul learns to rely more fully on God when feelings no longer carry it. Enduring faith presses on through the drought, believing that the same God who was present in the mountaintop moments is still faithfully working in the valleys.

A tree that grows deep roots can withstand powerful winds because its strength is not merely in what is seen above the ground, but in what is hidden beneath it. In the same way, the strength of a man is not measured by outward appearances but by the depth of their trust in God. When life's winds begin to blow those who have rooted their faith in the truth of God's Word remain standing. They are not easily shaken because their confidence is anchored in the unchanging character of God rather than the shifting circumstances of life. Faith that is cultivated through prayer, obedience, and a steady commitment to God grows deeper with every challenge faced. Storms may bend the man of God, but they cannot break the one whose life is grounded in the promises of God. In fact, the very storms that threaten to destroy faith often become the tools God uses to strengthen it - driving the roots even deeper into His truth, His presence, and His everlasting faithfulness.

Rooted faith develops slowly and deliberately as a man walks with God day by day. Just as a tree extends its roots deeper into the soil over time, faith grows deeper through consistent prayer, meditation on scripture, and a heart that chooses obedience even when the path is difficult. These spiritual disciplines anchor the soul in truth and strengthen the believer's connection to God. The more a man abides in God's presence and Word, the more stable and grounded his faith becomes. Seasons of testing are also part of the process that deepens faith. Trials press men to trust God beyond what they can see or understand. Each challenge faced with confidence in God's promises becomes another root pushing deeper into the foundation of faith. Over time, these experiences build spiritual resilience and unwavering trust. What once felt like a storm meant to uproot faith instead becomes the very thing that strengthens it, producing a life that stands firm, steady, and unshaken in God.

Trials deepen faith in ways comfort never could. When hardship arrives - when prayers seem unanswered, when strength feels insufficient, and when the path forward is unclear - men are drawn closer to God in a way comfort never demanded. In those moments of weakness, dependence on Him grows stronger. What once felt like a burden becomes an invitation to trust more deeply, pray more sincerely, and seek God with a greater hunger of heart. The very storm that once threatened to destroy faith often becomes the storm that strengthens it. Just as a tree grows stronger roots when battered by wind, a believer grows stronger faith when pressed by trials. Difficult seasons strip away self-reliance and reveal the steady faithfulness of God. What seemed like a breaking point becomes a turning point. In the end, the trial that looked like an enemy becomes a teacher proving that faith refined through hardship is stronger, deeper, and far more enduring than faith that has never been tested.

Enduring faith learns to wait. Waiting is one of the most difficult spiritual disciplines because it requires us to surrender control and trust in what we cannot yet see. In a world driven by speed, instant answers, and immediate gratification, the soul must learn a slower rhythm - the rhythm of God's timing. When God asks us to wait, He is not withholding goodness; He is preparing us for it. Waiting stretches our faith, deepens our dependence on Him, and reminds us that His plans unfold with wisdom far greater than our own hurried expectations. During seasons of waiting, faith becomes anchored rather than anxious. The heart learns to rest in the certainty that what feels like delay is often divine preparation. Roots grow deeper before branches reach higher. When we trust God's timing, patience becomes strength and hope becomes steady. Enduring faith does not panic in the storm of uncertainty - it stands firm, knowing that the God who began the work will complete it in His perfect time.

Waiting seasons often feel quiet, uncertain, and even discouraging. Yet in those moments, wisdom calls us to look back and remember the ways God has already proven Himself faithful. The same God who opened doors before, who carried you through trials, and who answered prayers you once thought impossible is still working today. Reflection becomes a powerful spiritual discipline, because when we rehearse the goodness of God, we remind our hearts that His character never changes. What He has done before becomes evidence of what He is able to do again. When believers pause to recall past victories, unexpected provisions, and moments of divine guidance, faith begins to rise again. Yesterday's testimonies become today's strength. The memory of God's faithfulness builds courage to trust Him in the present, even when the outcome is still unseen. Waiting is no longer empty when it is filled with remembrance. As you reflect on the goodness of God, your confidence grows that the same faithful hand that led you before will lead you through this season as well.

Enduring faith refuses to let disappointment redefine what we believe about God. There are moments when life unfolds in ways we did not expect, prayers seem unanswered, and the outcome does not resemble the picture we held in our hearts. Yet mature faith understands that just because something did not happen the way we imagined does not mean God has abandoned His purpose. Faith stands firm in the storm of unmet expectations and declares that God is still good, still faithful, and still working behind the scenes even when we cannot yet see the outcome. God sees the full landscape of our lives while we see only a small portion of the road ahead. In His wisdom, He may be strengthening our character, aligning circumstances, or preparing a greater blessing than we first envisioned. Enduring faith trusts that God's timing is never accidental and His plans are always purposeful, reminding us that the God who began a good work will complete it in His perfect time.

The man with enduring faith learns to stand firm when the skies darken and the winds of uncertainty begin to blow. Instead of demanding answers from every storm, he anchors his heart in the character of God. In moments when circumstances seem confusing, faith refuses to collapse. Instead, it steadies itself on the unchanging promises of God. This declaration transforms the heart. It shifts faith from fragile hope to resilient conviction. When a man of God chooses trust over explanation, something powerful happens inside him - fear loses its grip, peace begins to grow, and endurance takes root in the soul. Faith that once depended on favorable outcomes now rests in the faithfulness of God Himself. Such faith becomes enduring, able to handle the storms of disappointment, delay, and difficulty. And in the process, the man discovers a deeper strength: the quiet assurance that even when the path is unclear, the One who leads the journey is perfectly trustworthy.

Standing firm in difficult seasons becomes a testimony that words alone could never communicate. Anyone can praise God when the skies are clear and the path is easy, but true faith reveals itself when the winds rise and the storms refuse to pass. When a man continues to trust God through hardship - when he remains faithful in uncertainty and refuses to abandon hope - it reveals a strength that cannot be explained by circumstances alone. It shows that his confidence is built on the unchanging character of God. This kind of enduring faith becomes a living witness to everyone watching. People notice when a man remains steady while everything around him shakes. They see the perseverance that outlasts pressure and the quiet confidence that God is still in control. In a world that easily collapses under difficulty, steadfast faith shines like a beacon in the darkness. Your endurance may be the very evidence someone else needs to believe that God is real, faithful, and worthy of trust in every season of life.

Enduring faith is built upon a steadfast trust in the character of God. It reminds us that we do not walk alone through uncertainty. It calls us to lean on the wisdom and faithfulness of the One who sees the beginning and the end. When circumstances confuse us and explanations fail, trust becomes the bridge that carries us forward. Our confidence is not in our ability to understand every detail, but in God's ability to guide every step. Ultimately, enduring faith is not about perfect certainty - it is about unwavering trust in a perfect God. Faith does not demand that we solve every mystery or foresee every outcome. Instead, it invites us to rest in the assurance that God's purposes are greater than our perspective and His plans are wiser than our reasoning. Even when the path ahead is unclear, faith holds firmly to the truth that God remains faithful. In that trust, the heart finds peace, the soul finds strength, and the journey continues with quiet confidence in the One who already knows the way.

Storms are inevitable in every life. There will be moments when the winds rise, the skies darken, and the voice of God seems distant, yet these moments are opportunities for faith to grow stronger. Just as a tree develops deeper roots when battered by storms, the soul that clings to God in difficulty becomes firmly grounded in His promises. Faith that depends only on favorable circumstances is fragile, but faith anchored in the unchanging character of God becomes unshakable. Enduring faith is the kind that trusts God when silence fills the air. It believes that the same God who calms the storm is also working within it. When faith is rooted deeply in God's truth, no storm can uproot it. The winds may rage and the rain may fall, but the man who trusts beyond feelings and holds firmly to God's promises will still be standing when the clouds finally clear. Such faith does not merely survive the storm - it emerges stronger, proving that what is planted in God will endure every season.

| 11 |

"MORAL COURAGE"

Character is not truly revealed in moments of comfort; it is revealed in moments of pressure. When life is calm and the road is smooth, almost anyone can appear strong, confident, and unshaken. But the real measure of a person is discovered when the winds rise and the path grows difficult. It is in the storms of life that the true backbone of a man is exposed. Pressure does not create character as much as it reveals what was already living within the heart. Moral courage is the strength that refuses to bend when compromise would be easier. It is the resolve to stand for what is right even when no one is watching. A man of true character does not shift with the winds of culture or surrender to the convenience of the moment. Instead, he anchors his life in truth, conviction, and faith in God. And when the pressure comes - and it will - those who have built their lives upon righteousness will stand firm, proving that real strength is not found in comfort, but in unwavering obedience to what is right.

There comes a time when a man must decide whether his life will be governed by principle or convenience. Anyone can speak courageously when the room is quiet and the cost is low. But when opposition rises, when standing firm means standing alone, the true foundation of a person's life is revealed. Pressure has a way of exposing what is real. It reveals whether conviction is deeply rooted in the heart or merely resting on the surface of the lips. God often allows these moments because tested conviction becomes proven character. A faith that has never been challenged remains fragile, but faith that endures pressure becomes unshakable. When you stand firm in the face of difficulty - obedience over approval and righteousness over ease - you strengthen the backbone of your soul. In those moments, God forges courage within you. The test is not meant to break you; it is meant to prove that the principles guiding your life are strong enough to carry you through any storm.

Integrity begins in the unseen places of life. The true test of a person's character is revealed when no one else is in the room. Integrity is not built on public performance; it is forged in private decisions. It is the quiet commitment to honor God when no one would know if you didn't. A man of integrity understands that while the world may not see every action, God sees the heart. The life that is faithful in secret becomes powerful in the open. Every unseen choice for truth strengthens the soul and shapes the kind of person God can trust with greater responsibility. Integrity is the foundation upon which lasting character is built. It produces confidence before God, peace within the heart, and credibility before others. When a man consistently chooses what is right in the quiet places of life, he becomes unshakable in the public ones. For the man who walks with integrity does not live for applause - he lives to please the One who sees all things and rewards faithfulness in due time.

Long before character is revealed in front of others, it is quietly formed in the hidden places of the heart. The choices a man makes when no one is watching are the building blocks of the life he will eventually display to the world. What you repeatedly practice in secret becomes the natural expression of who you are in the open. A life of righteousness begins in the silent decisions of everyday moments where faithfulness is chosen simply because it honors God. A man who consistently chooses honesty is forging a moral backbone that cannot easily be broken when pressure comes. Trials, temptation, and public scrutiny reveal what private discipline has already built. When integrity has been practiced in the unseen places, courage and conviction will stand firm in the visible ones. God shapes strong men in hidden seasons so they can stand with strength in public moments. Guard your private life well, for the character you cultivate today will become the testimony the world sees tomorrow.

Integrity when no one sees is one of the greatest tests of character because it reveals the truth about who we really are. True character is not built in public but in private. It is formed in the silent decisions where doing right costs something and doing wrong appears easy. A man of integrity chooses righteousness not because it is noticed, but because it is right. He understands that the unseen moments of life are the very places where the foundation of his character is laid. God measures integrity by what happens in the hidden places of the heart. When no praise will follow and no consequence seems likely, the decision to walk in truth becomes an act of devotion. Those who pass this test develop an inner foundation that cannot easily be shaken. Their lives are anchored not in reputation, but in conviction. The man who stands firm in private will stand strong in public, because the character forged in secrecy becomes the pillar that supports a life of honor before God and men.

Convictions must always be stronger than convenience. Convenience whispers softly, promising an easier road if we bend just a little, overlook just a little, or delay obedience for a more comfortable moment. It tells us that compromise is harmless and that no one will notice. Yet the voice of conviction speaks from a deeper place within the soul. It reminds us that truth is not measured by comfort, and righteousness is not guided by what feels easiest. The path of integrity is often steeper, but it is the path that leads to strength, stability, and peace with God. The danger of convenience is that it erodes the foundation of our character one small compromise at a time. What begins as a minor surrender of principle slowly weakens the structure of our lives until the foundation itself begins to crack. But when men stand firmly on conviction, they build their life on solid ground. The storms of life will come, but a life anchored in conviction will stand strong, because it is built not on what is easy, but on what is right.

When men choose convenience over conviction, they slowly erode their own respect for themselves. Compromise whispers that it is easier to bend than to stand, easier to avoid conflict than to uphold truth. But each time a man surrenders conviction for comfort, something inside begins to weaken. Character is built on the decisions we make when the easy path and the right path stand before us. The more we choose convenience, the more we chip away at the foundation of our own integrity. But when someone stands firm in their convictions, they grow stronger within. Every difficult stand strengthens the backbone of the soul. It forms courage, deepens integrity, and builds a quiet confidence that cannot be shaken by circumstance. A man who honors conviction over convenience develops a character that is steady, trustworthy, and resilient. In the end, the temporary discomfort of standing firm produces a lasting strength that shapes a life of honor before both God and man.

The world often applauds the easy path. It praises flexibility when flexibility really means bending truth, lowering standards, or quietly surrendering convictions. Culture often suggests that the easiest route is the smartest route but the voice of God within the heart reminds us that not every open door should be entered and not every shortcut leads to a place worth going. The easy road may offer temporary comfort, but it often leaves a trail of weakened character and quiet regret. Men of true character understand that some lines must never be crossed. They know that integrity is built by the choices made when compromise would be convenient. Even when the harder path demands sacrifice, patience, or standing alone, they choose it because they value truth more than approval and obedience more than comfort. In the end, character forged through conviction becomes a foundation that cannot be shaken, and those who refuse the shortcut often discover that the harder road leads to a far greater destination.

Throughout history, those who chose to stand for what is right often discovered that conviction carries a cost. Speaking truth may cost popularity, because the crowd usually prefers comfort over correction. It may cost opportunities, because integrity sometimes closes doors that compromise would easily open. The price attached to truth is not punishment - it is proof that what you are standing for is precious and powerful. Many people recognize the truth when they see it but hesitate to embrace it because they fear what it will require of them. Truth asks a person to choose what is right over what is easy. But those who dare to stand firm discover something greater than approval - they gain strength of character, clarity of purpose, and the quiet confidence that comes from living with integrity before God. In the end, the cost of truth may be high, but the cost of abandoning it is far greater. A life built on truth may face resistance, but it will always stand on a foundation that cannot be shaken.

When a person chooses to stand firmly on what is right, their life becomes anchored to something deeper than circumstance or opinion. The winds of pressure, criticism, or opposition may rise, but a heart grounded in truth does not drift with every changing current. Like a tree planted beside living water, their roots run deep. Storms may shake the branches, but they cannot uproot the foundation. Truth steadies the soul and gives a man the courage to remain faithful when others bend to convenience. That kind of stability becomes a quiet but powerful witness to everyone watching. In a world where many shift with the culture, the person who stands on truth becomes someone others can lean on when confusion surrounds them. Their conviction strengthens the weak, encourages the weary, and reminds others that righteousness is still worth defending. By refusing to compromise, they become a pillar of strength for their family, their community, and the generation that follows.

History is filled with men who chose truth over comfort and conviction over convenience. They understood that standing for what is right often carries a cost, yet they refused to silence their conscience in exchange for an easier path. Their courage was not loud or boastful; it was steady, unwavering, and rooted in the belief that truth is worth defending. Because they stood firm when it mattered most, their lives became a beacon for others who were searching for the strength to do the same. Their bravery reminds us that the choices we make today echo far beyond our own lives. Every act of integrity plants seeds that future generations may one day harvest. When a person refuses to compromise their values, they create a path of freedom and clarity for those who follow. The courage of one faithful heart can shift the direction of many lives. So stand firm in truth, even when it costs you something because the backbone you show today may become the blessing someone else depends on tomorrow.

The desire to be liked, accepted, and praised can quietly influence the choices we make, often without us even realizing it. When the applause of people becomes the standard by which we measure our success, we begin to compromise small pieces of our character to maintain it. Truth may be softened, convictions may be silenced, and the courage to stand firm may slowly fade. In those moments, integrity is often the first thing sacrificed on the altar of acceptance. But a life anchored in God is not built on the shifting opinions of people. True strength comes from seeking the approval of the One who sees the heart and honors faithfulness over popularity. When you choose integrity over applause, you may lose temporary praise, but we gain something far greater - God's favor, inner peace, and unshakable character. Approval from people fades quickly, but a life lived with conviction before God builds a legacy that stands long after the voices of the crowd have grown silent.

Approval from people is one of the most fragile foundations a life can be built upon. The voices that celebrate you today may question you tomorrow, and the applause of the crowd can fade as quickly as it appeared. When a man measures his worth by the opinions of others, his identity rises and falls with every compliment and every criticism. Like a house built on shifting sand, a life anchored in human approval cannot stand firm when the winds of disappointment and rejection begin to blow. The opinions of people change, but the purpose God places within a man remains steady and true. Instead of chasing the unstable praise of the crowd, anchor your life in the unchanging approval of God. When your heart is fixed on pleasing Him, you gain a stability that the world cannot shake. Your direction will be guided by the quiet conviction of God's calling on your life. A man who lives for God's approval builds his life upon solid rock and is able to stand strong no matter how the winds of public opinion may shift.

Long-term respect is built through the quiet strength of consistent character. People recognize the difference between someone who bends with the wind and someone who stands firm on principle. Integrity has a way of revealing itself through steady actions, faithful decisions, and a life that remains anchored to what is right, even when the cost is high. While opinions may differ and voices may disagree, moral courage earns a deeper form of honor. When a person consistently chooses truth over convenience, righteousness over compromise, and faithfulness over popularity, respect begins to grow slowly but powerfully. Integrity becomes a testimony louder than words. It shows that character is not situational but foundational. In a world where many chase approval, the one who stands firm in truth reflects the strength of a life built on God's principles, and that kind of respect endures far beyond the shifting opinions of the moment.

When a man consistently chooses principle over popularity, something powerful begins to form within him. Integrity becomes the quiet foundation of his life. Over time, people begin to recognize that this person cannot easily be swayed by pressure, trends, or the opinions of the crowd. Their life becomes a testimony that truth matters more than approval. In a world where many bend to fit the moment, a man who stands firm becomes a steady voice that others instinctively respect. Eventually, their words begin to carry weight because their life supports their message. When they speak about courage, people see courage in the way they live. When they speak about faith, others have already witnessed their trust in God through difficult seasons. Their backbone becomes visible through quiet, unwavering strength. This kind of character reflects the heart of God who calls His people to stand firm in truth. And when a life is built on principle, it becomes a lighthouse in a culture often lost in the fog of popularity.

Life has a way of revealing what lies beneath the surface. When everything is comfortable, conviction is easy. But when opposition rises, when voices criticize, and when the cost of doing right becomes clear, character is tested. In those moments, a person must decide whether they will bend with the shifting winds of approval or stand firmly on the unchanging ground of truth. To stand with courage is not to be loud or defiant, but to be rooted deeply in what is right before God. Like a tree planted by living water, a person with spiritual backbone may sway in the storm, but they do not break. Their strength comes from knowing who they serve and why they stand. When pressure comes the faithful do not abandon their convictions for comfort. Instead, they rise with quiet confidence, knowing that the same God who calls them to stand also gives them the strength to remain standing. In the end, moral courage is not about winning approval from people, but about being faithful to the One who sees the heart.

Moral courage is not the absence of fear - it is the mastery of it. Every person faces moments when doing the right thing feels risky, uncomfortable, or costly. Fear whispers that it would be easier to remain silent, to look the other way, or to compromise what we know is true. Yet moral courage rises above that voice. It recognizes the fear, but it refuses to bow to it. Instead, it anchors itself in conviction, choosing integrity over convenience and truth over temporary safety. In those moments, courage becomes the quiet but powerful decision to stand firm when everything inside you is tempted to step back. True courage is measured not by how fearless a person appears, but by their willingness to act rightly despite the fear they feel. When a person chooses honesty over deception, justice over comfort, and faithfulness over popularity, they demonstrate a strength that shapes character and influences others. Each courageous decision strengthens the soul and builds a life of integrity.

Integrity is not merely a moral decision; it is a spiritual force that anchors the heart and steadies the mind. Each moment of courage plants deeper roots within the character of a man. Over time, those roots produce a quiet but unshakable confidence. A man who refuses to bend under pressure begins to realize that strength does not come from approval, popularity, or comfort - it comes from standing firmly in truth. With every decision to hold the line, spiritual strength increases. What once felt difficult becomes natural, and what once felt risky becomes a source of boldness. God shapes the backbone of a person through these moments of testing. Integrity becomes the steel that reinforces the soul, giving a man the courage to walk faithfully even when the path is lonely. The more a person practices unwavering conviction, the more their life reflects stability, authority, and spiritual maturity. In the end, having moral courage does more than prove character - it builds a life that cannot easily be shaken.

Character under pressure is not about pleasing the crowd, chasing applause, or bending to the expectations of the moment. It is about standing firmly on truth even when it would be easier to compromise. A man of character understands that integrity is not built in comfort but forged in the fires of testing. The man who chooses righteousness over convenience becomes stronger, deeper, and more grounded in who God has called him to be. In the end, true strength is not measured by popularity or temporary success but by the unwavering courage to live by conviction. The man who anchors his life in truth and integrity may face storms, criticism, and pressure from every side, yet he will not be broken. Instead, every trial becomes another stone laid in the foundation of his character. Such a life reflects the power of moral courage - a strength that stands firm. When the winds of pressure finally pass, what remains is a life that shines with authenticity, honor, and the unshakeable dignity of a soul that refused to bow.

| 12 |

"SPIRITUAL LEADERSHIP"

God never intended men to drift through life without direction. From the very beginning, He created man with purpose, calling him to rise with courage, conviction, and faith. A man who walks with God recognizes that life is not accidental - it is a divine assignment. Each day presents opportunities to stand firm in truth, to make decisions guided by wisdom, and to live in a way that honors the One who gave him life. Leadership in God's kingdom is not measured by power or control, but by faithfulness, humility, and the willingness to serve others with strength and integrity. A godly man understands that his words shape hearts, his choices set examples, and his character leaves a legacy. Because of this, he refuses to live passively or without direction. Instead, he seeks God's guidance, walks in obedience, and leads with a steady hand and a faithful heart. When a man commits his life to God's purpose, he becomes a living testimony that true leadership begins with surrender to God.

Passive men create chaos because when a man refuses to lead, he does not create peace; he creates a vacuum. In the home, that vacuum invites confusion. In the church, it invites weakness. In society, it invites instability. When godly men remain silent or inactive, other voices rush in to fill the space. Competing opinions, shifting values, and disorder begin to replace the steady influence that God intended a man to provide. Passivity may seem harmless, but its absence of direction quietly opens the door for chaos. God created men to provide spiritual direction, not through domination, but through responsibility. A man who walks with God understands that his presence sets a tone and his convictions create stability. The call of a godly man is not to lead his home with wisdom, to strengthen the church with courage, and to influence the world with righteousness. When men step into the role God gave them, the vacuum disappears and peace, clarity, and strength take its place.

The call of God has always been for men to rise, to stand firm, and to lead with humility, strength, and faith. History repeatedly shows the consequences of passive leadership. When men who are called to lead choose silence instead of courage, the void is quickly filled by confusion, disorder, and compromise. Families begin to fracture because no one is standing guard over the values that once held them together. Spiritual priorities slowly fade into the background when no one is willing to champion them. Leadership was never meant to be passive. God designed men to be watchmen over their homes and shepherds of the spiritual direction of their families. When that responsibility is neglected, the erosion may be slow at first, but over time the foundations weaken, and the consequences become painfully clear. Silence in moments of responsibility is not neutrality - it is surrender. Every moment that truth goes unspoken and every time conviction is withheld, something valuable is lost.

Leadership is often misunderstood as the ability to have all the answers, but true leadership begins with the courage to take a step when others remain still. A godly leader moves forward with conviction, trusting that God will guide his steps along the way. When a man is willing to stand up for what is right, even when the path is uncertain, he becomes a beacon for others who are searching for direction and strength. Real leadership is also a declaration of spiritual resolve. It is the bold decision to say, "As for me and my house, we will serve the Lord," even when the surrounding culture pulls in the opposite direction. In a world that often pressures people to compromise truth for comfort, a godly leader draws a line of conviction and stands firm upon it. His courage gives others permission to stand as well. When a man anchors his home, his character, and his decisions in devotion to God, he does more than lead - he establishes a legacy of faith that can guide generations.

A spiritual leader understands that leadership begins at home. Before a man ever stands before a crowd, speaks from a platform, or carries influence in the public eye, he must first lead within the walls of his own house. The home is the proving ground of character. It is there that faith is lived out in daily decisions, patience is practiced in ordinary moments, and devotion to God is demonstrated through consistent example. True spiritual leadership is established by the way a man loves, serves, protects, and guides those closest to him. When a man faithfully leads his household with wisdom and grace, he builds a foundation that cannot easily be shaken. From that strong foundation, his influence can extend outward into the church, the community, and the world. But if leadership is neglected at home, all other leadership becomes hollow. The man who learns to lead his family with courage, love, and godly conviction becomes the kind of leader God can trust with greater responsibility.

Leading your home spiritually does not require perfection. A man does not have to know every answer or have every weakness conquered before he can lead his family toward God. Spiritual leadership begins with a humble heart that is willing to place God first in the home. It is the father who opens the Word of God at the kitchen table and speaks about faith in everyday moments. When a man points his household toward the truth of scripture, he establishes a foundation that is stronger than circumstance and deeper than emotion. Spiritual leadership is praying over your family when they are hurting, thanking God together when He provides, and setting a visible example of faith that others can follow. Your children may not remember every sermon they hear, but they will remember the example they see. When a man establishes a standard of faith in his home, he creates an atmosphere where God is honored, love is strengthened, and character is shaped.

Children watch far more than they listen. When children see a father pray, walk in honesty, show kindness, and stand firm in conviction, they begin to understand what faith looks like in action. In many ways, a father becomes the first picture of authority and character that a child carries in their heart. If that picture reflects love, strength, and reverence for God, it can shape the way they view their Heavenly Father for the rest of their lives. When a man leads with faith, he is laying a spiritual foundation that can withstand life's storms. Trials will come, and seasons will change, but the lessons children absorb from a faithful father remain anchored deep within them. His example becomes a compass that points them back to truth when they feel lost. A father who walks with God plants seeds of courage, wisdom, and devotion that can grow for generations. By living a life of faith before his children, a man is strengthening the legacy that will carry them safely through tomorrow.

Spiritual leadership requires the courage to make decisions when others hesitate. Many men shrink back because they fear choosing the wrong path, yet God never called leaders to live paralyzed by uncertainty. Courageous leadership means seeking God, weighing wisdom, and then stepping forward with confidence that the Lord directs the steps of those who trust Him. Waiting for perfect clarity can become an excuse for inaction, but faith-filled leaders understand that obedience often begins with a single step. A godly leader knows that God honors a heart that is willing to act in faith. Decisions made prayerfully, with humility and integrity, place the outcome in God's hands rather than our own. Leadership is not about guaranteeing perfect results; it is about faithfully guiding others with courage, wisdom, and trust in the Lord. When a man chooses courage over hesitation, he becomes the kind of leader who inspires others to follow God boldly as well.

Decision-making with confidence comes from trust in God. A man who walks closely with the Lord learns that wisdom is something God gladly gives to those who seek Him. When a man places his choices before God and listens for His guidance, he does not have to live in constant doubt or fear. The peace of God becomes a quiet assurance within him that he is not walking alone, but that the Lord is directing his path. Because of this, confidence is not pride - it is faith in action. A man who trusts God can move forward boldly, not because he believes he knows everything, but because he believes God does. Even when the road ahead is uncertain, he knows that the steps of the righteous are ordered by the Lord. This kind of confidence produces calmness in the midst of pressure and clarity in moments of decision. When a man seeks God first, he can stand firm in his choices with peace in his heart, knowing that the God who guides his steps is faithful to lead him exactly where he needs to go.

Indecision quietly erodes the foundation of leadership. Families, teams, and communities are strengthened by clarity. They need to know that someone is willing to step forward and say, "This is the direction we will go." Leadership does not require perfection, but it does require courage. A man who trusts God and moves forward in faith becomes a steady foundation, bringing strength, direction, and security to everyone who depends on him. God never called men to lead by fear or endless hesitation. He calls them to seek His wisdom, make a decision, and walk forward with conviction. When a leader prays, listens to God, and then acts decisively, he creates an atmosphere of confidence and peace. People can rally around clear direction. Even when the path is challenging, decisive leadership strengthens those who follow. A man who places his trust in God can step forward boldly, knowing that the Lord is able to guide his steps and bless the direction he chooses.

Confidence does not appear overnight; it grows quietly as a man chooses to walk with God day by day. With every act of obedience, his heart becomes more aligned with God's voice. What once felt uncertain begins to grow clear. The more he listens, the more he recognizes the difference between truth and deception, wisdom and impulse, righteousness and compromise. In that steady walk with God, a man's spirit becomes grounded. His decisions are no longer driven by fear or confusion, but by a growing awareness that God is guiding his steps. When a man trusts that God is leading him, doubt loses its power to paralyze him. Courage begins to rise where uncertainty once lived. He may still face challenges and difficult choices, but he moves forward with confidence because he knows he does not walk alone. Each step taken in faith strengthens his resolve, shaping him into a man who stands firm, acts with courage, and follows the path God has set before him.

Spiritual authority is born out of humility before God. When a man bows his heart before the Lord, acknowledging his weakness and dependence, God entrusts him with influence that cannot be manufactured by human effort. The authority that carries weight in the kingdom of God flows from a spirit that listens and a heart that desires God's will above its own. Throughout Scripture, the men and women God raised up were those who walked humbly with Him. Moses led a nation not because he exalted himself, but because he continually sought the face of God. Jesus Himself demonstrated that true authority is expressed through servanthood, not self-exaltation. When humility anchors leadership, it keeps the heart pure, the motives right, and the focus on God's glory rather than personal gain. In this way, spiritual authority becomes a channel through which God works powerfully, because the vessel has learned that all strength, wisdom, and victory come from the Lord alone.

The greatest leaders in scripture were defined by humility. True spiritual leadership begins when a man understands that his strength, wisdom, and influence are not his own. When a leader bows his heart before God, he becomes a vessel through which God can guide, protect, and provide for others. Jesus Himself set the ultimate example of this truth. The One who commanded the winds and the waves, who held all authority in heaven and earth, knelt down and washed the dusty feet of His disciples. In doing so, He showed that greatness in God's kingdom is measured not by how many people serve you, but by how many people you are willing to serve. The man who walks humbly before God leads with wisdom, earns genuine respect, and guides others with a strength rooted in character rather than pride. When a leader walks in humility, his influence carries the fragrance of Christ, and his life becomes a living testimony that the highest calling is not to be served, but to serve.

Humility guards the heart of a leader from drifting into pride and control. Without humility, authority can easily become domination, and leadership can quietly transform into tyranny. But a humble leader knows that God entrusts people into a leader's care, not for personal power, but for faithful stewardship. The humble leader understands that every decision, every word, and every action will one day be measured by the One who gave the authority in the first place. When a man leads with humility, he does not see himself as the master of those he leads but as a servant of God and a guardian of those entrusted to him. He recognizes that people are not tools to advance his ambitions - they are souls created by God and deeply valued by Him. Humility keeps a leader teachable, accountable, and compassionate. It reminds him that the true purpose of leadership is not to rule over others, but to guide, protect, and serve them in a way that honors the Lord who placed them under his care.

A humble leader understands that wisdom does not come from pretending to have every answer. Instead, he listens carefully, learns continually, and seeks counsel from those who walk in truth. He values the voices God places around him, knowing that guidance often comes through the insight of others. Rather than guarding his pride, he guards his heart, remaining teachable and open to correction. In doing so, he reflects the spirit of Proverbs, where wise men welcome instruction and grow stronger because of it. Such a leader does not pretend to be flawless before God or before people. He walks honestly, acknowledging both his strengths and his weaknesses, trusting that God's grace is sufficient for every shortcoming. His transparency builds trust, and his humility invites God's favor upon his leadership. When a man leads this way, his authority is built on integrity. And in that posture of humility, God is able to use him to guide others with wisdom, compassion, and truth.

Leadership without humility easily drifts into control. When a man forgets that his authority is a stewardship from God, he begins to rule by force rather than by example. Pride hardens the heart, and conviction can slowly turn into domination. But the model of godly leadership is found in Christ, who possessed all authority yet washed the feet of His disciples. True strength does not need to shout, intimidate, or overpower. It stands firm in truth while remembering that every position of leadership is first a position of service before God. Yet humility without leadership can quietly become passivity. A man may avoid responsibility in the name of being gentle, when in reality he is shrinking back from the call to lead. Godly humility does not mean silence in the face of wrong or hesitation when courage is required. Instead, it produces a steady spirit that leads with conviction and authority. The man God raises up stands firmly for what is right while walking humbly with the God who entrusted him to lead.

The world today is desperate for men who will rise up and lead without apology. God never intended for men to shrink back from responsibility or hide from the call placed upon their lives. A godly man leads his home with love, protects what God has entrusted to him, and serves others with humility and purpose. When a man chooses courage over comfort and obedience over compromise, his life becomes a steady light in a dark and uncertain world. Men of faith must remember that when a man honors God with unwavering courage, he becomes a pillar for his family, a servant to his community, and a witness of God's strength in action. The world does not need passive men who drift with culture; it needs men who will stand on truth, walk in integrity, and lead with bold faith. When men live this way, their lives echo a powerful message that strength, conviction, and devotion to God can still shape homes, transform communities, and change the world.

When a man leads with faith, he anchors his life in something greater than himself. Faith steadies him when the road is uncertain and gives him the courage to step forward even when he cannot see the entire path. When that faith is joined with humility, it keeps his heart teachable before God and gentle toward others. And when it is strengthened by conviction, it gives him the resolve to stand firm in truth no matter the pressure of the world around him. Through that kind of leadership, the influence of one faithful man reaches far beyond himself. His example strengthens his family, giving them stability, direction, and hope. Those who watch his life learn what it means to trust God, to walk in integrity, and to stand firm in difficult times. In this way, one man's faithful leadership can shape generations, creating a legacy that echoes long after his lifetime. When men lead with faith, humility, and conviction, their lives help guide others toward the same path of truth, courage, and devotion.

| 13 |

"FINISH THE FIGHT"

Many people know how to start something with excitement. They step forward with vision, energy, and determination. The beginning of a journey often feels inspiring because hope is high and the path ahead seems full of promise. But faith is not proven in the excitement of the beginning - it is revealed in the endurance of the middle. When the road becomes difficult, when obstacles rise and enthusiasm fades, that is when true character is formed. The moments when progress feels slow and the reward seems distant are the moments when perseverance matters most. God is the God who strengthens us to continue when the initial excitement has passed. Those who finish strong understand that endurance is a spiritual discipline. They choose commitment over convenience and obedience over comfort. They keep walking when others turn back, trusting that the same God who inspired the vision will provide the strength to complete it. In the end, the greatest victories belong to those who refused to quit.

Starting strong is common. Anyone can be enthusiastic when the road is new and the dream is fresh. At the beginning of a journey, motivation is high, hope is strong, and the possibilities seem endless. But beginnings do not reveal the true depth of a person's character. The real test comes later when excitement fades, when obstacles appear, and when the path becomes steep and uncertain. It is in those moments that a person discovers whether their commitment is genuine or merely emotional. Character is forged in the difficult middle, where faith must replace feelings and perseverance must overcome discouragement. Many people start the race, but only those who refuse to quit finish it. When the journey becomes hard, remember that endurance is where strength is built and destiny is secured. Stay faithful when it is difficult, remain steady when others fall away, and keep walking when quitting seems easier because the reward belongs not to those who simply start, but to those who faithfully finish.

Every calling from God eventually leads through seasons of pressure. The excitement that once filled your heart when the journey began will not always remain at the same intensity. There will come days when the path feels long, the burden feels heavy, and the progress seems slow. Yet these seasons are not signs that you have stepped outside of God's will; they are often proof that you are walking deeper into it. Pressure reveals the depth of your commitment. It tests whether your faith was built on emotion or on conviction. When the excitement fades and the work becomes difficult, God is shaping endurance within you, forging a strength that excitement alone could never produce. In those moments, the real question is not whether you started the race, but whether you will keep running it. Many people begin with passion, but few continue when perseverance is required. The call of God is fulfilled not merely by those who begin well, but by those who remain faithful when the road grows difficult.

Finishing strong is rare. Many begin with passion and bold declarations of faith, but time has a way of wearing down enthusiasm, and hardship can shake even the strongest resolve. Disappointment, fatigue, and unexpected trials often cause people to step away from the very calling they once pursued with confidence. Yet the path of faith was never meant to be easy - it was meant to refine, strengthen, and mature those who walk it. The endurance required to continue when others quit is what separates a moment of inspiration from a life of true purpose. The one who stays the course when the excitement fades and the battle intensifies is the one who discovers the deeper strength that only perseverance can produce. Finishing strong is not about never feeling weary - it is about refusing to surrender when weariness comes. When you continue walking even when the road is long and the burden feels heavy, you are being forged into something greater than you imagined.

Many people start the journey with passion, vision, and enthusiasm, but when the road becomes steep and the path uncertain, their steps begin to slow. Obstacles appear, discouragement whispers, and the temptation to turn back grows stronger with every trial. Yet the men who truly shape history are the ones who refused to quit when the road became difficult. When others abandoned the journey, they lifted their eyes toward God and took one more step forward. Spiritual endurance is the quiet strength that carries a person beyond the moment of struggle into the place of purpose. These faithful souls kept walking when others turned back, trusting that God does His greatest work through perseverance. They understood that the road of calling is rarely easy, but it is always worth it. With every step forward they declared that difficulty would not define their destiny. Instead, their persistence became their testimony, proving that even the hardest roads can lead to a legacy that inspires generations.

Endurance is one of the greatest spiritual strengths a man can develop. Anyone can praise God when the sun is shining and the path is smooth, but endurance is revealed when the road becomes steep and the night seems long. In those moments, faith refuses to surrender. It chooses to trust God even when answers are delayed and relief has not yet arrived. Endurance reminds us that God is still working in the silence, shaping our character, strengthening our faith, and preparing us for victories that only perseverance can produce. Trials that once threatened to break us become the very tools that build spiritual strength within us. Each step forward in faith declares that our trust is not in our circumstances but in the unchanging character of God. Endurance keeps us standing when others fall away, pressing forward when quitting seems easier. And in the end, those who endure discover that what once felt like a battle was actually God forging them into stronger, wiser, and more faithful servants.

There will be days when quitting feels easier than continuing. The weight of the struggle presses hard, and the path ahead seems longer than the strength you feel inside. In those moments, the voice of discouragement will try to convince you that walking away is reasonable, that surrender is sensible, and that no one would blame you for stepping back. But those whispers are not the voice of faith - they are the echo of weariness trying to drown out the purpose God placed within you. Yet it is precisely in those moments that perseverance becomes sacred. When you continue even though everything inside you wants to stop, you step into the strength that God supplies beyond your own ability. Faith is not proven when the road is smooth, but when the journey is difficult and you refuse to abandon the calling placed on your life. The men who fulfill God's purpose are those who stand firm and trust that the same God who called them forward will also give them the strength to keep going.

Perseverance is the dividing line between those who merely dream about their calling and those who actually walk in it. God never promised that fulfilling your calling would be effortless, but He did promise strength for those who endure. The men who fulfill their calling are not always the most talented or the most gifted - they are simply the ones who refuse to quit when the battle intensifies. Anyone can abandon the mission when the fight grows fierce, but the faithful stay when the struggle becomes real. They remain when others retreat. They continue when progress seems slow. They trust God when circumstances appear uncertain. Perseverance is faith in motion - faith that refuses to surrender to fear, fatigue, or frustration. When you stay the course and remain committed to the calling God has placed upon your life, you prove that your purpose is greater than your pain. In the end, it is not the strongest who finish the race, but those who keep running when everything within them wants to stop.

God is not only honored by those who begin their assignment - He is honored by those who complete it. He is glorified not merely by our willingness to step forward, but by our determination to stay the course. When men refuse to abandon what God has entrusted to them, their perseverance becomes an act of worship and a declaration that God's purpose is greater than temporary struggle. Faithfulness through hardship becomes a powerful testimony of trust in God's purpose. When you continue serving, believing, and obeying even in seasons of fatigue, disappointment, or resistance, you demonstrate that your confidence rests in God rather than in comfort. Every step forward in the face of difficulty proclaims that His calling is worth the cost. Finishing what God has begun in you reveals a heart anchored in trust and obedience. In the end, it is not the loudest beginnings that honor God the most, but the steadfast lives that remain faithful until the assignment is complete.

Staying when quitting is easy requires courage. God does not place a calling in your life so it can be abandoned at the first sign of hardship. He plants it there so it will grow through perseverance. Courage is the decision to stay when every emotion whispers that leaving would be easier. It is the strength to say, "I will not abandon what God has entrusted to me." When you truly believe that the purpose God placed in your life is sacred, every sacrifice becomes meaningful. Long nights, difficult seasons, misunderstood efforts, and heavy burdens are no longer obstacles - they become part of the refining process. Just as gold is purified through fire, a calling is strengthened through endurance. Those who fulfill their God-given purpose are not always the most talented; they are the ones who refused to quit. They stayed when it was hard, trusted when it was uncertain, and continued walking forward because they believed that what God began in them was worth every sacrifice required to see it finished.

The Apostle Paul understood this truth when he declared that he had fought the good fight, finished the race, and kept the faith. His words were not the testimony of a man who avoided hardship, but of one who endured it. Paul knew beatings, imprisonment, rejection, and relentless opposition, yet none of these trials defined his defeat - they revealed his devotion. His life teaches us that faith is not proven in comfort but in conflict. Anyone can believe when the path is smooth, but true faith is forged when the road grows difficult and the outcome is uncertain. Paul did not measure success by ease or popularity; he measured it by faithfulness to the calling God placed upon his life. In the same way, every believer is called to run their race with endurance. When we refuse to quit, when we keep believing, and when we continue walking in obedience, we move closer to the moment when we too can say with confidence that we have fought the good fight, finished the race, and kept the faith.

Endurance is not about stubborn pride; it is about steadfast faith. Pride fights to prove something to people, but faith holds on because it trusts God. True endurance is born in the heart that believes the journey still matters even when the road becomes difficult. It is the quiet strength that refuses to give up when emotions grow weary and circumstances grow heavy. Faith whispers that God is still working, even when nothing seems to be changing. It is the quiet decision made day after day to continue moving forward even when progress feels slow. Many victories in the kingdom of God are not won in a single moment but through patient persistence. Step by step, prayer by prayer, act of obedience by act of obedience, the faithful soul keeps walking. In time, what once felt like small and unnoticed steps become the path that leads to breakthrough, growth, and lasting strength. Endurance transforms ordinary faithfulness into extraordinary testimony.

The greatest victories in life are rarely achieved in a single moment of triumph. More often, they are quietly built through long seasons of faithful obedience - days when nothing seems dramatic, yet everything important is taking place beneath the surface. Just as a tree grows strong through years of steady growth, so a life of faith is formed through daily choices to trust God, to stand firm, and to keep moving forward even when progress feels slow. In these long seasons, faithfulness becomes the true measure of strength. It is the willingness to keep praying when answers seem delayed, to keep believing when circumstances challenge hope, and to keep serving when recognition is absent. Every small act of obedience and every step taken despite difficulty becomes a brick in the foundation of a lasting victory. When the breakthrough finally comes, it may appear sudden to others, but those who walked the journey know it was built day by day and step by faithful step under the steady hand of God.

Many people search for greatness as though it were hidden in some dramatic moment, a sudden breakthrough, or a grand achievement that the world can see. Yet in the kingdom of God, greatness is often discovered in something far quieter and far less celebrated - simple persistence. It is the daily decision to keep believing when progress feels slow, to keep praying when answers seem delayed, and to keep walking the path God set before you even when the road is difficult. True greatness is found in the person who refuses to surrender their calling despite obstacles and delays. It is found in the man who stands firm when others walk away, a man who continues trusting God even when circumstances seem uncertain. When you remain faithful through the trials, the delays, and the disappointments, you prove that your calling is not driven by convenience but by conviction. In time, what looked like simple endurance will reveal itself as true greatness in the eyes of God.

Inspiration may start a journey, but perseverance is what finishes it. Many people feel a surge of passion when God first places a calling and a dream in their heart but passion without endurance fades when difficulty arrives. The truth is that every meaningful legacy is forged in the quiet days of faithfulness, when progress feels slow and obstacles seem heavy. It is in those moments when quitting would be easy that character is formed and destiny is secured. God does not measure legacy by how loudly we begin, but by how faithfully we continue. Perseverance is the steady determination to complete what God has placed in your hands. It is choosing to remain faithful when the excitement fades, when recognition is absent, and when the road grows long. A legacy worthy of remembrance is built one obedient step at a time through consistency and unwavering trust in God's purpose. When you keep moving forward in faith, you become a living testimony that what God begins, He is faithful to finish.

The people who leave a lasting impact are rarely the ones who simply begin with excitement; they are the ones who remain faithful when the excitement fades and the road becomes difficult. When others grow weary, distracted, or discouraged, they quietly continue the work God has placed in their hands. Faithfulness is proven in seasons of perseverance. The men who change the world are those who refuse to abandon their calling when the battle grows long. They trust that God is working even when the results are not immediately visible. Those who remain in the battle long enough eventually see the fruit of their labor. Seeds planted in obedience may take time to grow, but God never forgets the work done in faith. Every act of perseverance and every step taken when quitting seemed easier becomes part of the harvest that God brings forth in His perfect time. Lasting impact is not built by those who come and go, but by those who stay steadfast, patient, and committed until the purpose of God is fulfilled.

Strength is not formed in moments of comfort but in seasons of resistance. Every challenge you face becomes a tool in the hands of God, shaping your character and deepening your resolve. What once seemed like an obstacle becomes an opportunity for growth. The struggle that once felt overwhelming slowly becomes the very thing that strengthens your faith, sharpens your courage, and teaches your spirit to stand firm. Each difficulty you endure leaves a mark not of defeat, but of strength. Like iron in the forge, the heat of life's trials tempers your spirit and makes you unbreakable. With every obstacle overcome, you gain confidence that God's grace is sufficient and His power is working within you. What once shook you will no longer move you, because perseverance has built a deeper foundation in your soul. The person who refuses to quit becomes stronger with every storm they survive, and through endurance, God forms within them a strength that cannot be easily shaken.

Finishing the fight requires a strength that goes deeper than excitement or emotion. Many begin the journey of faith with passion and determination, but along the road come obstacles, weariness, disappointment, and moments when quitting seems easier than continuing. Yet God never called His people to simply start well - He called them to endure. The race of faith is not a sprint but a lifelong pursuit of obedience, trust, and perseverance. Those who keep moving forward demonstrate a devotion that goes beyond words. So finish the fight. Run your race with endurance and refuse to abandon the calling God has placed on your life. Many may start strong, but those who finish strong leave a legacy that honors God and inspires others to follow. When you remain steadfast, your life becomes a testimony that perseverance produces victory. In the end, it is not the one who begins the race who receives the crown - it is the one who refuses to quit until the finish line is crossed.

| 14 |

"SPIRITUAL TRAINING"

Every man who desires strength understands the value of the weight room. Muscles are built through resistance, strain, and repetition. In the same way, the spiritual life grows stronger through intentional training. Faith is not developed in moments of ease but in seasons that challenge our trust in God. Trials, discipline, prayer, and obedience act like spiritual resistance that stretches our character and deepens our dependence on the Lord. What feels difficult in the moment is often the very thing God is using to strengthen the soul. Just as a man who lifts weights gradually becomes stronger, a believer who consistently seeks God grows in spiritual endurance and confidence. God never intended for believers to live spiritually weak, exhausted, or defeated. He calls His people to rise in strength, maturity, and steadfast faith. The disciplined man learns to stand firm when pressures come and, over time, what once felt heavy becomes manageable because strength has been developed.

Paul understood that spiritual growth requires intentional effort. When he wrote, "Exercise yourself toward godliness" (1 Tim. 4:7–8), he was reminding believers that maturity in Christ is not the result of chance but of commitment. Just as an athlete trains consistently to build strength and endurance, a believer must cultivate habits that develop the soul. Prayer, time in God's Word, obedience, and worship become the spiritual exercises that shape a life devoted to God.

Through these disciplines, faith grows stronger and the heart becomes more aligned with the will of the Lord. Each challenge we face is like resistance that strengthens our endurance and deepens our trust in God. When we choose faith over fear and obedience over convenience, we are training our hearts in godliness. Over time, this daily discipline produces a life that reflects Christ more clearly. Spiritual strength is not built in a moment, but through a steady pattern of faithful living that prepares us to stand firm and finish our race well.

Many people desire spiritual strength, yet few are willing to enter the training ground where that strength is formed. They long for victory but resist the discipline that produces it. They pray for power yet avoid the preparation that makes a life usable in the hands of God. But just as muscles are strengthened through resistance, the spirit is strengthened through obedience, endurance, and daily surrender. God does not pour His strength into a passive life; He develops it in the heart of the believer who is willing to be trained, corrected, and refined. The weight room of the spirit is entered by those who are serious about walking with God. It is found in the perseverance that refuses to quit when trials come. Every act of faith, every moment of discipline, and every step of obedience adds strength to the soul. In time, the believer who trains with God becomes able to stand in storms, overcome temptation, and carry the weight of greater responsibility in the kingdom of God.

One of the most important exercises in this spiritual weight room is prayer. Prayer is the resistance training of the soul. Just as muscles grow stronger when they push against weight, the spirit of a believer grows stronger when it presses against the pressures, fears, and temptations of life through prayer. When a man bows before God, he is not retreating from the battle - he is preparing for it. In the quiet place of prayer, burdens are lifted, faith is strengthened, and the heart becomes steady even when the world is unstable. Prayer strengthens the inner man and aligns the heart with the will of God. As a man spends time in God's presence, his perspective changes, his courage rises, and his spirit becomes anchored in truth. In the spiritual weight room, prayer builds endurance, resilience, and spiritual authority. Those who consistently exercise this discipline become stronger in faith, steadier in character, and more capable of walking in the purposes God has prepared for them.

Resistance builds strength. Just as muscles grow stronger when they are pressed against the resistance of heavy weights, the spirit grows stronger when it presses through the resistance of life in persistent prayer. Every time a man kneels before God, he is lifting the weight of faith. In those quiet moments of surrender, trust is exercised, patience is stretched, and dependence on God deepens. The soul that continues to pray, is developing endurance that cannot be produced any other way. Through consistent prayer, the heart learns to rely on God's power rather than human strength. Each prayer becomes another repetition in the gym of faith, strengthening confidence in God's wisdom, timing, and provision. Persistent prayer reshapes the inner life, building resilience, humility, and unwavering faith. The more a person brings their burdens before God, the more their spirit is trained to stand firm, knowing that true strength is found not in self, but in the presence and power of God.

Prayer is also where battles are fought and victories are secured long before they ever appear in the natural world. What seems quiet and hidden to human eyes is often the place where the greatest spiritual work is taking place. When a men bow their heads in prayer, they are not retreating from the struggle - they are stepping onto the battlefield with heaven's authority. In prayer, burdens are lifted, wisdom is received, and strength is renewed. God begins to move in ways that cannot yet be seen, arranging circumstances, softening hearts, and preparing the path for the victory that will eventually appear. Every time men seek God, they are training their spirit to trust Him more deeply and stand more firmly. Prayer develops courage, endurance, and confidence because it reminds the heart that the battle does not belong to us alone - it belongs to the Lord. Those who pray consistently walk into life's challenges with a steady spirit, knowing that the victory has already begun in the presence of God.

Prayer opens the heart to God, but the Word of God feeds the soul with truth and strength. Just as an athlete cannot train effectively without proper nutrition, a believer cannot grow spiritually without the daily nourishment of scripture. The Bible supplies the wisdom, correction, encouragement, and direction needed for spiritual endurance. Each verse strengthens the inner man, sharpening discernment and renewing faith. When a man consistently feeds on God's Word, his spirit becomes resilient, his faith becomes steady, and his walk with God grows deeper and more confident. Without the steady intake of scripture, the soul becomes spiritually weak and vulnerable. Just as the body grows tired and frail without food, the spirit loses clarity, conviction, and strength when it is deprived of God's truth. The Word of God builds spiritual muscle, equips the man for life's battles, and keeps the heart aligned with God's will. It becomes the fuel that empowers a man to grow continually in the strength that comes from God.

Scripture is the steady light that fills the mind with truth and strengthens the heart with wisdom. When a man opens the Word of God, he is allowing divine truth to shape his thoughts, correct his attitudes, and guide his decisions. God's Word teaches what is right, exposes what is wrong, and gently redirects the heart back to the path of righteousness. In a world full of noise, confusion, and shifting opinions, the scriptures remain a firm and unchanging foundation. They bring clarity to the mind and stability to the soul, reminding believers of God's promises, His character, and His purposes. A man who feeds daily on God's Word develops a spiritual strength that cannot easily be shaken. As truth fills his mind, conviction settles into his heart, shaping the way he lives, speaks, and leads. The Word equips him for every challenge he faces. Over time, the man who consistently meditates on scripture becomes steady, wise, and courageous, because the voice guiding him is the voice of God.

When the Word of God becomes woven into the rhythm of daily life, it begins to renew the mind and reshape the heart from the inside out. The thoughts that once drifted toward fear, doubt, or confusion are gradually replaced with truth, clarity, and confidence in God's promises. As scripture takes root, you start to see life through a different lens - one guided not by emotions or circumstances, but by the wisdom of God. This transformation naturally flows into every area of life. Words become more life-giving, decisions become more discerning, and actions begin to reflect the character of Christ. The Word of God is the fuel that sustains a strong and resilient faith. When a believer consistently feeds on Scripture, discernment grows, courage rises, and the heart becomes steady even in difficult seasons. Over time, the Word forms a spiritual backbone within a man training him to stand firm, walk faithfully, and live with purpose as a reflection of God's truth in the world.

Another essential discipline in the weight room of the spirit is fasting. Fasting is a powerful exercise that trains the believer to place spiritual priorities above physical desires. When a person willingly sets aside food for a season, they are declaring that the voice of God is more important than the cravings of the body. Each moment of hunger becomes a reminder to seek the Lord, to listen more closely, and to depend more deeply on His presence. Through fasting, the believer learns that true strength is not found in what we consume, but in the One who sustains us. Fasting also sharpens spiritual focus and humbles the heart before God. It quiets the noise of the flesh so the spirit can hear more clearly. In those moments when the body longs for food, the soul is reminded of a greater hunger - the hunger for righteousness, truth, and the living word of God. As Jesus declared, "Man shall not live by bread alone, but by every word that proceeds from the mouth of God."

Fasting is a sacred discipline that teaches the believer the power of self-control and the beauty of complete dependence on the Lord. When a person willingly sets aside physical appetite, they are making a declaration that their spirit must lead their life, not their flesh. As the body grows quieter, the heart grows more attentive to the presence of the Lord, and the believer begins to recognize that true strength comes not from what we consume, but from the One who sustains us. Through fasting, the noise of daily desires begins to fade, and spiritual awareness becomes sharper and clearer. The temporary denial of food humbles the soul and opens the heart to hear the gentle voice of God that is often drowned out by the distractions of the flesh. In that quiet place, the believer learns to rely more deeply on the Lord's guidance. What begins as a physical sacrifice becomes a spiritual awakening, as God uses the discipline of fasting to refine the heart and draw His people into deeper communion with Him.

Discipline is the foundation of every successful training program. No athlete grows stronger through occasional effort or brief moments of enthusiasm. Real strength is built through daily practice, repeated effort, and the willingness to keep showing up even when the work feels difficult. Muscles grow because they are trained consistently, and skill develops because it is exercised regularly. In the same way, spiritual strength is not formed through sporadic moments with God, but through a steady life of devotion. When a believer commits to regular prayer, daily time in scripture, and continual fellowship with the Lord, the soul becomes stronger, faith becomes deeper, and character begins to reflect the heart of God. Just as an athlete trains the body with discipline, a follower of Christ must train the spirit with intentional devotion. Daily prayer aligns the heart with God's will, Scripture renews the mind with truth, and consistent fellowship with God builds endurance for life's challenges.

Discipline may not always feel exciting, but it produces powerful results in the life of a believer. Spiritual strength is rarely built in dramatic moments; it is formed in the quiet decisions made day after day. When a man chooses prayer instead of distraction, opens scripture instead of turning to entertainment, or walks in obedience instead of compromise, something powerful is happening beneath the surface. Just as physical muscles grow through consistent training, the spirit grows stronger through faithful practice. Each act of discipline deepens a man's connection with God and sharpens his ability to hear His voice. Over time, these small choices shape a life of stability, endurance, and spiritual authority. What begins as simple obedience becomes a well-trained heart that responds quickly to God's leading. Discipline teaches the soul to value eternal things, and it prepares a man to stand firm when trials arise because he walks confidently in God's purpose and reflects His strength in every area of life.

Over time, spiritual training produces endurance in the life of a man. Just as an athlete develops strength through repeated discipline, the soul grows stronger through consistent devotion to God. At first the growth may seem small, but every step of faith quietly strengthens the inner life until what once seemed insignificant becomes a deep and unshakable spiritual strength. Gradually, you develop a deeper trust in God, a steadier spirit, and a heart that is anchored in truth rather than circumstance. Because of this inner strengthening, when life inevitably brings trials, pressures, and challenges, the spiritually trained man does not collapse under the weight. Instead, he stands firm. The storms may rage around him, but within him there is stability, peace, and endurance. Consistent devotion has built a spiritual foundation that cannot easily be shaken, enabling him to persevere with faith, courage, and unwavering confidence in God's sustaining grace.

Spiritual muscles are formed over time through steady devotion and faithful practice. Every prayer whispered in faith, every verse of scripture read and pondered, and every step of obedience taken when it would be easier to turn away becomes a small but powerful investment in spiritual strength. These daily moments may seem simple or even unnoticed, yet they are shaping the heart, training the soul, and preparing the believer to stand firm when life's challenges arise. God often builds strength in quiet, ordinary ways rather than dramatic moments. Through perseverance and daily faithfulness, the man of God becomes rooted and resilient. Each act of trust deepens faith and each trial endured develops endurance and strengthens character. Over time, what once felt difficult becomes natural, and what once seemed impossible becomes achievable through God's grace. In this way, spiritual muscles grow stronger day by day, forming a life that is steady, faithful, and capable of carrying the weight of God's calling.

The Christian life was never meant to be a life of timid faith or fragile devotion. Throughout scripture, God consistently calls His people to grow stronger in Him - to stand firm, endure hardship, and rise above fear. Faith is strength formed through trust in God. When trials come, they are not signs that God has abandoned us, but opportunities for Him to develop endurance, wisdom, and spiritual stability within us. Just as muscles grow through resistance, the believer grows through challenges that demand deeper trust and greater perseverance. In the spiritual weight room, ordinary men are transformed into strong men of faith. Prayer becomes the discipline that builds endurance, obedience becomes the training that develops character, and trials become the resistance that produces spiritual power. God uses these moments to shape men who can stand firm when storms rise, who refuse to quit when life becomes difficult, and who carry the strength of heaven into a broken world.

Those who commit themselves to this spiritual training discover something remarkable over time. What once felt overwhelming slowly becomes manageable. The burdens that once seemed too heavy to carry are lifted with greater strength and confidence because they are no longer standing alone. God uses every challenge to build spiritual muscle within His people. Through this process, faith becomes more than a belief; it becomes a source of steady strength that carries a man through the pressures of life. As spiritual strength grows, a man's perspective begins to change. What once seemed impossible becomes achievable because faith sees beyond circumstances and anchors itself in the power of God. Instead of shrinking from adversity, the spiritually trained heart faces it with courage and stability. Spiritual strength transforms the way a man walks through life. He stands firm in trials, carrying burdens with grace, and lives with the quiet confidence that God has prepared him for every good work.

God's invitation to His people is not merely to believe, but to grow strong in Him. When a man enters the "weight room of the spirit," prayer becomes the lifting of the soul toward God, scripture becomes the nourishment that strengthens the heart, and fasting becomes the training that teaches the spirit to rule over the flesh. These practices are not empty rituals; they are the exercises through which God forms endurance, deepens faith, and builds spiritual resilience in those who pursue Him with sincerity. Over time, the transformation becomes evident. What once felt like struggle becomes steady strength. The man who consistently trains in prayer, scripture, fasting, and obedience begins to stand firm when trials come and remain faithful when pressures increase. His faith is no longer fragile but fortified. His spirit is no longer easily shaken but anchored in God's truth. Through this daily training, God shapes ordinary people into men whose lives reflect endurance and the quiet power of unshakable spiritual strength.

| 15 |

"THE COMFORT TRAP"

One of the greatest dangers a man can face is not failure but comfort. Failure has a way of shaking a man awake. It humbles him, strips away his pride, and often drives him to his knees before God. In those moments of weakness, a man begins to recognize how deeply he needs the Lord's wisdom, strength, and guidance. Many of the greatest seasons of spiritual growth are born in the soil of hardship, where a man learns to depend on God rather than on his own abilities. Comfort, however, is far more subtle. When life becomes easy and the pressure lifts, the urgency to seek God can quietly fade. Prayers become shorter, the Word becomes less central, and spiritual hunger slowly cools. What once burned as a passionate pursuit of God can settle into a routine habit. That is why a wise man guards his heart during seasons of blessing just as carefully as during seasons of struggle, choosing to remain hungry for God even when life feels comfortable.

Success can be a blessing, but it can also become a subtle test of the heart. When life grows easier and victories accumulate, the urgency that once drove a man to his knees can slowly fade. In seasons of struggle, a man often clings to God with fierce dependence, seeking wisdom, strength, and direction for every step. But when success arrives, the temptation is to lean on what has already been built rather than the One who made it possible. If he is not watchful, the fire that once pushed him toward God can begin to cool. A wise man understands that the very disciplines forged in hardship must be guarded even more carefully in times of success. Prayer must remain fervent and dependence on God must remain absolute. The strongest men are those who stay just as desperate for Him when everything seems to be going well. The man who keeps his heart humble before God will never allow success to weaken the character that God worked so hard to build.

Comfort itself is not evil. The Lord delights in blessing His people, and seasons of rest, provision, and peace are often evidence of His goodness. Rest restores the soul and peace allows a man to regain strength for the road ahead. These blessings are not meant to weaken a man, but to prepare him for continued faithfulness. When received with gratitude and humility, comfort becomes a reminder of God's kindness and a place where the heart can be renewed in His presence. Yet comfort was never meant to become the destination. A man's calling always requires movement, courage, sacrifice, and sometimes discomfort. When comfort becomes the goal, a man's vision shrinks and his purpose fades. But when calling remains first, comfort becomes what it was always intended to be - a temporary shelter along the journey, not the reason for the journey itself. A faithful man thanks God for seasons of rest, but he never allows comfort to replace the mission God has placed upon his life.

When life is difficult, a man naturally turns to God for strength, guidance, and endurance. Hardship reminds him of his need for the Lord. It humbles his heart and keeps his eyes lifted upward. But when comfort arrives - when success grows, problems fade, and life becomes stable - the danger quietly increases. In seasons of ease, the urgency to seek God can fade, and the heart begins to drift without even realizing it. The subtle shift happens slowly. Trust that once rested firmly in God begins to settle into personal achievement, financial security, reputation, or stability. A man may still believe in God, yet he quietly begins relying more on his own wisdom and resources. Scripture repeatedly warns of this danger, reminding us that prosperity can tempt the heart to forget the Lord who provided it. The wise man understands that comfort is not a time to loosen his dependence on God but a time to deepen it, remembering that every blessing and every season of peace ultimately comes from the hand of the Lord.

Comfort has a subtle way of dulling conviction. When life is difficult, a man feels the sharp edge of truth pressing against his soul. Trials strip away illusions and remind him of his deep need for God's righteousness, discipline, and obedience. Hard seasons expose weakness, awaken humility, and drive the heart back to prayer and dependence on the Lord. In struggle, the conscience becomes sensitive again, and the Spirit's voice is clearer because the soul knows it cannot survive without God. But when life becomes comfortable - when everything feels secure, predictable, and easy - the heart relaxes, discipline loosens, and the whisper of the Spirit becomes easier to ignore. Comfort can lull a man into spiritual complacency if he is not watchful. That is why a wise man chooses to remain tender before God even in seasons of blessing. He keeps his heart sharp through prayer, repentance, and obedience, refusing to let comfort silence the voice that calls him to holiness.

A man who once stood boldly for truth may slowly begin to compromise, not because he has abandoned truth, but because the weight of conviction can become costly. Standing for what is right often brings resistance, misunderstanding, or even loneliness. Speaking truth can create tension in relationships, and walking in discipline can demand sacrifices that comfort resists. Over time, the temptation arises to soften the edges of conviction just enough to avoid conflict. The heart still believes the truth, but the will begins to negotiate with convenience. Yet a man of God must remember that comfort has never been the measure of righteousness. The path of integrity has always required courage, endurance, and a willingness to stand when standing is unpopular. Peace purchased by compromise is not true peace, but a quiet surrender of the soul. God calls men to something higher - to love truth more than approval, purity more than ease, and obedience more than comfort.

The fading of conviction begins quietly, in moments that appear harmless. A prayer that once came naturally is postponed. A conviction that once felt urgent is softened to avoid inconvenience. The heart does not suddenly turn away from God; it simply drifts, little by little. What once stirred passion becomes routine, and what once demanded obedience becomes negotiable. The man who once felt the weight of truth strongly may not even notice the change, because the dulling happens slowly, like a flame that gradually loses its heat. Yet even when the fire has dimmed to a faint ember, it is not gone. God is always ready to breathe fresh life into the soul that turns back to Him. One sincere prayer can begin to reignite what compromise tried to extinguish. The embers of faith still hold the potential for a blazing fire if they are given fresh fuel through repentance and a renewed hunger for God's presence. What fades slowly can be restored powerfully when the heart chooses once again to draw near to Him.

Many men do not fall away from God in a single dramatic moment. More often, the drift begins quietly and almost unnoticed. From the outside, nothing appears different. Yet something subtle has changed within. The fire that once burned in his heart has grown dim and the urgency to seek God has softened. What once flowed from deep love and devotion becomes little more than spiritual routine. This is the tragedy of spiritual drifting: a man can maintain the appearance of faith while the intensity of his relationship with God quietly fades. The danger is not merely abandoning faith altogether but allowing passion to cool while outward activities remain the same. God never intended for a man's walk with Him to become mechanical or lifeless. He calls men to pursue Him with a whole heart, pressing forward with hunger, expectation, and devotion. When a man recognizes the early signs of drift, it becomes an invitation to rekindle the fire and once again seek God with the same fervor that once defined his faith.

Recognizing spiritual drift begins with the courage to look honestly into the mirror of the soul. Many men do not fall away from God suddenly; they simply drift a little at a time through comfort or quiet neglect. That is why honest self-examination is so important. A man must be willing to ask the hard question that exposes the true condition of his heart. "Am I still pursuing God with the same hunger I once had?" Spiritual maturity demands a living pursuit of God. When a man recognizes spiritual drift, he also opens the door for spiritual restoration. God is always ready to revive a heart that turns back toward Him. A faith that feels routine can become alive again when a man renews his hunger for God's presence, His Word, and His purpose. The question is not whether we have drifted at times but whether we will respond with humility and return with renewed passion. The man who chooses to pursue God again will find that spiritual fire can burn brighter than before.

Spiritual drift rarely happens all at once. It begins quietly, almost unnoticed, as the things that once ignited passion for God slowly lose their intensity. The Word that once stirred conviction now feels distant, prayer becomes brief and routine, and the urgency to seek God fades into the background of daily life. Yet these subtle changes are not insignificant - they are warning lights on the dashboard of the soul, gently alerting us that our hearts may be moving away from the closeness we once had with the Lord. When we notice the fading of hunger for His presence, it is an invitation to come back, not with guilt, but with renewed humility and desire. The same God who once stirred your heart is still calling you closer. When a man responds by opening the Word again with expectation, by seeking God in prayer with sincerity, and by choosing obedience over complacency, the fire of faith can burn again. Drift may begin subtly, but restoration begins the moment a heart turns back toward God.

Another sign of spiritual drift appears when a man begins protecting his comfort more than pursuing his growth. God never designed faith to flourish in the safe places of life; it is forged in the stretching, the testing, and the refining. When a man begins avoiding challenges that call him higher, he slowly trades transformation for temporary ease. Comfort quietly becomes the priority, and without realizing it, he begins stepping away from the very circumstances God intended to mature him. Scripture shows that God shapes strong men through pressure, challenge, and honest correction. But when a man resists these moments and instead chooses the path of least resistance, he delays the work God wants to do in him. True spiritual strength is built when a man leans into the difficult places, allowing God to stretch his character, deepen his faith, and enlarge his capacity. The man who chooses growth over comfort will always become the man God intended him to be.

The path of a faithful man is not designed to be easy, predictable, or sheltered. Instead, it is a journey where God steadily shapes the heart, strengthens the character, and deepens the faith of those who follow Him. The Christian life is not a padded chair where a man settles into ease, but a narrow road where God refines His sons through challenges that stretch them and moments that require courage. Every test, every correction, and every difficult step becomes part of the divine process by which God forms a man into the image of Christ. Trials become training grounds where faith matures and character takes root. The man who walks with God learns that transformation happens not in the absence of struggle, but in the middle of it. As he continues forward - trusting God, obeying His voice, and persevering through hardship - he discovers that purpose is far greater than comfort. In the hands of God, every challenge becomes a tool that shapes a life of impact, integrity, and eternal significance.

Complacency is one of the quietest enemies of a man's spiritual life. It whispers that he has already gone far enough, prayed enough, learned enough, and grown enough. Yet the heart that truly knows God understands that the journey never ends. The antidote to complacency is hunger - a deep, relentless desire for more of God. Spiritual hunger reminds a man that every step of growth only reveals greater depths still waiting to be discovered. A man must refuse to settle spiritually. No matter how far he has come, there is always more of God to know, more wisdom to gain, and more faith to develop. The greatest men of faith in scripture were not satisfied with yesterday's victories; they pressed forward toward a deeper walk with God. Spiritual hunger keeps a man humble, dependent, and expectant. When a man remains hungry for God, his faith stays alive, his vision stays clear, and his life continues to grow in strength, purpose, and devotion.

Staying spiritually hungry requires humility. A man who thinks he has arrived will soon stop growing, but a humble man understands that there is always more to learn from God. Humility keeps the heart open, the mind receptive, and the spirit eager for truth. When a man remains humble before the Lord, he continues to seek guidance, understanding, and the refining work that shapes him into a stronger vessel. A man who remains teachable will never stagnate, because he understands that spiritual maturity is not a destination but a lifelong journey. Each season brings new insights, new challenges, and deeper revelations of God's truth. Rather than becoming complacent, he continually pursues wisdom, allowing God to stretch his faith and enlarge his understanding. This hunger for growth keeps his spirit alive and his walk with God vibrant. The man who stays humble and hungry will always move forward, growing stronger, wiser, and more aligned with the purpose God has placed on his life.

Spiritual hunger is a powerful force in a man's life, but hunger alone is not enough. Hunger must be guarded by discipline. A man who truly longs for God understands that the fire of his spirit must be fed and protected. Just as the body weakens without food, the soul grows dull without consistent nourishment from the presence of God. Discipline is the decision to seek God not only when emotions are strong, but when life is busy, when distractions are loud, and when the heart feels tired. A man who disciplines himself to pursue God keeps the flame of his spiritual hunger burning bright. Through prayer he communes with the Father, through scripture he receives truth, through worship he refocuses his soul, and through obedience he walks in alignment with God's will. When these habits become part of a man's daily life, his hunger for God grows deeper rather than fading. Discipline protects that hunger, and hunger continually draws him closer to the heart of God.

A strong man understands that success is not a destination but a responsibility. When blessings increase, his humility must increase as well. Rather than allowing prosperity to lull him into complacency, he sees every victory as a reminder of God's faithfulness and grace. The strong man knows that the same God who opened the door is the One who must sustain him through it. Therefore, success does not make him independent - it makes him more dependent on the Lord. Gratitude fills his heart, and that gratitude draws him closer to God in prayer, worship, and obedience. Instead of drifting away from faith when life becomes comfortable, the strong man presses in even deeper. He treats being blessed as an opportunity to honor God with greater devotion. A wise man turns every blessing into an altar of thanksgiving. His success strengthens his faith, his gratitude fuels his devotion, and his life becomes a testimony that the greatest reward is not the blessing itself but the God who gave it.

Wise men understand that victory today does not guarantee strength tomorrow. They remain vigilant because they know that complacency quietly waits at the door, looking for an opportunity to enter when discipline relaxes. Instead of drifting into comfort, a wise man recognizes that spiritual strength must be maintained daily. Just as a warrior continues training even during times of peace, a man of God continues cultivating humility, prayer, and obedience so that his faith remains strong and steady. Seasons of peace are opportunities to grow deeper. Wise men use these quiet moments to sharpen their character, strengthen their faith, and draw nearer to God with renewed determination. They pray when there is no crisis, seek wisdom when life feels stable, and pursue righteousness when no one is watching. When challenges eventually come, they are not caught unprepared because their devotion to God never rested in comfort but remained active, watchful, and strong.

The man who escapes the comfort trap is the man who refuses to let ease replace pursuit. While many settle into routines that quiet their spiritual hunger, he guards the fire within his soul. He understands that comfort can dull the edge of devotion if left unchecked. Instead of allowing success, stability, or familiarity to slow his pursuit of God, he keeps pressing forward. His heart remains hungry for truth, his spirit alert to the voice of the Lord, and his life continues to stretch toward deeper faith and greater obedience. Such a man knows that earthly success is not the final destination - it is only a tool, never a master. Achievements never satisfy the deeper longing within his soul. His greatest desire is not recognition, security, or ease, but the presence and purpose of God. Day after day he chooses pursuit over comfort, devotion over complacency, and calling over convenience. In doing so, he becomes a man whose life continually grows stronger, wiser, and more aligned with the will of God.

| 16 |

"PROTECT WHAT MATTERS"

A godly man understands that life is not only about building, achieving, or pursuing dreams - it is also about protecting what God has entrusted to him. Protection is one of the highest expressions of love. When a man truly values something, he guards it with diligence and reverence. A man of God recognizes that what God has placed in his hands is precious, and he accepts the calling to stand watch over it. His protection flows from a heart that refuses to allow harm, corruption, or neglect to damage what God has given him to steward. A godly man guards the purity of his home, the peace of his mind, and the spiritual well-being of those he loves. Like a watchman on the wall, he remains alert and committed, knowing that his strength can bring safety and stability to others. Through prayer, wisdom, and steadfast character, he creates a covering of security around his family and community. In doing so, he reflects the very heart of God - the ultimate Protector who faithfully watches over His people.

God Himself is our ultimate protector. Throughout scripture, the Lord reveals His heart as a refuge, fortress, shield, and strong tower for those who trust Him. He surrounds His people with His presence, guards their steps, and provides safety in times of trouble. No earthly defense compares to the security found in the covering of God. When storms arise and enemies threaten, it is the Lord who stands as our defense, reminding us that our safety does not ultimately come from our own strength but from His faithful protection. When a man walks closely with God, that same protective nature begins to shape his character. As he learns to trust the Lord as his own shield, he also becomes a covering for others. He watches over his family, guards the purity of his home, and stands firm in protecting the values God has entrusted to him. With courage and faith, he becomes a steady presence for those around him reflecting the heart of the heavenly Father who watches over His children day and night.

A protector mindset begins with understanding the importance of spiritual covering. Families need far more than financial provision; they need spiritual leadership that invites the presence of God into the home. A godly man recognizes that his greatest responsibility is not only to work with his hands but to stand watch with his heart and spirit. He seeks God's guidance for decisions, prays protection over his family, and cultivates an atmosphere where peace, truth, and righteousness can flourish. A godly man understands that unseen battles are often fought in the spiritual realm, so he stands firm as a guardian over what influences his family. Through prayer, Scripture, and godly example, he shields his household from harmful influences and encourages faith to grow in every heart under his care. His leadership brings stability, safety, and direction. As he faithfully stands in that role, his home becomes a place where God's presence dwells and where every member of the family can grow strong in faith and purpose.

Spiritual covering means recognizing that many of life's most serious battles are unseen. Temptation, fear, doubt, and destructive influences quietly attempt to enter our homes, influence our thinking, and weaken our faith. A wise and godly man remains alert and watchful, refusing to allow negative influences to take root in his household. Through prayer, faith, and spiritual awareness, he stands like a guard at the gate of his family, inviting the presence of God while resisting anything that threatens their peace and purpose. A man who protects what matters becomes a spiritual shield for those he loves. His prayers become a covering of protection over his home. Even when challenges arise, his faith anchors the family in God's promises. In doing so, he fulfills one of the highest callings of manhood - to stand before God on behalf of those entrusted to his care and to ensure that his home remains a place where God's presence, peace, and protection dwell.

When a man prays for his family, he is engaging in spiritual warfare on their behalf. Every sincere prayer rises like a shield around the ones he loves. In the quiet moments when he calls upon God, he is asking heaven to guard their steps, protect their hearts, and guide their decisions. Though the world may not see it, a faithful man is building an invisible wall of protection through his prayers. His faith becomes a covering over his home, inviting God's presence to surround his family with peace, wisdom, and divine protection. A strong man understands that real strength is not only found in physical power but in spiritual authority. When he bows his head, he stands tall in the unseen realm. His prayers call upon the power of God to stand watch over his household, pushing back darkness and strengthening those under his care. A praying man becomes a guardian of the soul, a watchman for his family, and a faithful steward of the lives entrusted to him. Through prayer, he protects what matters most.

Protecting what matters includes protecting purity in the deepest places of the heart and mind. In a world that constantly celebrates compromise and blurs the lines between right and wrong, a godly man chooses a higher path. He understands that purity is not weakness, nor is it an outdated idea from another generation. It is the decision to guard his eyes, his thoughts, his words, and his actions so that nothing corrupts the character God is forming within him. A man who values purity understands that what he allows into his life today will shape the man he becomes tomorrow. Purity preserves the soul and keeps the heart sensitive to the voice of God. When a man walks in holiness, his mind becomes clearer, his spirit becomes stronger, and his influence becomes greater. His life begins to reflect integrity, discipline, and honor. In choosing purity, a godly man is not merely avoiding sin; he is actively building a life that honors God and leaves a legacy of strength and righteousness for others to follow.

A true protector understands that strength is not only demonstrated on the outside but also cultivated within. He refuses to allow destructive influences to gain access to his life because he knows that what he allows into his eyes, ears, and heart will eventually shape who he becomes. The protector is mindful of what he watches, what he listens to, and what he meditates on, because he understands that the mind is the gateway to the soul. Just as a guard stands watch over a city gate, a wise man stands watch over his thoughts and influences, allowing only what strengthens his character, faith, and purpose to enter. By guarding his purity, the protector preserves his spiritual strength and integrity. He knows that compromise weakens a man, but discipline fortifies him. When he chooses righteousness over temptation and truth over deception, he builds a life that is stable, honorable, and powerful. His vigilance not only protects his own heart, but also strengthens his ability to lead, protect, and guide others.

Protecting purity also means honoring the sacred relationships God has entrusted to us. A faithful husband understands that marriage is not merely a contract but a holy covenant before God. He guards his heart, his eyes, and his actions so that his devotion remains centered on his wife. His faithfulness is an act of love and reverence, demonstrating that purity strengthens the foundation of trust within the home. A godly father also protects purity by nurturing the innocence and spiritual growth of his children. He creates an environment where truth, respect, and godly values are modeled daily. Through his words and actions, he teaches them the importance of boundaries that preserve trust and dignity. A wise man understands that honoring these boundaries safeguards relationships and builds a legacy of integrity. When a man chooses purity in his thoughts, speech, and conduct, he becomes a protector of hearts, a guardian of trust, and a pillar of strength for those God has placed under his care.

The battle for purity often begins in the mind. Long before actions are taken, thoughts are planted like seeds in the soil of the heart. If those seeds are allowed to grow unchecked, they eventually shape attitudes, desires, and behavior. That is why guarding your thoughts is essential. Scripture reminds us to take every thought captive and bring it under the authority of Christ. A disciplined mind becomes a protected place where truth, wisdom, and righteousness can flourish. Your mind is the control center of your life. What you allow to live there will eventually influence your decisions, actions, and direction. When a man fills his mind with God's truth, he strengthens his ability to choose what is right even when temptation appears. By rejecting corrupt thoughts and replacing them with what is pure, honorable, and worthy, he builds a life anchored in integrity. A guarded mind leads to a guarded life, and a guarded life becomes a powerful testimony of God's transforming work within the heart.

Many spiritual battles are won or lost in the mind long before they ever appear in outward behavior. The battlefield is often invisible, fought quietly within thoughts, attitudes, and inner conversations. What begins as a small, unchallenged thought can eventually influence decisions, actions, and character. This is why scripture calls believers to guard their hearts and minds carefully, recognizing that what we continually think about eventually shapes the direction of our lives. A protector understands that the mind must be defended with vigilance and truth. Instead of entertaining thoughts that weaken the soul, a spiritually disciplined person confronts them with God's promises and truth. Doubt is replaced with faith, fear with courage, and discouragement with hope. By choosing what to dwell on, the believer builds inner strength and resilience. When the mind is guarded and anchored in truth, the enemy loses one of his most powerful avenues of attack, and the soul remains strong, steady, and protected.

Every voice you allow into your life, every image you linger on, and every message you entertain plants a seed in the soil of your heart. Over time those seeds grow into beliefs, attitudes, and actions. A wise man understands that his inner world determines the direction of his outer life, so he carefully chooses what he allows to influence him. Instead of feeding his mind with negativity, fear, or corruption, he fills his thoughts with truth, faith, wisdom, and the promises of God. When a man becomes intentional about what he feeds his spirit, he begins to grow stronger in faith and clarity. He surrounds himself with voices that build him up, scriptures that renew his thinking, and influences that point him toward righteousness. By guarding his mind, he protects the foundation of his character and keeps his heart aligned with God's purpose. The battle for a man's life often begins in his thoughts, but the man who fills his mind with truth will walk in strength, peace, and spiritual authority.

The Word of God becomes a powerful guard over the mind, shaping the way a man thinks and responds to the challenges of life. As the mind is saturated with His Word, it becomes anchored in wisdom, and the believer gains the ability to stand firm even when the world around him feels unstable. A man who consistently fills his mind with truth develops spiritual discernment and inner strength. The Word teaches him to recognize what is right, reject what is harmful, and pursue what honors God. Instead of being led by emotion or influenced by every passing voice, he becomes steady, thoughtful, and spiritually alert. The more he meditates on God's Word, the stronger his inner life becomes, and the more clearly he hears the guidance of the Holy Spirit. In this way, Scripture not only informs the mind but also fortifies the soul, creating a man who is wise, grounded, and prepared to walk faithfully in God's purpose.

Protecting what matters requires courage. It is not always easy to stand firm for what is right, especially when the pressure to compromise is strong or when doing so may bring criticism or discomfort. Yet a true protector understands that love is not passive - it is active, watchful, and willing to take a stand. Courage becomes the shield that protects what is precious. There will be moments when a man must rise above the fear of conflict and choose faithfulness over convenience. Standing firm may feel uncomfortable, but strength is often forged in those very moments. A protector recognizes that the safety and spiritual health of those he loves are worth defending. When he resists pressures that threaten their peace, he demonstrates not only strength but also deep devotion. Through courage, he becomes a steady presence - someone others can trust to guard what matters most. In doing so, he reflects the heart of a faithful guardian who refuses to let fear dictate his actions.

True strength is not measured by physical ability alone. Muscles may lift heavy burdens, but character carries the weight of life's most important responsibilities. Character forms the backbone of true manhood, and conviction gives a man the ability to hold his ground when circumstances try to shake him. Spiritual resolve is what anchors the soul, keeping a man steady when storms arise and pressures attempt to bend his values. A strong man stands firm for what is right even when the world encourages compromise. He understands that popularity is not the measure of righteousness, and that truth does not change simply because it becomes unpopular. When others drift with the current of culture, he chooses to remain anchored in God's principles. His strength is seen in his willingness to live by those convictions that honor the Lord. In a world that often rewards compromise, the man who stands firm becomes a pillar of stability, demonstrating that true strength flows from a heart fully surrendered to God.

God designed men with the capacity to carry burdens, to stand firm when others feel weak, and to create stability in uncertain times. Just as a strong tree provides shade and shelter during a storm, a godly man becomes a source of refuge for his family, friends, and community. His strength is not measured by how much he can dominate, but by how faithfully he can serve, protect, and uphold what is right. When a man walks in this calling, his strength becomes a blessing to others. He provides security through wisdom, courage through example, and peace through steady leadership. The protector understands that God entrusted him with influence not for selfish gain but for the good of those he loves. In this way, his life reflects the heart of Christ - the ultimate protector and shepherd - who laid down His life for others. A true protector stands watch, carries burdens, and remains faithful, knowing that his strength is a gift from God meant to uplift, defend, and care for the people placed within his reach.

When a man protects what truly matters, he becomes a shelter for those around him. His life becomes a steady wall others can lean on when storms arise. His leadership provides direction where confusion once lived, and his calm strength reminds others that someone is watching, guiding, and standing guard. A man who protects what matters does not simply talk about responsibility - he lives it in the quiet decisions he makes every day. Such a man becomes a source of trust in a world full of uncertainty. His integrity builds confidence in the hearts of those he leads, because his words and actions match. His family feels secure because they know he stands firm in both conviction and love. Friends and community members are strengthened by his example, seeing in him a man who refuses to abandon what is sacred. When a man chooses to guard truth, purity, and purpose, his life becomes more than personal success - it becomes a refuge for others, a place where strength and peace meet.

The world desperately needs men who embrace a protector mindset - men who understand that strength is not merely for personal success, but for the safeguarding of what God has entrusted to them. Families flourish when a man stands watch over the spiritual atmosphere of his home. Communities grow stronger when men choose courage over passivity and responsibility over indifference. Churches become pillars of hope when men step forward to defend truth, encourage the weak, and live with unwavering integrity. A man who embraces this calling becomes a shield of stability in an unstable world. When men rise to protect what truly matters entire generations are strengthened. Children grow up with confidence when they see a father who stands firm in conviction. Wives feel secure when they know the man beside them guards the spiritual direction of the home. Younger men gain a model worth following when they witness quiet strength paired with humility and conviction.

Protect what matters. Cover your family in prayer, because prayer builds a spiritual hedge of protection around the people you love. Protect your purity for it keeps your heart clear before God and your life aligned with His purpose. Guard your mind because the thoughts you allow to live there will shape the person you become. A disciplined mind becomes a fortress the enemy cannot easily penetrate. Stand strong not only for yourself, but for those who depend on your strength. A protector understands that his courage, faith, and integrity become a shield for others who may be weary or vulnerable. When you live with the heart of a protector, you reflect the very character of God, who faithfully watches over His people day and night. Just as the Lord guards, guides, and defends those who belong to Him, you are called to stand watch over the gifts He has entrusted to you - your faith, your family, your purity, and your mind. In doing so, you become a living example of God's protective love in action.

| 17 |

"HONEST CONVERSATIONS"

God did not design men to hide behind silence. From the beginning, the Lord spoke creation into existence, demonstrating that words carry power and purpose. Light appeared when God spoke, order formed when He declared it, and life came forth through His voice. In the same way, a man created in God's image is meant to use his words with intention and courage. A godly man understands that communication is part of his calling. His words bring clarity where there is confusion, encouragement where there is weariness, and truth where there is compromise. When a man refuses to speak truth, encouragement, or correction when it is needed, he abandons part of the responsibility God has given him. Leadership requires the courage to open one's mouth and speak with honesty, humility, and love. Godly communication is purposeful and constructive. When a man speaks with wisdom and conviction, his voice becomes a tool God can use to build, protect, and guide those entrusted to his care.

Many men believe silence protects them from conflict, but silence often creates deeper problems. When concerns are buried instead of addressed, misunderstandings multiply and relationships begin to weaken under the weight of what was never said. Silence may feel safe for the moment, but in the long run it can quietly erode trust, unity, and respect. Godly leadership requires the courage to use one's voice with wisdom, humility, and love. Speaking honestly does not mean speaking harshly; it means addressing matters with integrity and a heart that seeks restoration rather than victory. A strong man is the one who is willing to step into those moments with calmness and grace. When a man speaks truth with compassion, he brings clarity where confusion once lived and healing where tension once lingered. Leadership requires a voice that is willing to speak when it matters most, because words spoken with wisdom can build bridges, restore relationships, and guide others toward peace.

A man of God must recognize that his words are tools placed in his hands by the Lord Himself. God gives a man a voice so he can guide those entrusted to his care, protect them from danger, teach them truth, and inspire them to walk in faith. Just as a shepherd calls his sheep and they recognize his voice and follow, the people in a man's life need to hear his voice with clarity, wisdom, and conviction. When a man speaks with humility and purpose, his words can bring direction to confusion, peace to fear, and strength to weary hearts. A godly man seeks God for wisdom so that his voice becomes a source of encouragement, correction, and guidance. Through thoughtful, prayerful communication, a man can build trust, strengthen relationships, and lead others closer to the heart of God. When a man's words are shaped by faith and guided by love, they become instruments through which God works powerfully in the lives of others.

Honest conversations require courage because truth often exposes what comfort tries to hide. Many men would rather avoid difficult discussions than risk conflict, rejection, or misunderstanding. Yet God never called His people to live in avoidance. Throughout scripture, the Lord demonstrates that truth spoken in love brings clarity and healing. When a man chooses to speak honestly with humility and grace, he creates space for understanding instead of confusion. Difficult conversations, when handled with wisdom and patience, become instruments that strengthen relationships rather than weaken them. When people know that a man will speak truthfully while still showing compassion, they feel safe to open their hearts as well. In this way, courage in communication becomes a gift to those around him. It builds stronger families, deeper friendships, and healthier leadership. A man who learns to speak with honesty and grace becomes a builder of trust and a steward of relationships.

Many relationships do not crumble because love is absent, but because truth is withheld. When people avoid honest conversation, assumptions begin to grow, misunderstandings multiply, and hearts slowly drift apart. Silence can create a wall where there was once openness. A godly man understands that true strength is not found in avoiding difficult conversations but in approaching them with humility and courage. He recognizes that truth, spoken gently and sincerely, brings light into places where confusion once lived. Honest communication, when guided by love, becomes a tool that builds trust rather than destroys it. A godly man chooses words that heal, clarify, and restore. He does not weaponize truth, but he also refuses to bury it beneath fear or pride. By speaking with kindness, patience, and sincerity, he invites deeper understanding and stronger connection. In this way, truth becomes a bridge instead of a barrier, and relationships grow stronger because they are rooted in honesty and grace.

Speaking the truth in love requires both courage and compassion. Truth by itself can be harsh when it is delivered without tenderness, and words meant to correct can easily wound if they are spoken with pride or anger. Yet love that avoids truth becomes shallow and ineffective, offering comfort without guidance. A godly man understands that when he speaks honestly while maintaining a gentle spirit, his communication becomes a tool for healing, clarity, and growth. Learning to balance truth and love is part of spiritual maturity. A man who walks closely with God develops the wisdom to know when to speak firmly and when to speak softly, always seeking the good of others rather than the satisfaction of his own emotions. His goal is not to win arguments but to build people up. When truth is wrapped in genuine love, it becomes easier to receive and more powerful in its impact. In this way, a man who communicates with both conviction and compassion reflects the heart of Christ - steady in truth, yet rich in grace.

Honest conversations begin with humility. A strong man is not the one who always insists he is right, but the one who has the courage to admit when he is wrong. When a man humbles himself, he creates an atmosphere where honesty can flourish and where others feel safe to speak openly. Humility softens the heart and opens the door for understanding, reminding us that strength is not found in stubbornness but in the willingness to grow. When a man takes responsibility for his words and actions, he makes room for healing and reconciliation. Owning a mistake is not weakness - it is leadership. It shows integrity, maturity, and a desire for restoration rather than division. Honest humility disarms conflict and replaces it with respect, compassion, and renewed trust. In this way, a man who walks in humility becomes a builder of peace, using his words not as weapons, but as tools that repair what was broken and restore what once seemed lost.

Courageous vulnerability is another mark of godly communication. The world often tells men to hide their emotions, to appear tough and unaffected, as if strength means never letting anyone see your heart. But real strength is not found in pretending to be invincible - it is found in authenticity. A godly man has the courage to speak honestly about his struggles, his fears, and even his failures. When a man humbles himself enough to be transparent, he creates space for healing, growth, and deeper relationships. Vulnerability is not weakness; it is the doorway through which grace, wisdom, and restoration often enter. Jesus Himself demonstrated this kind of honest strength. He wept, He expressed sorrow, and He shared His heart with those closest to Him. A man who communicates like Christ does not hide behind pride or silence; he speaks truthfully and humbly. In God's kingdom, the strongest men are not the ones who hide their hearts, but the ones who have the courage to open them.

Vulnerability does not make a man weak; it makes him trustworthy. True courage is not found in pretending to have no wounds, but in having the humility to acknowledge them. When a man allows others to see his sincerity, he becomes real, approachable, and dependable. People instinctively trust a man who is authentic because his openness reveals integrity, and integrity builds confidence in those around him. When a man leads with this kind of honesty, he creates an environment where others feel safe to be genuine as well. In families, friendships, and communities, a man who is sincere with his heart encourages deeper conversations, stronger bonds, and lasting unity. Rather than weakening his influence, vulnerability strengthens it, because people follow those they trust. A man who is willing to be open, humble, and sincere becomes a source of stability, drawing others closer and building relationships that are rooted in truth, understanding, and mutual respect.

Courageous vulnerability is a powerful expression of faith. When a man humbly acknowledges his struggles, fears, and failures, he opens the door for God's grace to work within him. Pride tries to convince a man that he must appear strong at all times, but faith understands that true strength comes from surrender. By bringing his burdens into the light, a man invites God's healing, wisdom, and guidance into the areas of life where he needs it most. Vulnerability becomes an act of trust, declaring that God's power is greater than any weakness. When a man admits where he falls short, he allows the transforming work of God to take place. Honest confession breaks the chains of pride and replaces them with humility and dependence on the Lord. In that sacred place of transparency, God begins to rebuild confidence, restore courage, and strengthen character. A man who walks in courageous vulnerability does not rely on his own image of strength - he relies on the unfailing strength of God.

Words carry a quiet but profound power. God has placed within our speech the ability to shape hearts, strengthen spirits, and guide lives. A single sentence spoken with kindness can breathe hope into someone who feels defeated. A simple word of encouragement can remind a weary soul that they are not alone and that their story is not finished. Just as a gentle breeze can redirect a drifting sailboat, a timely word of wisdom can help someone find their way again. Every word we speak plants a seed in the hearts of others. Words filled with faith, truth, and love can inspire courage, restore confidence, and guide people toward God's purposes for their lives. When we choose our words carefully and speak with grace, we become instruments of encouragement and guidance in a world that desperately needs hope. A godly man understands this responsibility and uses his voice not to tear down, but to build up, strengthen, and lead others toward a better path.

A godly man understands that his words can either wound a soul or strengthen a heart. Instead of speaking out of anger, pride, or frustration, he chooses words that build others up. Harsh words may win an argument in the moment, but they often leave lasting scars and broken relationships behind. A man who walks with God realizes that his speech should reflect the character of Christ. He does not use his tongue as a weapon, but as a tool to encourage, guide, and restore. Wise words, spoken at the right moment, can breathe life into weary hearts. A timely word of encouragement can lift someone out of discouragement, restore hope, and remind them that they are not alone. A godly man listens carefully before he speaks, allowing the Spirit of God to shape his response. His goal is not simply to be heard, but to bring life, healing, and peace through what he says. In doing so, his words become a reflection of God's love, and those who hear them walk away strengthened, encouraged, and renewed.

Communication is the foundation of stability in every family. When a father speaks encouragement to his children, he plants seeds of confidence that will grow for years to come. A child who hears, "I believe in you," learns to face life with courage. In the same way, when a husband expresses appreciation and respect toward his wife, he strengthens the bond of love and security within the home. God designed the family to be a place where words lift, strengthen, and affirm the value of each person. A home filled with kind, thoughtful, and faith-filled words becomes a place of peace and spiritual strength. Encouragement builds faith in children, respect deepens love in marriage, and gentle speech invites the presence of God into daily life. When family members choose their words carefully, they help create a home where hearts feel safe and faith grows strong. In such an atmosphere, love flourishes and the family becomes a reflection of God's grace.

In leadership, clear communication brings unity and direction. God designed words to carry purpose, vision, and life. When a leader speaks with wisdom and sincerity, hearts align and people move forward together. Just as a shepherd calls his sheep and they recognize his voice, those who lead with clarity help others understand the path ahead. Clear communication removes uncertainty and replaces it with confidence. It reminds people not only what must be done, but why it matters in the greater purpose God has set before them. A leader who speaks with honesty, humility, and integrity creates an atmosphere of trust. When people know the direction and understand the vision, they are inspired to walk together in unity. Words guided by truth become instruments of peace, motivation, and faith. In this way, godly leadership does more than give instructions - it breathes life into a shared calling and points every heart toward the purpose God intends to fulfill through them.

A man who "says it like a man" does not speak with arrogance, aggression, or the need to overpower others. Instead, his words are steady, thoughtful, and purposeful. He understands that true strength is not measured by volume or force, but by clarity and honesty. When he speaks, people sense that his words are not driven by pride or ego, but by a desire to bring truth into the moment. A godly man chooses his words carefully because he understands that what he says has the power to build lives rather than tear them down. Such a man also speaks with conviction. He does not hide behind silence when truth needs to be spoken, nor does he manipulate others with clever words. Instead, he communicates with integrity, allowing his voice to guide, encourage, and strengthen those around him. His words become instruments of wisdom - correcting when necessary, uplifting when someone is discouraged, and pointing others toward what is right.

Discipline in speech is a mark of spiritual maturity. A wise man understands that words carry power and because of this, he learns to pause before speaking, allowing wisdom to guide his response. A disciplined man does not feel compelled to react to every situation; instead, he chooses his words carefully so that when he does speak, his voice carries clarity, grace, and purpose. Equally important is the discipline of listening. Listening demonstrates humility and respect, and it opens the door to understanding others more deeply. Many conflicts arise not from what is said, but from the failure to truly hear one another. A wise man listens first, seeking insight before offering his own thoughts. In doing so, he gathers wisdom, diffuses tension, and communicates with greater compassion. Meaningful communication begins not with speaking, but with listening, and the man who masters this discipline becomes a source of wisdom, peace, and strength to those around him.

When a man allows God to shape his words, his voice becomes a channel of blessing. Instead of reacting from pride, anger, or impatience, he speaks from a heart that has been surrendered to the Lord. His words begin to carry the fragrance of wisdom and grace. When confusion clouds the minds of those around him, his God-guided words bring clarity and direction. People feel strengthened because his voice reflects the heart of God rather than the impulses of the flesh. A man whose words are shaped by God becomes a builder of people. His encouragement lifts the weary, his counsel steadies the uncertain, and his kindness softens hardened hearts. Such a man understands that communication is not merely about expressing thoughts - it is about ministering grace. When the Spirit governs a man's words, every conversation becomes an opportunity for healing, hope, and strength, turning ordinary speech into a powerful instrument of God's blessing.

A godly man does not hide behind silence when courage is required. He understands that leadership often begins with a voice willing to speak what is right, even when it is difficult. His words are not reckless or harsh, but honest and guided by wisdom. He refuses the cowardice of avoiding hard conversations, choosing instead to communicate with clarity and integrity. In doing so, he reflects the character of Christ - firm in truth, yet rich in grace. When a man allows God to shape his heart, his words become instruments of life. He speaks in ways that strengthen the weary, encourage the discouraged, and bring direction to those who feel lost. His voice carries purpose because it is rooted in love and guided by wisdom. Rather than tearing down, his words build bridges, restore relationships, and inspire faith. A godly man understands that words have the power to change lives, and he accepts the responsibility of using his voice to lead, uplift, and bring light wherever he goes.

| 18 |

"LOVING WHEN IT'S DIFFICULT"

Marriage is not merely a romantic arrangement; it is a sacred covenant established before God. A covenant is stronger than emotion and deeper than convenience. Feelings may rise and fall, and circumstances may change, but a covenant stands firm because it is rooted in a promise made before the Lord. When a husband and wife join together in this holy bond, they are not simply agreeing to share life's pleasures - they are committing to walk faithfully together through every challenge that life may bring. When two people stand before God and vow to love one another, they enter a lifelong partnership designed to endure both sunshine and storms. True covenant love remains steady when emotions are strained and circumstances grow difficult. It chooses faithfulness over escape, forgiveness over bitterness, and unity over division. In honoring the covenant of marriage, a couple reflects God's enduring love - creating a foundation strong enough to sustain their family through every season of life.

Every marriage will eventually encounter storms. Life brings pressures that test even the strongest relationships - financial burdens, misunderstandings, disappointments, exhaustion, and seasons where hearts may feel distant. These challenges do not mean the marriage has failed. Rather, they reveal the true nature of the commitment two people made before God. A covenant is not built merely for easy days under clear skies; it is designed to endure the wind, rain, and thunder that inevitably come with life. When a couple chooses to remain faithful, patient, and loving during difficult seasons, their covenant grows stronger instead of weaker. Storms have a way of deepening trust, strengthening character, and reminding two people why they chose each other in the first place. With God at the center, even the fiercest trials can become opportunities for growth, grace, and renewed devotion. What once felt like a threat to the marriage can become the very storm that proves how firmly the foundation was built.

Covenant toughness means choosing commitment over convenience. In today's culture, people often walk away when things become uncomfortable, believing that difficulty is a sign that something is wrong. Yet the nature of covenant is different. Covenant love is not sustained by comfort but by character. It stands firm when emotions fluctuate and circumstances grow heavy. When two people enter into covenant before God, they are making a sacred promise that rises above feelings and temporary struggles. Covenant love remembers the vows spoken in sincerity and honors them even when the road becomes hard. This kind of toughness reflects the very heart of God, who keeps His promises even when His people fall short. Covenant love is a love that chooses perseverance over escape and faithfulness over convenience. Covenant toughness does not deny that challenges exist - it simply refuses to let those challenges break the promise that was made.

Marriage flourishes when both husband and wife understand that love is more than an emotion - it is a deliberate choice. Feelings are beautiful gifts, but they are not the foundation strong enough to sustain a lifelong covenant. Emotions can shift with circumstances, stress, or disappointment. True love, however, chooses to remain faithful even when emotions are quiet. This kind of love reflects the heart of God, who remains faithful to His promises regardless of the changing winds of human emotion. When disagreements occur and when life becomes overwhelming, the decision to remain devoted holds the relationship firm. Like an anchor that grips the ocean floor during turbulent seas, covenant commitment prevents a marriage from drifting into resentment or separation. A husband and wife who continually choose love through patience, forgiveness, and perseverance build a bond that grows stronger with time, proving that lasting marriages are sustained by faithful decisions made day after day.

The strongest marriages are not built on perfect circumstances but on unwavering commitment. When two people choose faithfulness, patience, and love through every season of life, their bond grows stronger than any challenge they face. A husband and wife who enter covenant with the understanding that leaving is not the first option create a foundation that can endure life's storms. Difficult seasons will come but couples who are committed remind themselves that the promise they made before God was not only for the easy days, but also for the hard ones. When couples face problems side by side with determination, they develop a bond that grows deeper with every trial they overcome. They understand that storms are temporary, but a broken covenant can leave wounds that echo through families and generations. A marriage that refuses to surrender to the storm becomes a testimony that love, when anchored in commitment and faith, can endure anything and emerge stronger on the other side.

Loving when it is difficult is one of the greatest tests of marriage. Anyone can be affectionate when life is calm, when words are gentle, and when hearts feel light. But real covenant love reveals itself when emotions are strained and patience feels thin. In those moments, love becomes a choice rather than just a feeling. True love is not proven during peaceful seasons, but during the storms when two people decide that protecting the relationship matters more than winning the argument. Choosing kindness when frustrations are high builds strength into the foundation of the relationship. It reminds both husband and wife that their commitment is deeper than temporary emotions. When a couple continues to love through disappointment, misunderstanding, and conflict, they are demonstrating the kind of faithful love that reflects God's own character - steady, patient, and enduring. Over time, those difficult moments become the very places where trust is strengthened and the covenant becomes unshakable.

Real love shines brightest during difficult seasons. Anyone can love when everything is easy but genuine love reveals its strength when circumstances are strained and emotions run high. True love chooses gentleness when harsh words are ready to spill out, remembering that words have the power either to wound or to heal. Real love is not driven by pride or momentary feelings; it is guided by a deeper commitment to care, protect, and uplift even when it requires sacrifice. True love also chooses grace when mistakes are made. It recognizes that no one is perfect and that relationships grow stronger through forgiveness rather than resentment. Grace restores trust and keeps the bond from breaking under pressure. In the hardest seasons, love becomes a steady light that refuses to fade. It reminds us that love is not merely an emotion - it is a daily decision. When patience replaces anger and gentleness replaces harshness, love becomes a reflection of the very heart of God.

Marriage requires learning how to love beyond mood and circumstance. Emotions rise and fall, and every relationship will pass through seasons of joy, stress, misunderstanding, and fatigue. If love depends only on how we feel in the moment, it becomes fragile and inconsistent. But true marital love is the daily choice to honor, respect, forgive, and remain faithful even when the heart feels tired or the situation feels difficult. In this way, love matures from a fleeting emotion into a steady commitment that reflects patience, grace, and perseverance. Love becomes truly powerful when it is rooted in character instead of emotion. Challenges may come, disagreements may arise, and life may test their resolve, but a love anchored in faith endures the storm. It stands firm because it is grounded in something deeper than feelings - it is built on conviction, devotion, and the belief that covenant love is meant to last. When love is anchored in faith and principle, it gains the strength to withstand almost anything.

Difficult moments reveal the true nature of love. When everything is easy and pleasant, almost any relationship can appear strong. But pressure exposes what lies beneath the surface. Conditional love quietly sets terms and expectations, but when those conditions are not met, affection begins to fade and commitment weakens. Yet trials serve a deeper purpose - they uncover whether love was built on convenience or on a sacred promise. Covenant love is different. Covenant love does not disappear when circumstances become difficult; it stands firm because it is rooted in a promise rather than a mood. This kind of love reflects the very heart of God, whose faithfulness does not waver when we stumble. Even when we fail, His love remains steady, lifting us up with mercy and calling us back with grace. In difficult seasons, covenant love becomes a stabilizing force, reminding us that real love is not proven when life is easy, but when we choose to remain faithful even when it costs us something.

Conflict is inevitable in every marriage because two imperfect people are learning to share one life. Differences in personality, expectations, habits, and communication styles naturally create moments of tension. One spouse may prefer quiet reflection while the other prefers open discussion. One may value structure while the other values spontaneity. These differences are not necessarily signs of a failing marriage; they are often simply evidence that two unique individuals are learning how to walk together. Marriage is not the union of two flawless people but the commitment of two growing people who must continually learn patience, understanding, and grace. When conflict arises, it becomes an opportunity rather than a threat. Healthy couples learn that disagreement does not have to lead to division. Instead, it can lead to deeper understanding when approached with humility and love. God uses these moments to shape character, teach forgiveness, and strengthen unity.

Conflict in marriage does not have to lead to collapse. In fact, when handled with humility and grace, it can become a pathway to deeper understanding and stronger unity. Two people who truly care for one another will inevitably see things differently at times, but disagreement does not have to become division. When couples choose patience over reaction and listening over defending, they create space for healing and clarity. In those moments, love proves itself not by avoiding conflict, but by navigating it with kindness and respect. The purpose of conflict should never be to win an argument, but to gain understanding. When victory becomes the goal, both partners lose; but when understanding becomes the goal, both partners grow. A godly marriage seeks reconciliation rather than domination. It asks, "How can we come closer through this?" rather than "How can I prove that I am right?" When two hearts remain committed to unity, even difficult conversations can strengthen the bond between them.

When couples approach conflict with the goal of winning, the relationship itself often becomes the greatest casualty. Words become weapons and the desire to be right overshadows the desire to be loving. In those moments, hearts close and walls begin to form. Yet God never designed marriage to be a battleground where one partner defeats the other. Instead, He calls husbands and wives to remember that they are on the same side, united in covenant. When both partners slow down, listen carefully, and speak with kindness, something beautiful begins to happen. Understanding replaces accusation and peace begins to grow where tension once lived. Conflict, when handled with patience and respect, becomes a tool that strengthens the bond rather than weakens it. In God's design, even disagreements can deepen love when both hearts are committed to humility, forgiveness, and unity. What once threatened the relationship can become a pathway to greater maturity, deeper trust, and a stronger marriage.

Words spoken in anger have a way of traveling farther than we intend and lasting longer than we expect. In a moment of frustration, sharp words may feel justified, but once released they cannot be taken back. Like a wound to the heart, they can leave scars that linger long after the argument itself has faded. Covenant love chooses restraint. It pauses before speaking, remembering that the person standing across from you is not an enemy to defeat, but a partner to protect. A strong marriage values the dignity of the other person, even in disagreement. Couples who understand covenant refuse to weaponize their words. Instead of tearing each other down, they choose language that preserves respect and honor. Disagreements will come, but when a husband and wife commit to speaking with grace, patience, and humility, they create a home where trust can grow and healing can flourish. In this way, guarding our words becomes an act of love that strengthens the covenant rather than weakening it.

Forgiveness is one of the strongest pillars that holds a marriage together when storms arise. Every relationship between two imperfect people will eventually experience mistakes, misunderstandings, and moments where words or actions cause pain. In those moments, bitterness can quietly grow if forgiveness is withheld. But when a husband and wife choose grace instead of resentment, they open the door for healing. Forgiveness reminds us that love is greater than pride, and that restoration is more valuable than being right. When forgiveness is practiced, wounds begin to mend and hearts soften again. It does not erase the mistake, but it removes the poison that would otherwise destroy the relationship. Just as God continually extends mercy to us, couples are called to extend that same mercy to one another. Forgiveness allows love and compassion to rebuild what was shaken. In this way, forgiveness becomes a lifeline that preserves the covenant and strengthens the bond between two hearts.

A stable marriage becomes the cornerstone of a healthy and thriving family. When a husband and wife remain committed to one another through every season of life, they create an atmosphere of strength and reliability in the home. Children may not understand every detail of life, but they quickly recognize consistency, love, and unity between their parents. When they see their mother and father choosing each other day after day, it builds a deep sense of security in their hearts. That security becomes the soil in which their confidence, character, and faith begin to grow. They know they are protected, valued, and supported. A strong marriage models commitment, forgiveness, patience, and love - lessons that children carry with them into their own future relationships. In this way, a stable marriage does more than strengthen a couple; it establishes a powerful spiritual and emotional foundation that blesses the entire household and shapes generations to come.

Children learn far more from what they see than from what they are told. When parents demonstrate loyalty, patience, and perseverance in their marriage, they give their children a living picture of covenant love. They show that love is a sacred commitment that remains steady through both joy and hardship. When children watch their parents forgive one another, speak with kindness, and remain faithful through challenges, they begin to understand that true love endures. In this way, the home becomes a classroom where the character of God's covenant love is quietly and powerfully displayed. The lessons children learn from their parents' marriage will shape their own relationships for years to come. A home where covenant love is practiced teaches children that relationships are worth protecting and nurturing. When parents model a marriage rooted in devotion and perseverance, they are preparing the next generation to build relationships marked by the same enduring love.

Marriage in the storm is not about pretending everything is perfect. It is not about hiding pain, avoiding conflict, or pretending that challenges do not exist. Every marriage will face moments when the winds of pressure blow and the waves of hardship rise. Financial strain, misunderstandings, disappointments, and seasons of exhaustion can test even the strongest relationships. Yet the strength of a marriage is not measured by the absence of storms, but by the commitment to remain standing together in the middle of them. When a husband and wife choose honesty, humility, and grace during difficult seasons, they demonstrate a covenant love that refuses to run when life becomes uncomfortable. When couples forgive quickly, the storm that once threatened them can actually strengthen their bond. In those moments, marriage becomes more than a relationship - it becomes a shelter where faith, perseverance, and commitment grow stronger than the storm around them.

There will be seasons when loving each other feels effortless and joyful, but there will also be moments when love must be a decision rather than an emotion. In those moments, covenant love rises above pride, frustration, and disappointment. It refuses to walk away when things get difficult. Instead, it holds tighter, prays deeper, and remembers the sacred vow that was made before God. A covenant marriage is not built on perfect people, but on two hearts that refuse to quit on each other. True covenant toughness also shows itself in how couples handle conflict and protect the stability of their home. Disagreements will come, but they do not have to destroy the relationship. A strong marriage learns how to forgive quickly and fight for the relationship rather than against each other. When a marriage is rooted in commitment and strengthened by faith, even the fiercest storm cannot tear it apart, because what God has joined together is held together by love and the unbreakable power of covenant.

| 19 |

"MODELING TOUGHNESS"

One of the greatest responsibilities God entrusts to a man is the sacred privilege of fatherhood. A father does far more than provide food, shelter, and clothing - he helps shape the heart, mind, and spirit of the next generation. Children watch their fathers closely, learning from the way they speak, work, pray, and handle life's challenges. A godly father models strength, integrity, and faith in everyday life. Through his example, he teaches his children that life is to be lived with courage, discipline, and trust in God. In a culture that often rewards constant complaining, fathers are called to raise warriors, not whiners. A warrior spirit is about resilience, responsibility, perseverance, and faith. Fathers build this spirit when they teach their children to face difficulty with courage, to work hard, and to rely on God in every season. When a father raises his children with strength and love, he is equipping them to stand strong in a world that desperately needs men of character, conviction, and unwavering faith.

Children are always watching. A father may speak many wise words, but the lessons that shape a child most deeply are the ones lived out in everyday life. When a father rises early, works faithfully, keeps his promises, and stands firm in his convictions, he becomes a living sermon his children can see. Courage, discipline, and integrity are not merely ideas to be explained - they are qualities to be demonstrated. As children observe their father choosing what is right over what is easy, they begin to understand what true strength looks like. In this way, a father's life becomes a blueprint for the character his children will one day carry into the world. Modeling toughness does not mean becoming harsh, distant, or cold. True strength is revealed in perseverance, patience, and faith when life grows difficult. When children watch their father endure hardship without bitterness, they discover that courage is not the absence of struggle, but the determination to keep moving forward with faith.

True toughness is rarely displayed in dramatic moments; it is most often revealed in the quiet faithfulness of daily life. A father shows real strength when he continues to stand firm through ordinary pressures - working hard when he is weary, remaining patient when frustration rises, and choosing integrity when shortcuts and compromise seem easier. These everyday decisions become living sermons that his children watch unfold before their eyes. They learn that strength is steady, dependable, and rooted in character. In these quiet acts of perseverance, a father becomes a powerful example of godly manhood. His refusal to quit teaches his children resilience, his commitment to righteousness teaches them integrity, and his faithful endurance shows them how to walk with courage through life's trials and challenges. What they witness day after day becomes the pattern they follow, shaping a generation that understands that true manhood is forged not in ease, but in faithful endurance.

A father's attitude quietly shapes the atmosphere of his home. When a father constantly complains about life, work, or circumstances, his children begin to see the world through the same lens of frustration and defeat. But when a father chooses faith over frustration and strength over self-pity, he teaches a far greater lesson. Children learn that difficulties are not excuses to quit but opportunities to trust God and grow stronger. A father who faces adversity with courage shows his children that challenges are the proving ground where character is built. If a father remains steady in spirit, anchored in faith and hopeful in the face of hardship, that stability becomes the foundation of the family. His calm strength reassures his children that storms can be endured and victories can be won. In this way, a father becomes more than a provider - he becomes the thermostat of the household, setting the tone of perseverance, faith, and resilience that shapes the next generation.

Spiritual toughness begins with faith in God. A warrior father understands that real strength is born from a humble trust in the Lord who guides every step. When children watch a father bow his head in prayer, seek God's wisdom, and place his burdens before the Lord, they learn that courage flows from faith. He teaches them that the strongest man is not the one who stands alone, but the one who stands firmly with God. Through his example, they see that trusting God provides a strength that no storm of life can shake. In a world that praises independence and pride, he demonstrates that true courage grows out of dependence on God. When challenges come, he turns to the Lord with confidence, knowing that God is his refuge and strength. His children learn that the greatest battles are won on their knees before they are ever fought in the world. By modeling faith, humility, and trust, he lays the foundation for a legacy of spiritual courage that will guide his children long after his voice has faded.

Discipline is one of the most powerful gifts a father can give his children. True discipline is not harshness, anger, or punishment for its own sake - it is loving training that shapes the heart and mind. Just as a warrior trains his body through repetition and correction, a child must be guided through consistent instruction and loving boundaries. When a father disciplines with patience and wisdom, he teaches his children that actions have consequences, that character matters, and that self-control is a strength. In this way, discipline becomes a form of love that prepares a child for the battles and responsibilities of life. When discipline is absent, children are left without direction, like soldiers sent into battle without training. They grow fragile, easily discouraged, and unprepared for hardship. But when discipline is rooted in love and guided by godly wisdom, it builds strength within them. It teaches them to stand firm, to correct their mistakes, and to pursue what is right even when it is difficult.

The Bible reminds us that the Lord disciplines those He loves. In the same way, a father disciplines his children because he cares deeply about who they will become. True discipline is not born from anger but from love and responsibility. A father who loves his children understands that correction today shapes character tomorrow. By guiding them firmly yet lovingly, he helps them understand the difference between right and wrong, preparing their hearts to walk in wisdom and integrity. Loving discipline prepares a child for life's realities. It teaches them that actions have consequences and that righteousness requires self-control. When discipline is given with patience and compassion, it becomes a powerful tool for growth rather than a source of resentment. Just as God corrects His children to lead them into greater maturity, a faithful father disciplines his children to help them grow strong in character, steady in faith, and prepared to face the challenges of life with courage and wisdom.

Discipline reaches its greatest purpose when it is rooted in love. Scripture reminds us that God disciplines His children because He loves them and desires their growth. In the same way, a wise father does not correct out of anger, frustration, or control, but out of a deep commitment to his child's future. Harshness without love can wound the heart and create resentment, but loving discipline communicates care, guidance, and protection. When children know they are loved, correction becomes a tool for growth rather than a source of fear. True fatherly wisdom balances firmness with compassion. Boundaries provide structure and direction, while love provides encouragement and security. When a father disciplines with patience, kindness, and consistency, he shapes character rather than crushing the spirit. Through loving discipline, a father helps his children develop strength, responsibility, and integrity - qualities that will guide them long after they leave his home.

When correction is given with patience, wisdom, and genuine love, the child begins to understand that every action carries a consequence. Discipline is not meant to shame or crush the spirit, but to guide the heart toward responsibility and integrity. Through consistent instruction, a young person learns that choices matter and that maturity is built through accepting responsibility for one's actions. This kind of loving guidance strengthens character and teaches the value of self-control. Over time, these lessons prepare a child to face life with courage rather than avoidance. Instead of running from mistakes or blaming others, they learn to stand up, make things right, and grow stronger through the process. Loving discipline forms a foundation of inner strength, helping a young person develop resilience, wisdom, and humility. In this way, accountability becomes a gift - one that equips them to walk through life with confidence, honor, and the maturity needed to overcome challenges.

Resilience is another vital trait a father must teach. Life will bring setbacks, disappointments, and trials, and no child grows into strength without encountering difficulty along the way. A wise father prepares his children for these realities by teaching them that hardship is not a sign of defeat, but an opportunity for growth. Through encouragement, guidance, and example, he shows them how to stand back up when life knocks them down. Instead of allowing failure to define them, he helps them see every struggle as a lesson, every obstacle as a chance to become stronger, and every challenge as a step toward maturity. Fathers who raise warriors help their children understand that hardship is not the end of the story - it is often the beginning of something greater. Trials refine character, build endurance, and deepen faith in God's purpose. When a father teaches resilience, he equips his children with the courage to keep moving forward when the path becomes difficult.

A wise father understands that failure is not the enemy of growth - avoiding struggle is. When a child faces disappointment, setbacks, or mistakes, the loving response of a father is not to remove every obstacle but to walk beside his child through it. Just as God patiently leads His children through trials, a godly father teaches that perseverance is born in the furnace of difficulty. Through encouragement, wisdom, and steady support, he helps his child rise again with greater courage than before. By allowing children to wrestle with challenges while offering guidance and strength, a father prepares them for the realities of life. Every struggle becomes a sacred classroom where God teaches resilience to endure, faith to trust His plan, and determination to keep moving forward. In this way, a father raises sons and daughters who face adversity with confidence and trust in God. The greatest gift a father can give is not a life free of struggle, but the character and faith needed to overcome it.

Resilient children learn early that falling down is part of the journey of growth. Every stumble becomes a lesson, every challenge an opportunity to become stronger. A warrior father understands this and refuses to raise children who fear failure. Instead, he teaches them to face life with courage, reminding them that setbacks are not the end of the story. When a child falls, a wise father does not rush to remove every hardship, but he guides them to stand again, dust themselves off, and keep moving forward. Through patience, encouragement, and example, he shows them that strength is not measured by how many times you fall, but by how many times you rise. More importantly, a godly father teaches his children that resilience is rooted in faith. Life will bring storms, disappointments, and moments of weakness, but God uses adversity to shape character and deepen wisdom. Just as a warrior becomes strong through battle, a child grows strong through trials faced with faith.

Teaching resilience also means cultivating courage. A wise father does not shield his children from every challenge but instead equips them to face life with faith and determination. He encourages them to attempt difficult things, to step beyond their comfort zones, and to confront fears rather than retreat from them. Whether it is standing up for what is right or pursuing a goal that requires sacrifice, these moments shape the character of a child. As children accept these challenges, they begin to discover they are capable of more than they imagined. Each obstacle overcome builds confidence and strengthens their spirit. They learn that setbacks are not the end of the journey but opportunities for growth and wisdom. A father who teaches resilience plants seeds of bold faith, reminding his children that God walks with them in every trial. In this way, courage becomes a lifelong companion, empowering them to pursue worthy goals and stand firm in the calling God has placed upon their lives.

A father must look beyond the present moment and think about the legacy he is building. Every word he speaks and every decision he makes is planting seeds in the hearts of his children. Fatherhood is not merely about guiding a child through the years of youth; it is about shaping the character of men and women who will one day guide others. When a father teaches integrity, faith, courage, and humility, he is laying a foundation that will influence not only his children, but also the families, communities, and churches they will one day lead. In this way, a father's influence stretches far beyond his own lifetime. The values he plants today can echo through generations, forming future fathers, leaders, and servants of God who carry those same principles forward. A godly father understands that he is helping shape the future of God's kingdom through the lives entrusted to him. When he leads with wisdom, love, and faith, he leaves behind a spiritual legacy that will continue to bear fruit long after he is gone.

A man who thinks about legacy understands that every word and action matters. He realizes that leadership in the home is not merely about providing material needs, but about planting spiritual seeds that will grow long after he is gone. His children are always watching

- learning how to respond to adversity, how to treat others, and how to walk with God by observing his example. When he prays, they learn the value of faith. When he shows integrity, they learn the importance of character. When he extends grace and love, they learn the heart of Christ. A father who lives with legacy in mind understands that the small, everyday moments are shaping the future of the next generation. He knows that the habits he models today will become the patterns his children follow tomorrow. Patience, discipline, humility, courage, and devotion to God are not just personal virtues - they are seeds being planted in young hearts. Over time those seeds grow into strong character, deep faith, and resilient lives.

When fathers raise warriors, they are shaping far more than the character of a single child - they are shaping the future of families, communities, and the church itself. A warrior-minded man stands firm when others compromise, holds to righteousness when the culture drifts, and chooses courage when fear would be easier. A father who models faith, discipline, and perseverance plants seeds that grow into men who will protect their families, strengthen their communities, and honor God in every arena of life. These men become pillars of stability in a world that often rewards weakness and confusion. Warrior-minded men defend what is right with humility and a servant's heart. They lead their homes with wisdom, stand guard over the values that matter most, and carry the quiet courage that refuses to bow to pressure or compromise. When fathers commit to raising warriors, they create a generation of men who walk in truth, lead with courage, and build a stronger, godly future for those who follow.

The world does not need another generation trained to complain about every hardship or retreat when life becomes difficult. Complaining weakens the spirit and clouds the vision God has placed within a person's heart. Scripture consistently reminds us that growth often comes through trials. Hardship is not meant to destroy us but to shape us. When men choose faith over frustration, they discover a strength that cannot be shaken by circumstance. Instead of becoming victims of adversity, they become overcomers who trust that God is working even in the difficult moments. What the world truly needs are men who stand firm in their faith, rise above adversity, and carry forward the timeless principles of courage and responsibility. These are the men who refuse to surrender their character when pressure comes. They understand that faith is not proven in comfort but in challenge. By choosing perseverance, integrity, and trust in God, they become examples for others to follow.

A father who embraces the sacred calling of leadership in the home plants seeds that will grow long after he is gone. His words, his discipline, his example, and his unwavering faith become the foundation upon which future generations build their lives. When a father chooses courage over comfort and truth over convenience, he teaches his children that strength of character matters more than temporary ease. His legacy is not measured in possessions or achievements, but in the spiritual strength he leaves within the hearts of those he has raised. The values he lived - faith in God, resilience in hardship, and integrity in all things - echo through the lives of his children and grandchildren. When fathers raise warriors instead of whiners, they prepare the next generation to stand firm in a world that often encourages weakness and compromise. They teach their children to trust God when life is difficult, to persevere when challenges arise, and to walk boldly in the purpose God has placed on their lives.

| 20 |

"IRON SHARPENS IRON"

From the very beginning, God made it clear that men were never meant to walk the path of life alone. When the Lord looked upon Adam in the garden, He declared that it was not good for man to be alone. God understood that isolation weakens the heart, dulls conviction, and leaves a man vulnerable to battles he was never meant to fight by himself. A man standing alone becomes an easy target for discouragement, temptation, and despair. But when men stand together - encouraging one another and praying for one another - they become stronger in spirit, clearer in purpose, and steadier in faith. Brotherhood is one of God's greatest gifts to men because it forms a sacred bond that builds character, reinforces faith, and keeps a man accountable to the life he is called to live. True brothers challenge one another to rise higher, to live with integrity, and to remain faithful when the road grows difficult. They remind each other of God's promises and stand shoulder to shoulder when storms come.

Many men today pride themselves on independence, believing strength means standing alone. But the truth is that God never designed a man to live in isolation. Lone wolves may appear strong for a season, but storms eventually reveal the weakness of solitude. When a man walks alone, there is no one to sharpen his thinking or help him rise when he falls. What feels like independence can quietly become a prison where pride replaces wisdom and silence replaces accountability. God's design for men has always included brotherhood. Strength grows when men stand shoulder to shoulder, encouraging one another, praying for one another, and challenging each other to live righteously. In true brotherhood, a man finds hands that lift him when he stumbles, and hearts that refuse to let him quit when the road becomes hard. When men walk together in faith, they become stronger, wiser, and more resilient, proving that real strength is not found in isolation but in the power of godly fellowship.

God never intended for men to walk the path of faith alone. From the beginning, He called men to walk together - encouraging one another, strengthening one another, and standing side by side in the journey of faith. When men gather in brotherhood, they create an environment where truth is spoken, burdens are shared, and courage is renewed. In that kind of fellowship, faith becomes stronger because it is reinforced by the prayers and wisdom of others who are walking the same road. Just as iron sharpens iron, men grow sharper, stronger, and wiser when they surround themselves with godly companions who challenge them to rise higher. Honest accountability protects a man from drifting and keeps his heart aligned with God's purpose. Through shared experiences - both victories and struggles - men build one another up and become spiritual pillars for each other. In this sacred bond of brotherhood, faith is strengthened, refined, and prepared for the battles and blessings that lie ahead.

The Bible reminds us that "iron sharpens iron, and one man sharpens another" (Prov. 27:17). Just as two blades rubbing together remove dull edges and produce a sharper tool, godly relationships refine the character of a man. When men walk together in faith, they speak truth, share wisdom, and help each other see blind spots that would otherwise go unnoticed. Through honest conversation, encouragement, and accountability, each man becomes stronger, wiser, and more prepared for the battles of life. Genuine friends care enough to challenge complacency, confront weakness, and call one another to a higher standard of living. They remind each other of God's truth, lift one another up during struggle, and celebrate victories along the journey. In this kind of fellowship, character is refined, faith is strengthened, and courage is renewed. Just as iron grows sharper through friction, a man becomes stronger when surrounded by brothers who are willing to sharpen him with truth, loyalty, and love.

Brotherhood is not about casual friendship or shallow connection. It is built on a shared commitment to see one another grow, succeed, and fulfill the calling God has placed upon their lives. It is a bond where men stand together in faith, encouraging one another to become better husbands, fathers, leaders, and servants of God. These relationships are not formed through convenience, but through sincerity, honesty, and a shared pursuit of righteousness. In true brotherhood, men speak truth to one another with humility and respect. They celebrate victories, confront weaknesses, and offer strength during moments of struggle. This kind of relationship creates an environment where character is sharpened and purpose becomes clearer. When men walk together in this spirit, they become stronger than they could ever be alone. Their unity reflects God's design for community, where encouragement, accountability, and mutual support help each man walk faithfully in the life he was created to live.

A true brother will tell you what you need to hear, not merely what you want to hear. Real brotherhood is not built on flattery, silence, or comfortable agreement - it is built on truth spoken in love. When a man begins to drift, compromise, or lose focus, a godly brother refuses to stand by quietly. Instead, he steps forward with courage and care, speaking words that may be difficult but are necessary. The book of Proverbs reminds us that "faithful are the wounds of a friend," because a brother who loves you enough to confront you is helping protect your future. He is not attacking you; he is fighting for you. Accountability acts as a shield that guards a man's character from the slow erosion of compromise. Small compromises rarely look dangerous at first but left unchecked they quietly weaken a man's convictions and cloud his judgment. A faithful brother helps keep your vision clear and your path straight. He reminds you of who you are, what God has called you to be, and the standards you must live by.

One of the greatest dangers a man faces is not always loud, obvious temptation but the quiet influence of the wrong voices. The people a man allows into his inner circle slowly shape the way he thinks, what he believes, and ultimately the decisions he makes. Conversations, attitudes, and opinions repeated over time begin to mold a man's mindset. If those voices are negative, cynical, careless, or spiritually weak, they gradually pull a man away from strength, purpose, and faith. Scripture reminds us that "bad company corrupts good character," because influence works quietly but powerfully in the heart. But the opposite is also true. When a man surrounds himself with strong, godly influences, those voices call him upward instead of pulling him downward. Wise friends challenge him to grow, hold him accountable, and encourage him to live with courage and integrity. Just as iron sharpens iron, the presence of strong men strengthens a man's resolve to walk the right path.

Choosing the right brotherhood is one of the most important decisions a man can make, because the men you walk beside will shape the man you become. When you surround yourself with men who pursue God with sincerity, honor their families with devotion, work with integrity, and refuse to settle for mediocrity, you place yourself in an environment where growth is inevitable. Their discipline becomes a mirror that reflects your own potential, and their faith becomes a steady reminder that a higher standard of living is not only possible but expected. When the men around you strive to be better husbands, fathers, workers, and disciples of Christ, their example quietly challenges you to rise higher. Their prayers strengthen you in weakness, their accountability keeps you aligned with truth, and their courage inspires you to live boldly for God. Choose brothers who push you toward purpose, because the right brotherhood will not just walk with you through life - it will help shape the man God created you to be.

When men walk together with shared values and faith, something powerful begins to unfold among them. Courage multiplies because each man sees strength reflected in the others. When one grows weary, another stands firm. When one faces fear, another reminds him of who he truly is. Faith shared among brothers becomes a steady fire that refuses to burn out. Just as iron sharpens iron, strong men refine one another, shaping character, strengthening resolve, and pushing each other to live with greater purpose. They challenge one another to rise higher, stand stronger, and remain faithful even in difficult seasons. Together they overcome weakness, resist compromise, and pursue the calling God has placed upon their lives. A brotherhood built on faith does more than support its members - it elevates them. United in purpose and conviction, these men climb heights they could never reach alone, lifting each other toward strength, courage, and lasting impact.

When a man stands alone, he becomes an easy target for discouragement and defeat. But when godly men walk together, they become a wall of strength around one another. Brothers in faith speak truth when lies try to creep in, they pray when another is weary, and they remind each other of God's promises when doubt begins to whisper. Just as soldiers in battle guard each other's blind spots, spiritual brothers watch over one another's hearts, helping each other stay alert, disciplined, and faithful. In true brotherhood, men lift one another when someone begins to stumble and call each other back to purpose when distractions appear. Accountability strengthens character, and shared faith builds courage. A man surrounded by strong, faithful brothers becomes far more difficult for the enemy to defeat, because he is no longer fighting alone. Together they stand firm, sharpen each other, and move forward with greater strength, protecting not only themselves but the mission God has placed before them.

When men stand together, they become a wall of strength that the enemy cannot easily penetrate. In true brotherhood, men lift one another up in prayer, speak courage into weary hearts, and remind each other of God's promises when faith begins to waver. Just as soldiers stand shoulder to shoulder in battle, spiritual brothers stand together against temptation, discouragement, and fear. Their unity forms a barrier that protects each man from isolation, which is often where the enemy does his greatest damage. Brotherhood becomes a powerful spiritual defense system because every man brings strength to another man's weakness. When one grows tired, another steps in to carry the burden. When one begins to drift, another lovingly pulls him back toward truth. Through prayer and encouragement, brothers in faith sharpen one another and build resilience for the storms of life. In this kind of unity, men become stronger than they could ever be alone, standing firm together as a living wall built by God Himself.

True brotherhood is more than friendship; it is a spiritual alliance where men stand shoulder to shoulder, encouraging one another to remain faithful, to rise when they fall, and to keep moving forward until the victory God promised becomes reality. In moments of struggle, a brother reminds you who you are and what you stand for. When your vision becomes clouded with discouragement, a faithful brother reminds you that you are not defined by your current battle but by the calling God has placed upon your life. Like iron sharpening iron, his words restore courage and help you remember that God never intended for men to fight their spiritual battles alone. When fatigue sets in, a brother steps beside you and helps carry the load. His presence becomes a reminder that the journey of faith is meant to be walked together. And when the path grows dark and uncertainty surrounds you, a brother helps carry the light - lifting your eyes back to God's promises and pointing you toward hope.

A man who walks alone can easily drift into compromise, distraction, or complacency, but a man who surrounds himself with strong brothers gains a powerful advantage. When others are watching his life, encouraging his progress, and believing in his calling, it awakens a deeper level of discipline within him. He rises earlier, works harder, and guards his character more carefully because he understands that his life influences those around him. Brotherhood keeps a man focused on the life he was created to live. True brothers remind one another of their purpose when temptation tries to pull them off course. They challenge each other to grow stronger, wiser, and more faithful. Like iron sharpening iron, their presence refines character and strengthens resolve. When a man commits to walking with brothers who pursue God, excellence, and integrity, he finds the courage to live at a higher level. Through brotherhood, he discovers the strength to become the man he was always meant to be.

Throughout history, the greatest leaders surrounded themselves with trusted voices - friends, mentors, and brothers who challenged their thinking and strengthened their resolve. These relationships acted like iron sharpening iron, refining character, exposing weaknesses, and encouraging growth. God never intended for a man to walk his path alone. Wisdom multiplies when it is shared, and strength grows when faithful companions stand beside you. No lasting legacy is built in solitude. The men who leave a powerful mark on the world understand the value of a strong circle - people who speak truth, offer accountability, and encourage perseverance when the road becomes difficult. Behind every strong leader is a fellowship of voices that helped shape his journey, reminding him of his purpose and calling him to something greater. When men stand together in faith and purpose, they create an environment where courage rises, character deepens, and destinies are fulfilled.

When men strengthen, encourage, and challenge one another to grow, the effects ripple outward into every area of life. A man who is supported by faithful brothers becomes a better father, a better husband, and a better leader. When a man builds his life on godly character, his heart grows steadier, his decisions become wiser, and his example becomes a guiding light that strengthens everyone around him. When men stand together in faith, families grow stronger, communities become healthier, and future generations inherit a clearer picture of true manhood. Sons and daughters learn what integrity, loyalty, and courage look like by watching men who support and uplift one another. Brotherhood builds a foundation of strength that lasts for generations. In this way, the legacy of a faithful brotherhood is not measured merely by individual accomplishments, but by the lives transformed and the enduring example of godly character passed down to those who follow.

When a man surrounds himself with strong, godly brothers, he places himself in an environment where wisdom is sharpened, character is refined, and courage is strengthened. Each man brings a different perspective, a different testimony, and a different strength to the table. Through honest conversation, accountability, and shared experience, a man gains insights he could never discover by himself. In this way, brotherhood becomes a place where men grow stronger together and where one man's victory becomes a victory for all. When men stand together in faith, they build legacy, strength, and spiritual impact that reaches beyond themselves. One man may plant the seed, another may water it, and another may help it grow, but together they advance the purposes of God in powerful ways. A man who invests in brotherhood becomes part of a force that strengthens families, encourages faith, and changes communities. Alone a man can go far, but together men can transform the world around them.

When you surround yourself with brothers who love God deeply and pursue excellence in their lives, their strength begins to call out the strength within you. Their discipline challenges your complacency and their commitment to God reminds you of the standard you are called to live by. Walking with men who refuse to settle for mediocrity helps you rise above your own limitations and step more fully into the man God created you to be. Choose companions who challenge you to grow, not those who quietly accept your weaknesses. True brotherhood is not built on comfort but on accountability and the shared pursuit of God's purpose. When men walk together with a common commitment to honor God, they become a powerful force against compromise and spiritual drift. Stand beside men who will pray with you, speak truth to you, and push you toward greater faith. In that kind of brotherhood, strength multiplies, character deepens, and purpose becomes clearer with every step forward.

Brotherhood makes a man better because God never designed us to walk the road alone. When men surround themselves with strong, faithful brothers, accountability keeps their hearts sharp and their character strong. A brother will speak truth when pride tries to rise, offer correction when the path begins to drift, and remind a man of who he is called to be. Just as iron sharpens iron, godly brotherhood refines courage, strengthens conviction, and protects a man from the quiet dangers of isolation. Courage grows when men stand together, and shared strength helps a man keep moving when the road becomes difficult. In true brotherhood, burdens are carried together, victories are celebrated together, and no man is left to fight his battles alone. A man who walks with strong brothers will not only survive the journey, but he will also finish it with power, honor, and lasting impact, leaving behind a testimony of faith, strength, and unwavering commitment to the path God set before him.

| 21 |

"OWNING YOUR MISTAKES"

Every man faces battles in life, but the fiercest battles are fought within. Before a man ever conquers mountains, builds a legacy, or influences others, he must first confront the unseen struggles of his own heart. Pride, fear, doubt, anger, and temptation all wage war within the soul. Yet it is in these quiet, hidden moments that a man chooses who he will become. When he chooses truth over excuses, humility over pride, and obedience over impulse, the foundation of true strength is laid. The man who wins the inner battle learns to bring his thoughts, motives, and desires under the authority of God's truth. This requires honesty with oneself, humility before God, and the courage to face weaknesses rather than hide them. The heart becomes a training ground where faith grows stronger and character becomes refined. When a man consistently wins the battles within, he becomes wise and resilient. Out of that quiet victory flows a life of integrity, strength, and purpose that no outward storm can easily shake.

Excuses may soothe the conscience for a moment, but they quietly rob the soul of strength. Every time a man shifts blame or rationalizes his shortcomings, he builds a wall between himself and the growth God desires for him. Scripture consistently calls men to truth, humility, and accountability. When we hide behind excuses, we avoid the refining work of God that shapes our character. Excuses may protect pride, but they also imprison potential, keeping a man stuck in the very place he longs to escape. True strength begins when a man chooses honesty over comfort. The moment he stops explaining away his failures and starts owning them, transformation begins. God cannot reshape what we refuse to acknowledge, but when a man humbly admits his weaknesses, the Lord begins a deeper work within him. Responsibility is the doorway to maturity, wisdom, and spiritual victory. When excuses die, growth begins, and a man rises stronger, wiser, and more aligned with the purpose God has placed within him.

Blame is a subtle form of weakness because it quietly transfers responsibility away from the heart that needs to change. It is easier to point at circumstances, other people, or fate than it is to examine our own choices. Yet every time a man blames others, he unknowingly gives away the very power God placed within him - the power to grow, to learn, and to rise above adversity. Blame creates the illusion of relief, but in reality it chains a man to the same problems, keeping him trapped in cycles of frustration and disappointment. A strong man, however, chooses a different path. Instead of blaming, he accepts responsibility for his attitudes, actions, and responses. This mindset transforms him from a victim of life into a steward of it. When a man owns his failures, he also claims the authority to change his future. Growth begins where excuses end. In the hands of a humble and honest man, responsibility becomes a powerful tool God uses to shape character and lead him into maturity and wisdom.

A mature man does not hide behind explanations or shift the blame onto others when things go wrong. Instead, he looks honestly at his own actions and accepts responsibility for them. This kind of ownership requires courage, because it means facing our weaknesses without excuses. Yet it is in that very moment of honesty that a man begins to grow. When he stands tall and says, "The responsibility is mine," he steps out of the shadows of denial and into the light of transformation. That moment of ownership becomes the doorway to real change. God cannot reshape what a man refuses to acknowledge, but He eagerly works with the heart that is humble and honest. Accountability clears the ground for wisdom, discipline, and spiritual maturity to take root. The man who accepts responsibility gains the power to correct his course, learn from his failures, and rise stronger than before. True strength is found in the humility to admit wrong and the determination to grow beyond it.

Blaming others may soothe the ego for a moment, but it robs the soul of transformation. When a man shifts responsibility away from himself, he builds a wall between who he is and who he could become. Excuses may provide temporary comfort, but they quietly weaken character and stall spiritual growth. The path of maturity requires humility - the courage to look inward and say, "There is something in me that must change." In that moment of honesty, a man stops running from the truth and begins walking toward it. True growth begins when excuses end. When a man accepts responsibility for his actions, he opens the door for God to shape his character and renew his mind. Ownership creates fertile soil where wisdom, strength, and transformation can grow. Instead of remaining trapped in cycles of blame, he steps into the freedom of accountability. A man who embraces responsibility does not become smaller - he becomes stronger, wiser, and more aligned with the purpose God designed for his life.

Radical responsibility is the antidote to a life filled with excuses. A man who embraces this mindset refuses to hide behind blame, circumstances, or the failures of others. Instead, he stands firm and acknowledges that his choices, attitudes, and responses belong to him alone. Life may present difficulties, injustice, or unexpected setbacks, but a man of strength understands that his character is revealed in how he responds. By taking ownership of his actions and reactions, he shifts from being a victim of circumstances to becoming a steward of his own growth. This perspective creates power and freedom in a man's life. When he accepts radical responsibility, he learns from his mistakes, corrects his course, and grows wiser with every challenge. Even when he cannot control what happens around him, he chooses integrity, discipline, and faith in how he responds. In that moment, responsibility becomes more than a burden - it becomes the pathway to maturity, strength, and transformation.

Ownership of one's life requires a deep well of humility. Pride fights to protect the ego, searching for excuses and shifting blame so that the heart never has to face the truth. But humility has the courage to stand in the light and say, "I was wrong." In that moment, a man stops defending his failures and begins learning from them. He recognizes that mistakes are not the end of his story but the beginning of his refinement. Just as gold is purified through fire, a humble heart allows God to shape, correct, and strengthen it through every misstep. When a man lowers his defenses and honestly admits where he has fallen short, something powerful happens within him. The walls of pride crumble, and the door to transformation opens wide. Instead of being trapped by denial, he becomes teachable and ready to grow. Humility turns failure into instruction and weakness into wisdom. Through this posture, a man becomes stronger in character, deeper in integrity, and more aligned with the man God is calling him to become.

When a man accepts responsibility for his choices, attitudes, and actions, he is not tearing himself down; he is positioning himself to rise higher. Denial keeps a man stuck, but honesty sets him free. When you recognize your role in your failures, you gain the power to change direction. Instead of blaming circumstances, people, or the past, you step into the authority God has given you to grow, learn, and correct your course. There is great strength in facing the truth about yourself. Weakness hides, excuses, and deflects, but strength stands in the light and says, "I will own this, and I will become better because of it." Radical responsibility is not about shame - it is about transformation. It is the courage to confront your flaws, the humility to admit your mistakes, and the determination to become the man God created you to be. The strongest men are not those who pretend they are perfect, but those who are brave enough to face the truth and rise stronger because of it.

Owning your mistakes is one of the most powerful steps in personal growth because it opens the door to transformation. When a person humbly acknowledges where they have fallen short, they stop wasting energy defending the past and begin investing strength into building a better future. The man who is willing to say, "I was wrong," is not weak - he is courageous. Through humility comes clarity, and through clarity comes the opportunity to grow, mature, and walk in greater wisdom. When you acknowledge your failures honestly, you reclaim the ability to change them. What you own, you can improve; what you deny, you remain bound to. Refusing responsibility keeps a person trapped in cycles of frustration, but accepting responsibility places the steering wheel back in your hands. With God's grace, yesterday's mistakes can become today's lessons and tomorrow's strength. A man who faces the truth about himself is a man who is preparing to rise stronger than before.

Many men delay their progress because they refuse to confront their shortcomings. Instead of facing the truth, they construct explanations that soften their responsibility and protect their pride. These stories may bring temporary comfort, but they quietly imprison the soul. Every excuse becomes another brick in a wall that separates a man from the strength, wisdom, and maturity God desires to build within him. What feels like self-protection often becomes self-limitation, keeping him from stepping fully into the life he was created to live. True growth begins the moment a man stops defending his weaknesses and starts confronting them with honesty before God. A man who humbly acknowledges his faults opens the door for transformation, because God works most powerfully in hearts that are willing to be corrected. The walls built by excuses can be torn down by courage and humility, and on the other side stands the man he who is stronger, wiser, and shaped by truth rather than self-deception.

A man of integrity does not run from his errors; he faces them with courage and humility. Instead of hiding behind excuses or shifting blame, he pauses and reflects on his actions. He asks the hard questions, "What did I do wrong? What must I change? How can I grow from this?" These questions are not signs of weakness but marks of maturity. In the quiet moments of honest self-examination, the heart begins to align with truth, and character is strengthened through accountability. Through that process of reflection, wisdom begins to emerge. Each mistake becomes a teacher, and every failure becomes an opportunity for refinement. God often uses these moments to shape a man's character, teaching him patience, discernment, and humility. When a man chooses growth over denial, his integrity deepens and his path becomes clearer. In time, the very lessons born from his errors become the foundation for greater wisdom, stronger leadership, and a life that reflects both strength and grace.

When a man stands honestly before God, he stops hiding behind excuses and begins opening his heart to correction, grace, and guidance. God does not require perfection - He requires sincerity. When a man admits where he has fallen short, where he has been weak, or where he has wandered from the right path, he invites God's transforming power into those very places. Honesty becomes the doorway through which mercy enters and change begins. That same honesty must extend inward. A man who refuses to lie to himself becomes capable of real growth. When he acknowledges his faults, confronts his habits, and takes responsibility for his choices, he breaks the chains of self-deception. In that moment, transformation becomes possible. Truth clears the ground where character is built, wisdom grows, and strength is formed. The man who walks in honesty with God, with others, and with himself is a man who is steadily becoming the person God designed him to be.

The inner battle demands courage because the truth is not always comfortable. When a man begins to look honestly into his own heart, he often discovers things he would rather ignore - pride that resists correction, laziness that avoids responsibility, fear that shrinks back from calling, and decisions that were driven by impulse instead of wisdom. Facing these realities requires humility and bravery. Yet this honest confrontation is not meant to condemn us; it is meant to awaken us. God does not reveal weaknesses to shame His people, but to invite them into transformation. What is exposed in the light can be healed, strengthened, and redeemed. Each moment of conviction is an opportunity for growth, each admission of weakness a doorway to strength. When a man stops hiding from the truth and begins to face it with faith, God begins refining him like metal in a furnace. The process may be uncomfortable, but the result is powerful - clearer vision and a heart that grows more aligned with God's purposes.

When excuses die, responsibility comes alive awakening the strength, discipline, and God-given authority within a man to take ownership of his life and walk boldly in his purpose. A man who once blamed circumstances, other people, or past failures begins to see the truth - his life is not dictated by what happens to him, but by the choices he makes in response. This realization is both sobering and empowering. The moment a man stops defending his excuses, he begins unlocking the strength, discipline, and purpose that God placed within him from the beginning. From that point forward, every decision becomes a doorway to growth. Each step of obedience, humility, and honesty moves him closer to the man God designed him to be. Responsibility awakens purpose, and purpose fuels transformation. Instead of waiting for life to change, he becomes the man who changes his life by aligning his choices with God's truth. And in that moment, the inner battle begins to turn into inner victory.

Ownership empowers a man to rebuild what has been broken because it shifts his focus from blame to responsibility. Instead of dwelling on past failures or pointing fingers at circumstances or other people, he stands up and says, "This is mine to fix." That moment of honest acceptance becomes the turning point of transformation. When a man owns his mistakes, he gains the authority to change them. Walls that were torn down can be rebuilt, trust that was fractured can begin to mend, and paths that were lost can be rediscovered. Responsibility transforms regret into resolve. Regret alone only looks backward and keeps a man trapped in guilt, but responsibility looks forward and asks, "What can I do now?" God honors this spirit of accountability because it reflects a heart that remains humble, teachable, and ready for the growth that He desires to produce. When a man embraces responsibility, he uses his past as a foundation to build a stronger, wiser, and more faithful future.

The man who kills his excuses becomes dangerous in the best possible way. No longer does he hide behind blame or comfortable illusions. He confronts truth with courage and accepts responsibility for the direction of his life. When excuses die, clarity is born. A man begins to see where he must grow, where he must change, and where he must stand stronger. The fog of self-deception lifts, and in its place rises a man who is honest with himself and accountable before God. Such a man becomes focused, disciplined, and determined to grow. Instead of wasting energy defending his weaknesses, he invests that energy in strengthening his character. Each challenge becomes an opportunity to rise higher, and every mistake becomes a lesson that sharpens his wisdom. This kind of man is powerful because he refuses to remain the same. With humility before God and determination in his spirit, he moves forward with purpose, becoming a living example that growth begins the moment excuses end.

In the inner battle of a man's soul, excuses quietly become chains that bind him to a life far beneath his potential. They whisper comfortable lies - blaming circumstances, people, or past failures - while slowly draining courage and conviction. Yet excuses never produce freedom;

they only protect weakness. The moment a man chooses honesty over justification, he begins to see clearly. He recognizes where he has fallen short, where discipline has been lacking, and where responsibility has been avoided. When a man breaks the chains of excuses through truth and responsibility, he steps into a new kind of freedom. No longer trapped by denial, he becomes empowered to change what must be changed and rebuild what has been broken. Honesty plants the seed of growth deep within his character, and from that seed rises strength, discipline, and maturity. Growth then becomes inevitable, because truth has taken root in his heart, and a man who walks in truth cannot remain the same.

Excuses weaken the soul because they shift responsibility away from the place where growth begins. When a man who walks with God confronts his failures, admits his shortcomings, and lays them before the Lord, he begins to break the chains that once held him back. Truth becomes his ally, and integrity becomes the foundation upon which his character is built. When a man embraces radical responsibility, he steps into the authority and purpose God designed for him from the beginning. Ownership awakens strength, maturity, and clarity of direction. Instead of being controlled by circumstances, he becomes a man who leads his life with faith, discipline, and conviction. God works powerfully through the man who refuses excuses and chooses accountability, because such a man is ready to grow, ready to change, and ready to fulfill the calling placed upon his life. In that moment, responsibility becomes not a burden, but the doorway to the man God created him to be.

| 22 |

"THE PATH OF FAITH"

Fear often arrives quietly, whispering its warnings into the heart of a man. It rarely announces itself as fear. Instead, it disguises itself as caution, logic, or even wisdom. It tells a man to stay where it is safe, to avoid the unknown, and to protect himself from possible failure. Yet beneath that calm voice often lies a deeper enemy - the subtle attempt to keep a man from stepping into the calling God has placed upon his life. What appears to be wisdom can sometimes be hesitation, and what feels like protection can become a prison. Fear narrows a man's vision until he begins to measure his future by risk instead of by faith. But the life of faith has never been built on safety; it has always been built on trust. God calls men to move forward even when the path is uncertain and the outcome is unseen. When a man listens more closely to the voice of God than to the whisper of fear, he discovers that faith opens doors fear would have kept closed.

Fear often disguises itself as wisdom. It whispers warnings, paints vivid images of failure, and convinces the heart that caution is the safest path. Yet many of these warnings are only shadows cast by imagination rather than reality. Fear exaggerates the dangers before us while diminishing the possibilities God has prepared, but faith restores our vision and reminds us that with God the path forward is always greater than the obstacles we face. What appears on the surface to be careful thinking may actually be hesitation rooted in doubt, quietly persuading us to step back from the very opportunities where faith could lead us forward. But faith calls us to see beyond the illusions fear creates. When we trust Him, we refuse to let fear dictate our decisions. Courage grows when we move forward in obedience, even when uncertainty remains. Often the door that fear warns us to avoid is the very doorway through which God intends to lead us into growth, purpose, and victory.

The enemy of the soul understands the power of fear, because when fear fills the heart it weakens faith, clouds judgment, and attempts to silence the courage that God has placed within us. If he can fill a man's mind with uncertainty, he can paralyze his progress and cloud the clarity of his calling. Fear whispers lies that exaggerate danger and diminish faith, convincing a man that he is weaker than he truly is and that the obstacles before him are greater than the God within him. Under the weight of fear, courage fades, vision narrows, and purpose begins to stall. Yet God did not create man to live in the prison of fear. Scripture reminds us that God has not given us a spirit of fear, but of power, love, and a sound mind. When a man anchors his heart in truth, fear loses its grip and faith begins to rise. Instead of retreating, he steps forward with confidence in the Lord, advancing when it is time to move. Faith breaks the paralysis of fear and restores the boldness that God intended for every man to walk in.

Scripture repeatedly reminds us that fear is not the voice of God. Fear paralyzes, clouds judgment, and causes people to shrink back from the purposes God has placed before them. But the Lord does not motivate His children through dread or intimidation. His voice brings clarity, courage, and peace. Even when He calls someone into something difficult or unknown, His presence brings a quiet confidence that He will walk with them every step of the way. Instead of pushing us forward with fear, God calls us forward through faith and trust. Faith opens the door to obedience, and trust anchors the heart in God's character. When a person learns to recognize the difference between fear and faith, they begin to move with boldness rather than hesitation. The voice of God invites us to step beyond our worries and into His promises. In that place of trust, we discover that courage is not the absence of difficulty - it is the result of believing that the God who calls us is faithful to guide us, strengthen us, and carry us through.

Many of the greatest moments in biblical history required men and women to move beyond fear and step forward in faith. Abraham left the security of his homeland simply because God told him to go. He did not know the destination or the challenges that would arise, yet he trusted God more than the comfort of familiarity. In the same way, David walked onto the battlefield when every seasoned soldier shrank back from Goliath. Where others saw an impossible threat, David saw an opportunity for God's power to be revealed. Their courage was not the absence of fear; it was the decision to trust God more than their fears. Faith often asks us to step into moments that feel uncertain and intimidating. The path God calls us to walk may not always be clear, but obedience opens the door for His miracles to unfold. Just as Abraham discovered a new future through obedience and David witnessed God's victory over a giant, we too experience God's faithfulness when we move forward despite our fears.

Courage does not mean a person never feels fear. Even the strongest men and women of faith have faced moments when their hearts trembled and uncertainty whispered in their minds. Throughout scripture, God often spoke the words, "Do not be afraid," not because fear would never appear, but because faith gives us the strength to move forward in spite of it. True courage is born when a person refuses to allow fear to control their obedience. It is the quiet resolve that says, "I will trust God and step forward anyway." When a person chooses to act in faith while fear is present, something powerful happens within them. Their confidence grows, their character strengthens, and their trust in God deepens. Courage becomes a testimony that faith is greater than fear. The brave are not those who never tremble, but those who refuse to let fear stop them from doing what is right. In that moment, faith rises, and the person becomes stronger than the fear that once tried to hold them back.

Every man will face moments when fear rises up and attempts to dictate his choices. Fear whispers that the challenge is too great and the risk too high. Yet fear itself is not the enemy - allowing it to rule is. God never promised a life without moments of trembling, but He consistently calls men to walk forward in faith rather than retreat in intimidation. When fear appears, it becomes a crossroads: one path leads to shrinking back, the other to trusting God and stepping forward despite the pounding heart. A godly man learns that courage is not the absence of fear but the decision that faith will have the final word. When a man anchors his heart in God's promises, fear loses its authority over his choices. Instead of allowing anxiety to control his direction, he chooses obedience, conviction, and trust in the Lord's strength. In those moments, fear becomes a proving ground where character is forged, faith is strengthened, and a man discovers that God's presence is greater than any fear that tries to stand in his way.

Fear whispers to a man that he should stay quiet and stay safe. It fills his mind with doubts and questions meant to paralyze his courage. Fear tries to shrink a man's vision until he settles for comfort instead of calling. Yet God did not create men to live confined by fear. He created them to walk by faith, to rise above doubt, and to trust that His strength is greater than their weakness. Fear focuses on the possibility of failure, but faith focuses on the presence of God. Faith steps forward even when the path is uncertain. When a man remembers that the Lord walks beside him, fear loses its power and a quiet, unshakable courage begins to rise within his heart. Faith does not promise an easy road, but it assures a man that through every trial, valley, and storm, the faithful presence of God will walk beside him every step of the way. And when a man moves forward trusting God, his life expands beyond the limits of fear into the strength, purpose, and destiny that God prepared for him.

Fear often disguises itself as wisdom. It whispers words like "be careful," or "wait for the right time," or "don't move too quickly" and these phrases can sound responsible and thoughtful. Yet when God has already spoken, hesitation is not wisdom - it is resistance. Scripture shows again and again that God calls His people to step forward in faith before they feel ready. Fear tries to cloak itself in logic, convincing a man that delay is maturity, when in reality it is simply a reluctance to trust God enough to act. True wisdom listens for God's voice and responds with obedience. A courageous man understands that faith often requires stepping into uncertainty while trusting the One who called him. Waiting can sometimes be wise, but when waiting becomes an excuse to avoid the challenge God has placed before us, it becomes a prison. The man who grows in strength and character is the one who refuses to let fear masquerade as wisdom - he chooses obedience, trusting that God will meet him on the path of faith.

God's wisdom does not operate by the same rules as the world's wisdom. The world values what can be proven and controlled, but God often calls His people to move forward before the full picture is visible. His wisdom asks a man to step beyond comfort and rely on faith rather than certainty. Throughout scripture, men were called to act before they understood everything. They trusted the voice of God more than the evidence around them, and in doing so they stepped into the purposes God had prepared for them. God's wisdom often requires bold steps of faith. It invites a man to walk where there is no clear path yet, trusting that God will guide each step as it comes. Faith is not the absence of questions - it is the courage to obey God despite them. When a man learns to trust what he cannot yet see, he begins to live by a higher wisdom. In that place of bold obedience, God reveals His power, strengthens a man's character, and leads him into victories that human wisdom alone could never achieve.

Courage is the bridge between fear and faith, empowering us to step forward in obedience even when uncertainty surrounds us, trusting that God will carry us safely to the other side. Every man will face moments where fear whispers that he is not strong enough, not capable enough, or not prepared enough for the road ahead. Fear tries to paralyze the heart and cloud the vision of what God has called him to become. But courage steps forward in the presence of fear and declares that God's promises are greater than the doubts within. When a man chooses courage, he refuses to allow fear to dictate his future; instead, he allows faith to guide his steps and trust in the One who goes before him. Each brave decision strengthens his faith and builds the character God desires within him. As he walks across that bridge of courage, he leaves fear behind and steps into the life of purpose, strength, and destiny that God prepared for him long before the battle began.

When a person chooses to obey God, they are often stepping into situations where the outcome is not fully visible. Faith rarely comes with complete explanations or guaranteed comfort. Instead, it invites us to trust the character of God more than the certainty of circumstances. Abraham left his homeland without knowing where he was going, Peter stepped onto the water without knowing how long it would hold. The path of faith frequently leads into unfamiliar territory, but it is there that God reveals His power most clearly. When we move beyond our comfort and follow His voice, we discover that courage is not the absence of fear but the presence of trust. Each step into uncertainty becomes an opportunity for God to guide, provide, and strengthen us. What feels risky from a human perspective is often the very place where God's promises unfold. Those who walk with Him learn that the safest place in the world is not where everything is predictable, but where obedience leads and God goes before them.

When Jesus walked along the shore and called His disciples, He invited them into a life far greater than the one they knew. Their nets represented security, familiarity, and a predictable future. Yet when

Christ said, "Follow Me," they chose obedience over comfort. In that moment, they stepped away from the ordinary rhythms of life and into a divine calling that would transform not only their own lives, but the lives of countless others. Their willingness to leave what was safe revealed a deep trust that the One who called them was worthy to be followed. The same principle still speaks to believers today. God often calls people beyond the boundaries of comfort and into a deeper purpose. Like the disciples, faith requires the courage to loosen our grip on what feels secure so we can embrace the greater destiny God has prepared. When a person answers Christ's call, the journey may be uncertain, but the reward is a life shaped by purpose, growth, and eternal impact.

Risk and obedience often travel together because the path of faith rarely unfolds in places of safety and certainty. When God calls a man forward, He often leads him beyond the boundaries of what feels comfortable or predictable. Obedience may require stepping into unfamiliar territory, trusting God when the outcome is unclear. In those moments, a man must loosen his grip on control and security, believing that God's wisdom is greater than his own understanding. Faith grows strongest not when everything is safe, but when a man chooses to trust God in the unknown. A man who walks with God learns that surrender is not weakness - it is strength. Releasing comfort and control allows God to shape his character, deepen his courage, and expand his faith. Every act of obedience becomes a declaration that God is trustworthy, even when the road ahead is uncertain. Though risk may accompany obedience, the reward is a life guided by divine purpose rather than human limitation.

Fear magnifies problems, predicts failure, and questions God's goodness. Yet faith rises with quiet strength and declares that God's word is more reliable than our emotions and more trustworthy than our circumstances. When a person anchors their heart in what God has spoken, they refuse to let temporary worries drown out eternal truth.

Faith listens carefully for the voice of God and holds tightly to it, even when the winds of uncertainty blow. Faith also believes that God's promises are stronger than the doubts that echo in the mind. Doubt may question, but promise answers. Doubt may tremble, but promise stands firm. Every promise of God carries the weight of His character, and because He is faithful, His word cannot fail. When a believer chooses faith, they silence the inner voices of despair and replace them with the assurance that God will do what He has said. In that confidence, the heart finds peace, courage grows stronger, and hope begins to rise again.

Feelings often change like the weather. One day the heart feels strong and confident, and the next it may feel uncertain or afraid. Circumstances can stir emotions that rise and fall with the challenges of life. Fear may whisper doubts, and discouragement may try to cloud the mind. But faith does not rest on the shifting ground of emotions. Faith looks beyond the moment and chooses to trust the steady voice and promises of God. True faith remains steady in every storm because it is firmly anchored in the unchanging character, promises, and faithfulness of God. While feelings may drift with the tide of circumstances, God's nature never changes. His faithfulness remains constant, His promises remain sure, and His love remains steadfast. When faith is rooted in who God is rather than how we feel, it becomes a firm foundation that cannot be shaken. In every season, faith holds steady, trusting that the same God who was faithful yesterday will be faithful today and forever.

A courageous man does not wait until he feels fearless. Courage is not the absence of fear, but the decision to move forward in spite of it. Faith-filled courage is rooted in trust that God is greater than every obstacle, stronger than every enemy, and wiser than every path we must walk. The man who walks with God understands that feelings are unreliable guides, but the voice of the Lord is steady and sure. When fear whispers that he is not ready, faith reminds him that God is already there, preparing the way before him. Because of this trust, a courageous man steps forward even when the path is uncertain. He moves not because he feels strong, but because he knows the One who leads him is strong. God does not call men to a life of comfort, but to a life of obedience and faith. When a man anchors his heart in the leadership of God, fear loses its power to paralyze him. Step by step, decision by decision, he advances with quiet confidence, knowing that the One who guides him will also sustain him.

The battle between fear and faith happens in the mind, but the victory is won in the heart when a man chooses to believe what God says rather than what fear suggests. Fear has a quiet way of whispering lies into the heart of a man. It tells him he is not strong enough and not capable enough to step into the purpose God has placed before him. Fear paints the future with doubt and shadows the path with uncertainty. But the man who chooses faith over fear begins to walk differently. Courage rises within him not because the obstacles disappear, but because he trusts the One who walks beside him. Each step of faith unlocks doors that fear would have kept closed. Opportunities emerge, strength grows, and purpose becomes clearer with every act of trust. In the end, courage is not the absence of fear, but the decision that God's promises are greater than fear's lies. And the man who walks in that courage will discover that faith leads him straight into the life God intended for him all along.

| 23 |

"FREEDOM THROUGH DISCIPLINE"

Every man fights battles that no one else can see. Beneath the surface of daily life, within the quiet chambers of the heart, cravings, impulses, and desires struggle for control. Lust calls for indulgence, greed whispers for more, and laziness invites a man to surrender his discipline. These unseen conflicts shape a man far more than the battles others witness. The man who acknowledges this inner war and chooses to confront it is already stepping onto the path of spiritual maturity, because he understands that the true battlefield of life lies within. The man who learns to conquer his cravings discovers a powerful form of mastery. Through prayer, self-denial, and disciplined obedience to God, he trains his desires instead of being ruled by them. What once controlled him becomes subject to his will, and what once weakened him becomes the very ground where strength is forged. In mastering his appetites, he experiences a deeper freedom - the freedom to live according to purpose rather than impulse.

Cravings themselves are not unusual. God created human beings with desires, appetites, and longings. The problem is not that a man feels desire, but that desire must be trained and brought under the authority of wisdom and the Spirit of God. When desires are left undisciplined, they grow louder, stronger, and more demanding until they begin to control a man's decisions. Instead of directing his life with purpose and conviction, he becomes pulled by impulse - chasing whatever promises the quickest satisfaction rather than what produces lasting strength and righteousness. A disciplined man learns to master his desires rather than be mastered by them. Through prayer and self-control, he trains his heart to pursue what is good, honorable, and pleasing to God. In doing so, cravings lose their power to dominate his life. True freedom is not found in indulging every appetite, but in developing the strength to say no when necessary and yes to the higher calling God has placed upon his life.

Lust, greed, and laziness are subtle enemies of the soul. They whisper promises of pleasure, ease, and quick satisfaction, but their true outcome is far different from what they advertise. Lust clouds judgment and reduces people to objects rather than souls created in God's image. Greed convinces the heart that more possessions will bring peace, yet it only deepens dissatisfaction. Laziness quietly steals time, potential, and purpose, persuading a man to settle for comfort rather than calling. Though these cravings may begin as small indulgences, they gradually tighten their grip until they shape habits, weaken discipline, and erode character. Yet God calls every man to mastery over these desires rather than slavery to them. Through spiritual discipline, renewed thinking, and reliance on God's strength, a man can train his appetites instead of being ruled by them. Self-denial is not weakness but a powerful act of freedom, proving that the spirit is stronger than the flesh.

Lust seeks immediate gratification and blinds a man to the long-term consequences of his choices. It narrows his vision until he sees people not as souls created in the image of God, but as objects to satisfy temporary desires. Instead of building relationships rooted in honor, patience, and genuine love, lust replaces depth with impulse and commitment with craving. In doing so, it slowly erodes the ability to see others with dignity and to value the holiness of connection that God designed between people. A man who refuses to master lust will eventually find that other areas of his life begin to unravel as well. The same lack of discipline that gives lust power will weaken his judgment, dull his character, and compromise his integrity. But when a man learns to govern his desires, he grows in strength, clarity, and honor. Self-control restores vision, reminding him that true fulfillment is not found in momentary indulgence but in living with purpose, purity, and reverence for the sacred bonds God intended.

Greed whispers a dangerous lie to the human heart: that more is always better. It quietly convinces a man that fulfillment lies just beyond the next possession, the next achievement, or the next gain. What begins as a desire for provision can grow into an endless hunger that no amount of success or wealth can satisfy. The greedy heart becomes restless, always chasing but never arriving, because it seeks fulfillment in things that were never meant to fill the soul. God calls His people to a different way of living - a life rooted in contentment and trust in His provision. When a man learns to be grateful for what God has already given him, he discovers a deeper richness than greed could ever offer. Contentment frees the heart from constant striving and opens the door to generosity, integrity, and peace. True fulfillment is not found in accumulating more, but in recognizing that God Himself is the greatest treasure, and His provision is always enough.

Laziness rarely announces itself as a great moral failure; instead, it whispers gentle excuses that seem harmless in the moment. It persuades a man that comfort is a reasonable substitute for effort. Yet every delay quietly weakens the muscles of character. What begins as a small compromise gradually becomes a habit of avoidance, and the man who was meant to grow strong in purpose slowly drifts away from the life God intended him to build. Over time, laziness erodes the very things that give a man meaning - his strength, his opportunities, and his sense of calling. While diligence builds momentum and opens doors, complacency quietly closes them. God designed men to rise, build, serve, and lead with purpose, but laziness dulls that calling and replaces it with stagnation. The man who refuses the lure of comfort and embraces discipline, however, begins to reclaim his strength, rediscover his purpose, and step boldly into the opportunities God places before him.

It's a fact of life that what you feed will grow, and what you starve will weaken. The desires of the flesh gain strength when they are continually satisfied without restraint. Every time a craving is indulged, it learns to demand more, and the voice of the flesh becomes louder. But when a man begins to discipline his appetites and refuse every impulse that seeks to rule him, the power of those cravings begins to fade. Like muscles that weaken without use, unhealthy desires lose their grip when they are no longer fed. When a man trains his desires through prayer, self-control, and obedience to God's Word, he begins to reshape the inner life of his heart. The Spirit grows stronger as the flesh grows weaker. Over time, the cravings that once dominated him lose their authority, and new desires begin to rise - desires for righteousness, purity, and purpose. True freedom is not found in giving in to every urge, but in gaining the strength to say no and choosing the life that honors God.

Training your desires is a form of spiritual conditioning. Just as muscles grow through resistance, character grows through restraint. The inner life is strengthened each time a person chooses discipline over impulse and purpose over pleasure. God calls us not to be ruled by our appetites, but to rule them through the power of His Spirit. Every decision to pause, pray, and choose what is right builds spiritual endurance, shaping a heart that is steady, focused, and aligned with God's will. Over time, these small victories of self-control transform the inner man. What once felt like sacrifice becomes strength, and what once felt like denial becomes freedom. The more a person trains their desires, the more their character reflects maturity, wisdom, and spiritual authority. Just as a trained athlete develops power through repeated effort, a disciplined believer develops a resilient spirit capable of standing firm in temptation and walking confidently in God's purpose.

A disciplined man understands that feelings are powerful, but they are not meant to be the ruler of his life. Emotions rise and fall like waves, but truth remains steady. A man who walks with God does not allow temporary feelings to dictate permanent decisions. Instead, he anchors his life in values shaped by scripture, convictions forged through experience, and faith rooted in trust in God's wisdom. When temptation whispers or comfort calls him to take the easy path, he remembers that character is built when a man chooses what is right rather than what is convenient. Rather than asking, "What do I feel like doing?" a disciplined man asks, "What is right?" That simple shift changes everything. It places obedience above impulse, purpose above pleasure, and faith above fear. A man who lives this way becomes a powerful example to others, showing that true strength is not found in following feelings, but in faithfully following the path that God has set before him.

Scripture teaches that the spirit must rule over the flesh. The flesh represents our natural appetites - impulses driven by comfort, pride, lust, fear, and self-gratification. When these desires dominate a person's life, they create confusion and instability. Decisions become reactive rather than wise, emotions begin to rule the heart, and a man is pulled in many directions at once. The flesh promises satisfaction but often delivers turmoil, leaving a person restless and divided within himself. A life governed by the flesh lacks the steady compass that God intended for the human soul. But when the spirit takes its rightful place of leadership, life begins to align with God's design. The spirit, guided by God's truth, brings discipline to desire and purpose to daily choices. Instead of chaos, there is clarity. Instead of weakness, there is strength. Instead of inner conflict, there is peace. As the spirit grows stronger through prayer, obedience, and surrender to God, it begins to govern the impulses of the flesh.

A man who can restrain his own desires possesses a strength that many never develop. Anyone can follow an impulse, but it takes discipline and character to pause, evaluate, and say no -even to something that may be good - so that something greater can be pursued. This kind of mastery reflects a heart that understands purpose. It shows that a man is not ruled by his appetites, emotions, or cravings, but instead governs them with wisdom and conviction. This is the kind of strength that separates mature men from childish ones. Children chase whatever feels good in the moment, but mature men understand that lasting reward often requires present sacrifice. When a man denies himself for the sake of growth, calling, or obedience to God, he is not losing power - he is demonstrating it. Through self-denial he sharpens his character, strengthens his spirit, and aligns his life with a higher purpose, proving that true freedom is found not in indulgence, but in disciplined devotion.

Many people misunderstand discipline as restriction, as if it were a chain that limits joy or suppresses desire. In reality, discipline is the pathway to freedom. It is the quiet strength that enables a man to govern his impulses rather than be governed by them. Scripture reminds us that "he who rules his spirit is greater than he who takes a city." True power is not found in giving in to every urge, but in mastering the heart, the mind, and the will. A man who cannot say no to himself will eventually become a prisoner to his own appetites. Lust, greed, comfort, and indulgence slowly tighten their grip until they control his decisions and weaken his resolve. But when a man learns the sacred practice of self-control, he breaks those chains and walks in strength. Discipline teaches the soul to pursue what is right rather than what is easy. In that process, God forms a man who is steady, trustworthy, and free to live with purpose, free to walk in integrity, and free to become the man he was created to be.

A man who is ruled by his impulses becomes a prisoner to them, constantly pulled in whatever direction his appetites demand. Lust, greed, anger, and laziness promise satisfaction but quietly tighten their grip on the soul. God calls men to a higher life - one where desires are not dictators but servants. Through discipline, prayer, and self-control, a man learns to govern his inner world rather than be governed by it. When a man gains control of his desires, he gains control of his direction. His decisions become guided by purpose instead of impulse, by conviction instead of craving. This kind of mastery builds strength of character and clarity of vision. The man who can say no to himself becomes capable of saying yes to the greater calling God has placed on his life. In that discipline there is real freedom - the freedom to walk the path of wisdom, to pursue righteousness, and to live a life that is steady, strong, and led by the Spirit rather than by the flesh.

Training the soul is not accomplished through occasional moments of inspiration, but through the steady rhythm of daily choices. A man grows stronger in spirit each time he chooses prayer over distraction, turning his attention toward God rather than the noise of the world. He matures when he chooses responsibility over laziness, stepping into the duties God has placed before him instead of shrinking back from them. Character is forged in these quiet decisions, when no one else is watching but God sees the direction of the heart. The soul is shaped when a man chooses purity over temptation and generosity over greed. Each act of self-control strengthens the inner man and weakens the grip of the flesh. Over time these choices build a life of freedom, discipline, and spiritual authority. What begins as small decisions becomes a powerful testimony, because the man who trains his soul daily becomes a vessel through which God's strength, wisdom, and goodness can flow into the world.

The choices we make each day often appear small and insignificant, yet they carry far greater weight than we realize. A decision to resist temptation, to stay faithful to what is right, or to remain disciplined when it would be easier to give in may seem minor in the moment.

But in the kingdom of God, small acts of obedience are never wasted. They are like stones carefully laid into the foundation of a house. One stone may not look impressive, but over time those stones form something solid, unshakable, and enduring. Every act of discipline strengthens the inner man. Each time a person chooses patience over anger, diligence over laziness, or purity over compromise, spiritual muscle is being built. What begins as a simple choice becomes a pattern, and that pattern becomes character. Over time, those steady acts of faithfulness produce tremendous strength. A life built on daily discipline becomes a life that can withstand storms, because its foundation has been formed through countless quiet victories.

In a world where many are ruled by impulse and appetite, the man who disciplines his heart and mind stands apart. He understands that true strength is not found in dominating others but in governing his own desires. When a man humbly turns to the Lord and asks for help, God supplies the strength he cannot produce on his own. Even the strongest cravings can be brought into submission when a man walks closely with God. The Lord reshapes the heart, strengthens the will, and renews the mind of those who seek Him sincerely. What once felt like an overpowering temptation begins to lose its grip as a man feeds his spirit with truth and disciplines his life according to God's ways. Through prayer, self-denial, and obedience, he discovers that freedom is not the absence of struggle, but the victory of the Spirit within him. In this way, the man who pursues mastery under God becomes a living testimony that grace can transform even the deepest desires.

The disciplined man walks with confidence because he is not ruled by every passing impulse or emotion. Instead of reacting to every desire, he chooses wisdom, restraint, and self-control. His heart is anchored in truth, and his mind is guided by purpose rather than pressure. Because he has learned to master himself, he is not easily shaken by temptation or distraction. Discipline builds strength within him, and that strength allows him to move forward knowing that his steps are directed by conviction rather than impulse. When a man brings his desires under control, his heart becomes steady, his mind grows focused, and his path becomes purposeful. He no longer wanders aimlessly through life but walks deliberately in the direction God has placed before him. Through discipline he gains the freedom to pursue righteousness, fulfill his calling, and live with integrity. A disciplined life produces confidence because it reflects a heart aligned with God and a spirit determined to live wisely.

When a man conquers his cravings, he rises above the tyranny of impulse and begins to walk in true spiritual authority. The appetites of the flesh no longer dictate his decisions. Instead, he learns to rule over them with wisdom, discipline, and reverence for God. In that moment, he stops living as a captive to desire and begins living as a steward of his own life. Self-control becomes the evidence of inner strength, and his choices start to reflect the character of a man who is guided by purpose rather than pressure. This mastery over cravings opens the door to genuine freedom. A man who governs his appetites cannot easily be manipulated, distracted, or defeated by temptation. His spirit grows stronger, his focus sharper, and his walk with God deeper. What once ruled him now serves him, and the discipline he develops becomes the foundation of lasting victory. In learning to say no to destructive desires, he gains the power to say yes to the higher calling God has placed upon his life.

| 24 |

"CONTINUOUS REFINEMENT"

Every man eventually faces the mirror. Not the mirror that reflects his face, but the mirror that reflects his heart. In that sacred moment, a man is confronted not by what others think of him, but by who he truly is before God. The titles, the accomplishments, and the outward appearances fall away, and what remains is the condition of the soul. Yet this moment is not meant to condemn him - it is meant to awaken him. For when a man dares to look honestly into that spiritual mirror, he discovers the places where pride must bend, where wounds must heal, and where God is calling him to grow. The man who humbly receives what the mirror reveals walks away refined. With repentance, courage, and renewed faith, he begins the work of becoming the man God intended him to be. Each honest look into that mirror shapes his character, deepens his humility, and strengthens his integrity. In time, what once revealed flaws begins to reveal wisdom, maturity, and a heart that has been steadily molded by truth.

When a man looks honestly into the reflection of his own heart, he begins to see what God already sees: the progress that grace has produced and the places where growth is still needed. The mirror reveals the strength that has been forged through trials and the character that has been shaped through obedience. In that reflection, a man recognizes that God has already been at work in him, quietly building courage, wisdom, and resilience. Yet the mirror also exposes the areas where weakness still lingers, and this is where humility becomes powerful. Truth may be uncomfortable, but it is always necessary, because transformation begins with honesty. When a man refuses to hide from the truth, he positions himself for refinement. Instead of shrinking from what he sees, he allows God to shape, correct, and strengthen him. In this way, the mirror of self-examination becomes a doorway to growth where a man becomes stronger, wiser, and more aligned with the purpose God placed within him.

Many men spend their lives avoiding the mirror of honest self-examination. It is far easier to blame circumstances, criticize others, or defend our own behavior than it is to face the truth about ourselves. Yet the greatest barrier to growth is not what happens around a man, but what he refuses to confront within. When a man constantly looks outward for someone else to blame, he remains trapped in immaturity. But the moment he becomes brave enough to examine his own heart, acknowledge his flaws, and accept responsibility for his choices, he takes the first real step toward transformation. Spiritual growth begins the moment a man turns the mirror toward his own soul. In that moment, pride gives way to humility, excuses give way to honesty, and defensiveness gives way to repentance. When a man stops pointing outward and begins looking inward, he opens the door for God to shape his character, deepen his wisdom, and lead him into the strength and maturity he was created to possess.

Brutal self-assessment requires courage. It takes strength to admit where pride has quietly taken root, where discipline has slipped, and where character has been weakened by compromise. Most people avoid this kind of honest reflection because it exposes uncomfortable truths about the heart. Yet a man who is willing to stand before the mirror of truth without excuses or defenses demonstrates a rare strength. He refuses to hide behind blame, denial, or appearances. Instead, he chooses honesty, recognizing that true growth begins when a person stops pretending and starts acknowledging what must change. The man who confronts his weaknesses with humility opens the door for God to reshape his character and restore what has been lost. Honest reflection becomes the starting line for renewal. When a man sees clearly where he has fallen short, he can begin to rebuild with purpose, discipline, and integrity. In that moment, he becomes more aligned with the man God created him to be.

Strength is not proven by pretending to be perfect; it is revealed in the courage to face the truth about oneself. Many men try to hide their weaknesses believing that admitting fault will make them appear weak. Yet real strength begins the moment a man stands honestly before God and himself and acknowledges where he has fallen short. When a man can say, "This must change," he steps out of illusion and into transformation. That moment of honesty becomes the doorway through which wisdom, humility, and maturity begin to enter his life. God does not expect flawless men; He works through willing ones. The man who humbles himself, confronts his faults, and invites God to reshape his character is the man who grows stronger with every season. Each honest self-examination becomes a refining fire that removes pride and replaces it with purpose. In that sacred moment of truth, weakness turns into strength, failure becomes a teacher, and the journey of real growth begins.

Self-examination strips away the comforting illusions we often build around ourselves. It removes the mask of appearance and exposes the distance between who a man claims to be and who he truly is in his heart, his motives, and his actions. This moment of honest reflection can be uncomfortable because it confronts pride, excuses, and hidden weaknesses. Yet it is in this sacred place of truth that real growth begins, for God cannot refine what a man refuses to see. Though the discovery may sting at first, the clarity it brings is a profound gift. When a man has the courage to see himself truthfully before God, he discovers the clarity, humility, and direction needed to walk faithfully into the purpose that lies ahead. Instead of wandering in self-deception, he can move forward with humility, repentance, and renewed purpose. What once felt like exposure becomes transformation, because the man who is willing to examine his soul is the man God can shape into strength, integrity, and lasting character.

Humility is the faithful companion of honest reflection. When a man is willing to look into the mirror of his soul and admit what he truly sees, he begins the process of genuine growth. Instead of defending his weaknesses or hiding behind excuses, he lowers his defenses and acknowledges that he is still a work in progress. This posture of humility opens his heart to truth, softens his spirit, and allows God to shape his character in deeper and more meaningful ways. Pride resists correction because it fears exposure, but humility welcomes correction because it desires transformation. A humble man understands that every rebuke can become a lesson and every mistake can become a steppingstone toward maturity. Rather than shrinking from truth, he leans into it, knowing that wisdom often arrives through honest confrontation with his own shortcomings. In this spirit of teachability, a man grows stronger, wiser, and more aligned with the person God is calling him to become.

Humility is the quiet confidence of a man who understands that true power does not need to shout, boast, or prove itself to others. A humble man is secure enough to face the truth about himself. He does not hide behind pride or pretend to be flawless. Instead, he looks honestly into the mirror of his own heart, recognizing both his strengths and his shortcomings. This kind of humility frees a man from the exhausting burden of pretending, allowing him to walk in authenticity before God and others. Such humility becomes the foundation for real growth. When a man is willing to acknowledge where he falls short, he positions himself for transformation. The humble man understands that admitting weakness is not defeat - it is the first step toward becoming stronger. With a teachable spirit and a determined heart, he continues refining his character, trusting that God honors those who walk in humility and steadily shapes them into men of greater wisdom, strength, and purpose.

A humble man understands that truth is not his enemy but his teacher. While pride tries to protect the ego and hide weakness, humility opens the heart to correction, instruction, and revelation. A man who walks with God knows that every truth uncovered is an invitation to become better. Whether the truth exposes a flaw, reveals a blind spot, or challenges a comfortable habit, he accepts it with gratitude because he knows God is refining him into a stronger and wiser man. For this reason, a humble man actively pursues truth rather than avoiding it. He reads the Word, listens to wise counsel, and examines his own heart honestly before God. Each revelation becomes another tool in the hands of the Master Craftsman who is shaping his character. Truth chisels away pride, strengthens integrity, and builds the kind of character that reflects the heart of God. In this way, humility becomes the doorway to continual growth, and every truth received becomes another step toward the man God created him to be.

The mirror of God's truth does more than reveal who we are - it gently invites us to become who we are meant to be. When a man looks honestly into that mirror, he may see attitudes that need correcting, habits that need breaking, and motives that need purifying. Yet this moment of clarity is not meant to condemn him; it is meant to awaken him. The mirror exposes what is wrong so that grace can begin its work of restoration. God does not reveal our flaws to humiliate us, but to guide us toward a better path. That is why repentance is not a word of shame - it is a word of change. Repentance simply means turning away from what is wrong and stepping toward what is right. It is the courageous decision to realign the heart with God's will and walk in a new direction. When a man embraces repentance, he is not admitting defeat; he is choosing transformation. In that turning, the soul grows lighter, the conscience grows clearer, and the path forward becomes brighter with the promise of renewal.

Repentance is the moment a man refuses to let yesterday define tomorrow. Instead of hiding from his failures, he faces them with honesty and humility. He acknowledges where he was wrong, not to condemn himself, but to grow stronger and wiser. A repentant heart understands that mistakes are not the end of the story - they are lessons that shape a better future. By turning away from what was wrong and embracing what is right, a man steps out of the shadow of regret and begins walking again in the light of purpose. When a man truly repents, the weight of the past no longer holds his spirit captive. Repentance restores movement to the soul; it breaks the chains of guilt and replaces them with renewed direction. Instead of being stuck in shame, he rises with determination, choosing a better path and trusting God for the strength to walk it. In that moment, momentum returns to his life, and what once felt like defeat becomes the very ground where transformation begins.

There is a powerful freedom that comes through honest repentance. When a man stops pretending, stops defending his mistakes, and humbly brings his failures before God, the heavy burden of guilt begins to lift from his soul. Repentance is not meant to crush a man but to restore him. It is the moment when truth replaces denial and grace replaces shame. God does not ask a man to carry the weight of his past forever; He invites him to lay it down and receive mercy. The courage to admit wrong is not weakness - it is the doorway to healing and renewal. When a man brings his failures into the light, their power begins to fade. Secrets lose their grip when they are confessed, and regret no longer rules the heart when forgiveness is received. Instead of hiding in the shadows of shame, he can walk forward with a clean conscience and a renewed spirit. Honest repentance breaks the chains of the past and opens the path toward growth, maturity, and deeper fellowship with God.

God does not ask men to pretend they are perfect. He asks them to be honest. Too many people spend their lives trying to maintain an image - appearing strong, spiritual, and flawless on the outside while quietly struggling within. But God is not impressed by polished appearances or carefully managed reputations. He searches the heart. A man who is willing to admit where he has fallen short, who refuses to hide behind pride or excuses, is already walking in a place of spiritual strength. Honesty before God opens the door to transformation because it allows His truth and grace to reach the places we once tried to hide. A repentant heart is far more valuable than a polished image. Repentance is not weakness; it is courage. It is the humility to step into the light and say, "Lord, I need You to change me." When a man brings his failures before God with sincerity, he finds mercy instead of condemnation and restoration instead of shame. God can rebuild, refine, and strengthen a heart that is honest before Him.

Self-examination also produces continuous refinement. When a man honestly evaluates his thoughts, motives, and actions before God, he begins to see where growth is needed. This kind of reflection is not meant to condemn the heart, but to shape it. Just as a craftsman studies his work and carefully removes imperfections, a wise man allows the Spirit of God to reveal areas that require adjustment. Through humility and honesty, he becomes teachable, and every moment of reflection becomes an opportunity for transformation. In the same way that metal is purified in fire, a man's character is strengthened through repeated reflection and correction. Each time he confronts his weaknesses and chooses to change, the impurities of pride, selfishness, and carelessness are burned away. Over time, the process produces a stronger, steadier, and more disciplined character. What begins as self-examination ultimately becomes refinement, and what is refined becomes valuable.

The wise man does not wait for a crisis to examine the condition of his heart. He understands that growth requires honest reflection, and so he regularly steps back from the noise of life to measure his actions, motives, and direction. Like a traveler checking his compass, he pauses to ensure that he is still walking the path God has set before him. Through prayer, humility, and self-examination, he allows the light of truth to reveal both his strengths and his weaknesses. This discipline is not a sign of insecurity but of wisdom, because the man who is willing to look within is the man who is willing to grow. By making reflection a regular habit, he prevents small cracks in his character from becoming devastating fractures. A careless word, a drifting attitude, or a neglected responsibility can quietly grow into something destructive if left unchecked. But the wise man adjusts his course early. He corrects small errors before they become great failures and realigns himself with God's principles.

Every honest look in the mirror sharpens a man's character because it forces him to confront the truth about himself. Instead of hiding from his weaknesses, the wise man studies them, learns from them, and submits them to God for refinement. Through this process, discipline grows stronger, integrity becomes deeper, and the inner life begins to align with the values he claims to hold. What begins as honest reflection becomes the forge where a stronger character is formed. The man who practices this kind of self-examination grows steadily stronger with time because he refuses to live blindly. Each day he evaluates his words, his choices, and the condition of his heart. He asks God for wisdom and guidance. Over time his purpose becomes clearer, his convictions firmer, and his life more focused. By continually looking within and adjusting his course, he becomes a man whose strength is built on humility, growth, and unwavering commitment to becoming the man God created him to be.

The mirror never lies. It reflects what is truly there - strengths, flaws, victories, and failures. Yet the purpose of the mirror is not to shame the man who stands before it. God does not reveal truth to crush the heart but to awaken it. When a man has the courage to examine himself honestly, he steps onto the path of growth. What he sees may not always be comfortable, but it is necessary. Self-examination becomes a sacred moment where pride falls away, humility rises, and the heart becomes willing to change. The mirror also never condemns the man who is willing to grow. Instead, it becomes a tool of refinement, revealing what must be removed so something stronger can emerge. Just as a craftsman shapes steel by removing impurities, God shapes character through honest reflection and repentance. The man who humbly embraces this process of growth and refinement does not remain the same; he becomes wiser in judgment, steadier in character, and more resilient in the face of life's trials.

When a man learns to face the mirror with courage, humility, and repentance, he steps into the refining work of truth. Instead of hiding from his weaknesses or defending his faults, he allows God's light to reveal what must change. Courage gives him the strength to be honest, humility gives him the grace to admit where he has fallen short, and repentance gives him the power to turn and grow. In that process, his character is steadily shaped, his motives are purified, and his heart becomes more aligned with the will of God. As truth continues to shape his life, he becomes a man marked by strength and integrity. His words carry weight because they are rooted in honesty, and his actions reflect the convictions of a transformed heart. The man who consistently walks in truth develops a quiet but powerful spiritual authority - an influence that comes not from position or title, but from a life that has been forged in humility, obedience, and unwavering commitment to what is right.

| 25 |

"QUIET STRENGTH"

One of the quiet battles in the human heart is the desire to be noticed. Deep within us is a longing for recognition, praise, and affirmation. We want our efforts acknowledged and our sacrifices seen. While appreciation is not wrong, the craving for applause can slowly become an addiction that shapes our behavior and decisions. When a person begins to measure their worth by the approval of others, their identity becomes fragile and unstable. Every compliment lifts them up, but every silence or criticism pulls them down. God never designed the human soul to be sustained by the applause of people, because human approval is temporary and inconsistent. The freedom of the Spirit comes when a person learns to live for the audience of One. When our identity is rooted in Christ rather than the opinions of others, we no longer need constant recognition to feel valuable. We can serve faithfully even when no one is watching and give our best even when no one applauds.

Approval addiction quietly enslaves the heart by tying a person's sense of worth to the reactions of others. When compliments come, confidence rises for a moment, but when criticism appears - or when silence replaces applause - the soul can quickly sink into discouragement. Living this way places a fragile foundation beneath one's identity, because human approval is inconsistent and constantly shifting. If a person measures their value by praise, they will spend their life chasing affirmation instead of walking in the steady confidence that God desires for them. True spiritual strength begins when a person roots their identity in who God says they are rather than in what people say about them. The applause of others may come and go, but God's approval is constant, unchanging, and secure. When a heart learns to serve faithfully whether seen or unseen, it develops a quiet strength that no criticism can destroy and no silence can diminish. A life grounded in God's truth becomes steady, confident, and free.

A life driven by approval slowly drifts away from the anchor of truth. When a person begins to measure their worth by applause, they become vulnerable to the shifting opinions of the crowd. What is right is quietly replaced by what is popular, and conviction is traded for acceptance. Yet the voice of God is not always the loudest voice in the room - it is the truest. The danger is that when a heart constantly seeks validation from people, it gradually becomes deaf to the gentle but powerful guidance of the Spirit. True strength is found in choosing obedience over approval. A person who lives for God understands that popularity is temporary, but truth is eternal. The opinions of people will change with the wind, but the Word of God remains steady and unshakable. When a man decides that pleasing God matters more than pleasing the crowd, he regains clarity, courage, and direction. In that place of surrender, his life is no longer steered by the noise of human praise but by the quiet authority of divine truth.

Many people move through life like actors on a stage, constantly looking for approval from the crowd. Every action becomes a performance, every decision becomes an attempt to impress someone, and every success is measured by how loudly others applaud. Yet living this way slowly drains the soul. The applause of people is temporary, and the validation of the world fades quickly. What once felt satisfying soon becomes hollow, forcing a person to perform again and again just to feel valued. A life built on the opinions of others becomes exhausting because the stage is never empty and the pressure to impress never truly ends. God never intended His children to live for the applause of people. True peace comes when a person steps off the stage and begins living for the approval of the Lord alone. When identity is rooted in Christ, there is freedom from the exhausting need to impress others. A man can serve quietly, love sincerely, and walk faithfully even when no one is watching.

Jesus warned His followers about the subtle trap of performing good deeds merely to be seen by others. In His teaching, He described those who give, pray, or serve publicly in order to gain admiration. Their actions may appear righteous on the outside, but the true motive of the heart is revealed by the desire for applause. When recognition from people becomes the goal, the reward is limited to the fleeting praise of human approval. The crowd may notice, compliments may come, and reputations may grow but the deeper, eternal reward that comes from God is missed. True devotion is not measured by how loudly our actions are seen, but by the sincerity of our hearts before God. Jesus taught that when we give, pray, and serve quietly, our Father who sees in secret takes notice. In those unseen moments, character is formed, humility grows, and the soul learns to seek God's pleasure rather than man's approval. The greatest reward is not public recognition but the quiet affirmation of heaven.

When a man constantly needs applause, he becomes controlled by it. The craving for approval quietly shifts his focus away from truth and toward acceptance. Instead of standing firmly on conviction, he begins measuring his choices by how others will react. Hard truths become uncomfortable to speak, righteous decisions become easier to compromise, and the fear of disappointing people grows stronger than the desire to honor God. What once was a strong, steady spirit becomes vulnerable to the opinions of the crowd, and the applause that once felt empowering slowly becomes a chain that limits courage and integrity. Spiritual strength grows when a man learns to value God's approval above human applause. When his identity is rooted in

Christ rather than in public praise, he gains the freedom to live with quiet conviction and unwavering purpose. He can speak truth even when it is unpopular, stand firm even when he stands alone, and pursue righteousness without needing recognition.

True freedom begins the moment a person loosens the grip of human approval on their heart and turns their attention toward the pleasure of God. When someone lives for the applause of people, their identity becomes fragile and constantly shifting, rising and falling with every compliment or criticism. But when a person anchors their life in God's opinion, they step into a deeper stability. They no longer measure their worth by public recognition or social acceptance, but by the quiet assurance that they are walking in obedience to the One who sees every motive and knows every intention of the heart. When God's approval becomes the highest authority, the noise of human opinion begins to fade. The need for applause loses its grip, and a quiet strength replaces the craving for recognition. A person who lives for God's pleasure can serve faithfully whether they are celebrated or unnoticed, because their reward is not found in the cheers of the crowd but in the smile of their Father.

When a person's identity becomes rooted in Christ, everything begins to change from the inside out. The restless need for approval slowly loses its power, because worth is no longer determined by the shifting opinions of people but by the unchanging love of God. This shift transforms motivation, decisions, and priorities. Life is no longer lived to impress the crowd, but to please the One who created, redeemed, and called us. When identity is anchored in Christ, freedom replaces insecurity. A person can walk with quiet confidence, serve without needing recognition, and remain steady whether praised or criticized. Their value is not found in applause but in obedience. In this place of spiritual maturity, character grows stronger and purpose becomes clearer, because the soul is no longer chasing approval but pursuing faithfulness. Identity rooted in Christ truly changes everything - it turns a life driven by validation into a life devoted to honoring God.

Scripture teaches that our identity is not based on public recognition, applause, or the opinions of others, but on our relationship with Christ. In Him we discover a deeper truth about who we are. We are accepted not because of what we have done, but because of what He has done for us. Through His grace we are forgiven, through His sacrifice we are chosen, and through His love we are made new. When a person understands this, the need for constant validation fades because their worth is already secured in the One who knows them completely. Living from this identity produces a quiet confidence that does not depend on recognition. Christ calls His followers to rest in the assurance that they are deeply loved and fully accepted in Him. When this truth settles into the heart, it frees a person from chasing applause and allows them to live with humility, peace, and purpose, knowing that their true identity is safely anchored in Christ.

When a man truly understands who he is in Christ, he is no longer driven by the need for constant approval. The world trains people to chase applause, recognition, and affirmation, but a man whose identity is rooted in Christ knows that he is chosen, called, and accepted by God. Because of this, his worth is not determined by how loudly the crowd cheers or how many people agree with him. His confidence flows from the unchanging truth that he belongs to God and has been given a purpose that cannot be shaken by human opinion. This kind of man walks with a quiet strength. He serves faithfully whether anyone notices or not because his motivation is not the praise of people but the pleasure of God. When criticism comes, it does not crush him, and when praise comes, it does not control him. His heart is anchored in the calling God has placed on his life. Secure in Christ, he moves forward knowing that the only approval that truly matters is the approval of the One who called him.

Faithfulness is never measured by the size of the audience but by the sincerity of the heart before God. When a person understands that their identity and purpose come from the Lord, they no longer need applause to remain committed. A heart that belongs to God finds joy in obedience itself, not in the approval that may or may not follow. The most meaningful acts of obedience are often performed in quiet places, where no applause is heard and no spotlight shines. A prayer whispered in private, a sacrifice made without recognition, or a kind deed done with no expectation of reward carries great weight in the kingdom of God. These unseen moments shape character and deepen spiritual strength. When a person learns to live this way, their faith becomes steady and genuine, rooted not in attention but in love for God. And though the world may never notice these quiet acts, God honors them, and in His perfect time He reveals the beauty of a life faithfully lived before Him.

Some of the greatest spiritual victories do not happen on stages or in front of crowds. They are born in quiet rooms, whispered through private prayers, and expressed through simple acts of kindness that no one else notices. In those hidden moments, a soul draws near to God without the need for applause or recognition. The world may overlook these small acts of faithfulness, but heaven never does. Every sincere prayer, every unseen sacrifice, and every quiet decision to do what is right becomes a powerful testimony before God. When a person remains faithful in the unseen places, they develop a strength that cannot be manufactured in public. Character is forged in solitude, and devotion is proven when no one is watching. The Father who sees in secret honors those hidden victories and stores them as treasures in eternity. What the world may consider insignificant, God often considers sacred. In the stillness of faithful obedience, heaven records victories that will echo far beyond this life.

Serving unseen develops a deeper kind of character because it shifts the focus from personal recognition to faithful obedience. When a person learns to serve without applause, without praise, and without anyone noticing, their motives are purified. Pride begins to lose its grip because there is no audience to impress. In the quiet places where no one is watching, the heart learns that true faithfulness is not measured by public approval but by devotion to God. It is in these hidden moments of service that character is forged, integrity is strengthened, and the soul grows steady and sincere. This kind of unseen service also strengthens humility and teaches the heart to love obedience more than recognition. When a person continues to serve faithfully even when their efforts go unnoticed, they begin to understand that God sees what others overlook. The desire for applause fades, replaced by a deeper satisfaction in simply doing what is right. Quiet obedience becomes its own reward.

Quiet strength is formed in the hidden places of the soul where a person learns to stand firm without the need for applause or recognition. It is the strength that chooses integrity when no one is watching, faithfulness when no one is cheering, and perseverance when no one is rewarding the effort. When a person learns to walk faithfully without the need for validation, they develop a character that is steady, resilient, and deeply rooted in purpose. Though the world may overlook such quiet faithfulness, heaven does not. God sees every unseen act of obedience, every silent sacrifice, and every moment when a person chooses righteousness without recognition. What goes unnoticed by people is fully honored by God, for He values the heart that serves Him sincerely rather than the one that seeks applause. Quiet strength may not receive a standing ovation on earth, but it earns the approval that matters most - the smile of God and the affirmation of a life lived faithfully before Him.

A man who no longer depends on applause becomes steady and secure because his identity is no longer anchored in the shifting winds of human approval. He understands that praise and criticism are often influenced by opinions, emotions, and circumstances that change from day to day. Instead of chasing validation, he roots his worth in the unchanging truth of who God says he is. When a man lives from that deeper foundation, praise does not inflate his ego, and criticism does not shatter his confidence. He becomes calm in success and humble in correction because his sense of value is not built on the reactions of others. This kind of man walks with quiet strength. He serves faithfully whether he is noticed or overlooked, celebrated or misunderstood. In that freedom his character grows stronger, and his spirit becomes more stable, and his life reflects a maturity that cannot be shaken by public opinion. Because his heart is anchored in God's approval, he is free from the need to impress people.

True spiritual strength is rarely loud or celebrated, because it is forged in the quiet surrender of the ego. The world often applauds those who seek recognition, influence, and applause, but the kingdom of God measures greatness differently. Real strength is the ability to step out of the spotlight and say, "Not my will, but Yours be done." It is the courage to let go of pride, personal ambition, and the need for approval, trusting that God sees what others may never notice. This kind of humility requires deep faith, because it believes that God's reward is greater than human recognition. When a person chooses faithfulness over fame and obedience over popularity, they walk the same path that Christ walked. Jesus did not pursue the praise of crowds; He pursued the will of the Father. In the same way, spiritual maturity grows when a believer becomes more concerned with pleasing God than impressing people. The world may overlook this kind of life, but heaven celebrates it.

The person who walks this path discovers the freedom that comes when a man no longer lives for the approval of others but for the approval of God. Such a person is no longer controlled by public opinion, trends, or the shifting expectations of people. He can choose what is right even when it costs him popularity, comfort, or recognition, because his identity is rooted in something far greater than human praise. This freedom produces a quiet but unshakable faithfulness. A man who walks with God learns to do what is right even when no one is watching and to serve faithfully even when no one applauds. He understands that heaven sees what the world overlooks and that God honors the integrity of a hidden life. In that place of unseen obedience, character grows stronger, conviction grows deeper, and the soul becomes steady because true strength is not built on recognition, but on faithfulness to the One who sees all.

When your identity is rooted in Christ, your worth is no longer measured by the applause of people or the recognition of the crowd. In Christ, you are already accepted, already loved, already chosen. You do not have to chase approval because your value was settled at the cross. When a man understands that his identity is anchored in the unchanging love of God, he is freed from the exhausting cycle of trying to please everyone around him. In that quiet place of divine approval, a deeper strength begins to grow. You learn to serve faithfully even when no one notices, to stand firm even when no one applauds, and to obey God even when it costs you something. The quiet approval of God becomes more satisfying than the loud praise of people. And from that place of security, humility, and devotion, true strength is born - a strength that is steady, grounded, and unshaken because it draws its confidence not from the crowd, but from Christ.

| 26 |

"SPIRITUAL AGGRESSION"

Prayer was never designed to be timid, weak, or hesitant. It is the place where faith finds its voice and where the believer stands boldly before the throne of God. When a man of God prays with courage and conviction, he is not merely speaking words into the air - he is engaging in a spiritual battle. Heaven listens, angels move, and the power of God is released into situations that once seemed impossible. Bold prayer rises from a heart that knows God is faithful, powerful, and attentive to the cries of His people. On the battlefield of prayer, victories are often won long before they appear in the natural world. Circumstances begin to shift, atmospheres begin to change, and the forces that oppose God's purposes begin to lose their grip. A man who learns to pray with boldness steps into a realm where faith confronts fear and truth confronts darkness. Through courageous prayer, he partners with God's power, standing firm until heaven's will is accomplished on earth.

Many men approach prayer like beggars, whispering timid requests and hoping something might happen. Yet the Word of God paints a far different picture. Prayer was never intended to be the weak murmur of uncertainty; it is the bold language of faith spoken by those who know their position in Christ. When a man understands who he is in the Kingdom of God, prayer becomes confident and purposeful. Prayer is the weapon of the warrior. Through it a man calls upon the power of heaven and advances with courage knowing that God fights beside him. It pushes back darkness, breaks spiritual resistance, and releases the power of heaven into earthly situations. Through prayer, men engage, contend, and stand in authority through Christ. Faith-filled prayer rises with expectation, knowing that God hears and moves on behalf of those who seek Him. When a believer prays with this understanding, prayer becomes a powerful act of spiritual warfare that advances God's purposes in the world.

Bold prayers are born from bold faith. When a man truly understands the greatness of God, his prayers begin to change. He no longer approaches God with hesitation or doubt, but with confidence in the character and promises of the Almighty. Faith reminds him that the God who created the universe is not limited by human weakness, circumstances, or impossibilities. Because of this assurance, his prayers grow larger, stronger, and more courageous. Instead of asking only for what seems reasonable, he begins to pray for what only God can accomplish. These bold prayers honor God because they declare His limitless power. When a man prays with confidence, he is acknowledging that nothing is too difficult for the Lord. Mountains can move, broken lives can be restored, and impossible situations can be transformed when faith calls upon the name of God. Bold prayers are not arrogance - they are trust. They reflect a heart that believes God is faithful to His Word and mighty in His works.

Throughout scripture, the greatest men of faith approached God with boldness because they knew who He was. Elijah prayed and the heavens closed, demonstrating that the prayers of a righteous man carry authority before God. Moses lifted his voice and the Red Sea parted, proving that when God's servant calls upon Him, the impossible can become reality. Joshua commanded the sun to stand still, and heaven responded. These men were not timid in prayer because their confidence was in the power and sovereignty of the God they served. This same boldness is available to every believer today. Prayer is not meant to be weak, hesitant, or uncertain; it is the language of faith spoken to a mighty God. When we understand His character and trust His promises, our prayers begin to carry courage and expectation. Bold prayer confidently seeks God's will with unwavering faith. The God who answered Elijah, Moses, and Joshua still responds to those who call upon Him with hearts full of faith.

Bold prayer flows from a heart that knows God not merely as a distant ruler, but as a loving Father. A stranger approaches cautiously, unsure of his welcome, but a son comes with confidence because he belongs. When a man understands his identity as a child of God, his prayers begin to carry a different tone - no longer timid or uncertain but filled with trust and expectation. Bold prayer is the natural expression of a heart that has learned to rest in the faithfulness and goodness of the Father. When you truly know your Father, you approach Him with confidence, not fear. You pray knowing that He listens, that He cares, and that He delights in the faith of His children. Your words are not empty wishes thrown into the air; they are conversations with the One who loves you and has invited you into His presence. Faith grows strongest in the soil of a close relationship with God, and from that living connection springs a bold courage that approaches Him in prayer with confidence and trust.

A true prayer warrior refuses to be intimidated by circumstances because he understands that what he sees with his eyes is not the final authority. Storms may roar, pressure may mount, and obstacles may appear immovable, but the man who prays knows that heaven governs what earth experiences. He remembers that the same God who calmed the raging sea, toppled the walls of Jericho, and delivered His people time and again still rules with unmatched power. Because of this confidence, he does not allow fear to silence his voice before God. Instead, he kneels with boldness, knowing that every sincere prayer invites the authority of heaven into the struggles of earth. Rather than retreating from the battle, the praying man steps directly into it through faith-filled prayer. He understands that prayer is not passive resignation but active spiritual engagement. While others panic or surrender to discouragement, the prayer warrior stands firm, lifting his voice with persistence and authority in Christ.

Persistence is the heartbeat of powerful prayer because it reveals a heart that truly believes God hears and responds. Spiritual warriors understand that prayer is not a one-time request but an ongoing pursuit of God's presence and promises. When answers seem delayed, they do not withdraw in frustration or doubt. Instead, they press deeper into faith, continuing to knock, seek, and ask with confidence that heaven is listening. Each prayer becomes another declaration that God is faithful, and every moment of waiting becomes an opportunity to strengthen trust in His perfect timing. Persistence in prayer is faith refusing to quit when circumstances appear unchanged. Just as a warrior refuses to abandon the battlefield, a believer refuses to abandon the place of prayer. Breakthrough often comes to those who stay faithful long after others would have walked away. With every repeated prayer, the soul grows stronger, hope grows steadier, and the man aligns more closely with God's will.

Jesus illustrated the power of persistence through the parable of the persistent widow. Though she had no social influence or power, she refused to stop seeking justice from the unjust judge. Day after day she returned with the same request, unwilling to surrender to discouragement or silence. Eventually the judge granted her request - not because of compassion, but because of her relentless persistence. Through this story, Jesus revealed a profound spiritual truth: faith that refuses to quit will eventually see heaven move. Persistence in prayer demonstrates a heart that truly believes God hears and cares. Prayer is not meant to be a single request quickly abandoned when answers seem delayed. Instead, it is a continual pursuit of God's intervention and will. When a person keeps seeking, knocking, and asking, they demonstrate unwavering trust in God's justice and goodness. God honors the faith that keeps praying, keeps believing, and keeps expecting His answer to come in the perfect time.

Many prayers fail not because they are misguided, but because they are surrendered too quickly. The spiritual battlefield of prayer often requires endurance, patience, and unwavering trust in God's timing. Just as a warrior does not abandon the field at the first sign of resistance, a believer must refuse to retreat when answers seem delayed. God is often working behind the scenes and what appears to be silence is frequently divine preparation. A warrior understands that persistence is part of the victory. Jesus taught that men ought always to pray and not lose heart, because faithful prayer demonstrates trust in the One who hears. When others grow weary and walk away, the prayer warrior presses deeper. Many breakthroughs occur just beyond the moment where discouragement whispers the loudest. Those who stay in the fight, standing firm in faith and continuing to seek God with bold persistence, will often witness the very answer that would have been missed had they given up too soon.

Persistent prayer develops spiritual endurance in the life of a believer. Just as physical muscles grow stronger through repeated exercise, faith grows stronger through consistent communion with God. Every moment spent in prayer stretches the heart to trust Him more deeply. When a person continues to pray even when answers seem delayed, their faith becomes steadier and their spirit becomes more resilient. Prayer trains the soul to rely on God rather than circumstances, building a quiet confidence that He hears and responds according to His perfect will. Through persistent prayer, spiritual awareness becomes sharper and dependence upon God becomes deeper. The man begins to recognize God's presence, guidance, and strength in every situation. Over time, this steady practice of prayer forms an unbreakable spiritual foundation where faith is strengthened, courage is renewed, and the soul learns to draw continually from God's endless supply of strength.

Authority in Christ changes the way a man approaches prayer. No longer does he come timidly as someone begging from a position of defeat. Instead, he comes boldly before the throne of grace, standing firmly in the victory that Jesus Christ has already won through His death and resurrection. With faith in his heart and confidence in God's promises, he prays with boldness, knowing that heaven listens and responds to those who stand in Christ. Through Christ, believers have been given authority over darkness and every force that opposes the purposes of God. This authority does not come from human strength, but from the finished work of the cross and the power of the risen Savior. When a believer prays with this understanding, his prayers carry conviction, courage, and expectation. He resists fear, confronts spiritual opposition, and declares the truth of God's Word with confidence. In Christ, the warrior does not pray as a victim of the battle, but as a servant of the King who already holds the victory.

Jesus declared that all authority in heaven and on earth had been given to Him, revealing the limitless power that rests in His name. When men pray in the name of Jesus, they are not simply attaching a religious phrase to the end of a request. They are approaching God under the authority of the risen King. Just as an ambassador speaks on behalf of the nation that sent him, the follower of Christ speaks under the authority of the One who conquered sin, death, and the grave. Prayer in His name means we stand aligned with His will, His character, and His purpose We pray knowing that Jesus has already established victory and that His authority opens doors no human power can shut. When men pray in faith, fear gives way to boldness, doubt gives way to assurance, and uncertainty gives way to expectation. Standing under the authority of Christ transforms prayer into a powerful act of faith, trusting that the King who holds all authority hears and responds.

A warrior of faith understands that prayer is far more than quiet conversation with God; it is spiritual confrontation. When a man bows in prayer, he steps onto a battlefield where the will of God challenges the resistance of darkness. Prayer is the moment when faith speaks, authority rises, and heaven's purposes are declared over situations that seem impossible. Through prayer, the man of faith aligns his heart with God and boldly stands against fear, deception, and opposition, knowing that the presence of God is greater than any force that stands against His promises. When men pray, they release divine power into circumstances that once seemed unchangeable. Chains begin to break, wisdom begins to flow, and spiritual resistance begins to weaken. The warrior who prays understands that victory is often won on his knees before it is seen with his eyes. In prayer, heaven's authority is unleashed, and God's will advances in the lives of His people and in the world around them.

Prayer is not merely a defensive practice for the believer; it is a powerful offensive weapon in the spiritual battle. When a man of God prays with faith and authority, he confronts fear, doubt, temptation, and spiritual oppression head-on. In prayer, the man of God is not retreating from the battlefield but stepping forward with spiritual authority, inviting the power of God to intervene in earthly circumstances. A spiritual warrior understands that prayer moves him from reaction to action. Instead of waiting for problems to overwhelm him, he advances in prayer, speaking truth, claiming God's promises, and calling upon divine strength. Prayer shifts the atmosphere, strengthens the soul, and releases the presence of God into situations that once seemed impossible. When a warrior prays, heaven responds, courage rises, and the enemy's influence weakens. In this way, prayer becomes a mighty weapon - one that pushes back darkness and opens the door for God's power, peace, and victory to flow.

Through prayer, a man steps into a battlefield that exists beyond what human eyes can see. Long before challenges surface in the physical world, the battle has already begun in the unseen realm. When men bow their heads before God, they are not retreating from the fight

- they are advancing into it. Prayer invites heaven's authority into earthly circumstances, releasing wisdom, strength, and divine intervention. What looks like quiet devotion is actually powerful spiritual engagement, where God prepares the way, dismantles hidden obstacles, and positions His people for victory before the conflict ever becomes visible. Victories are often born in secret moments with God. Every sincere prayer weakens the grip of darkness and shakes the foundations of spiritual strongholds. When faithful believers stand boldly before the throne of grace, heaven moves on their behalf. Chains begin to loosen, hearts begin to change, and circumstances begin to shift long before the results are seen.

A life of powerful prayer does not merely change circumstances - it transforms the one who prays. In the presence of God, the soul is strengthened and the heart is steadied. Confidence replaces doubt when a man understands that the Almighty hears his voice and walks beside him through every challenge. Prayer shifts the focus from human weakness to divine strength, reminding the believer that God's power is greater than any obstacle that stands before him. As time in prayer deepens, peace begins to settle where anxiety once ruled. The mind becomes quiet, the spirit becomes steady, and the heart becomes anchored in trust. The warrior who kneels before God rises stronger, clearer, and more determined, because time spent in the presence of the Almighty refines his character and renews his strength. Prayer becomes the place where burdens are lifted, vision is restored, and courage is reborn. In that sacred place, the warrior emerges prepared for the fight by the power of God who equips him.

Unbreakable faith is not formed in moments of comfort, but in the quiet discipline of the prayer room. It is there, away from the noise and distractions of life, that a man learns to trust God beyond what the natural eyes can see. Prayer becomes the place where fears are confronted and confidence in God begins to rise. As the heart pours itself out before the Lord, faith is strengthened by the realization that

God hears, God cares, and God is already at work even when circumstances appear unchanged. In the place of prayer, the soul becomes anchored to the promises of God rather than the shifting winds of emotion or circumstance. Each moment spent seeking Him deepens spiritual resolve and builds a quiet certainty that God is faithful to fulfill His word. The more a man prays, the more steadfast his heart becomes, learning to stand firm in hope and expectation. Through prayer, faith grows unbreakable because the man of God becomes stronger in trusting the One who holds all things in His hands.

When a man learns to pray like a warrior, he steps into a dimension of spiritual authority that reaches far beyond what the eyes can see. Prayer is no longer a quiet ritual but a powerful act of faith that confronts darkness and invites the presence of God into every situation. Through bold and persistent prayer, he stands in the gap for his family, his community, and his calling. His words become weapons of faith that drive back fear, break strongholds, and release the light of God into places that once seemed hopeless. Though the world may never witness the battles he fights on his knees, heaven records every moment of his faithfulness. Each prayer offered in humility and trust moves the heart of God and shifts the atmosphere of the unseen realm. Hope is released, miracles begin to unfold, and lives are quietly transformed. The praying man may walk through life unnoticed by many, but in the Kingdom of God he is a mighty force, advancing God's purposes and leaving a trail of spiritual victories behind him.

| 27 |

"INTEGRITY IN ISOLATION"

Conviction is the backbone of a godly life because it anchors a man to truth when everything around him is shifting. Opinions change, culture drifts, and pressure from the crowd can be relentless, but conviction provides a steady foundation that does not move. It is not loud or boastful; it is a quiet strength rooted deep in the heart of a man who has settled what he believes before God. When storms come - and they always do - conviction keeps him from being tossed back and forth by every new idea or demand. It steadies his steps and gives him the courage to remain faithful when compromise would be easier. A man who lives by conviction does not measure his life by the approval of the crowd but by the standard of truth. He understands that integrity sometimes requires standing alone, refusing to bow to pressure, and holding firmly to what is right. History and scripture are filled with men who walked this lonely road, yet their unwavering commitment became a light for others to follow.

The call of God has never been about blending in. Scripture reminds us that we are called to be set apart, transformed by the renewing of our minds, and courageous enough to walk a path that may not always be popular. A man who follows God must sometimes stand alone, choosing conviction over convenience and truth over acceptance. Spiritual maturity requires the strength to resist the invisible pull of cultural pressure. The world rewards agreement and punishes conviction, but God honors those who remain faithful when it would be easier to compromise. The faithful man learns that approval from people is temporary, but the approval of God carries eternal weight. When your identity is anchored in Christ, you no longer need the permission of the crowd to live righteously. Instead of conforming to the pressure around you, you become a quiet example of courage, integrity, and faith - proving that true strength is not found in fitting in, but in standing firm.

The world often rewards those who blend in. It celebrates those who stay quiet when truth is inconvenient and who soften their values when standing firm might cost them something. But the call of God has never been a call to quiet compromise. Throughout scripture, the men and women God used most powerfully were those who refused to bow to pressure. They chose conviction over comfort and truth over popularity. Daniel would not defile himself in Babylon, Elijah would not stay silent before a corrupt king, and the apostles boldly proclaimed Christ even when threatened. Faithfulness to God often means standing where others step back and speaking when others remain silent. God calls His people to a higher standard - a life anchored in truth, courage, and unwavering devotion. When a believer refuses to bend with the shifting winds of culture, he becomes a light in a darkened world. Integrity may not always bring applause from people, but it always earns the approval of heaven.

A man of conviction does not allow the noise of the crowd to drown out the quiet voice of truth. Popularity shifts like the wind, changing direction with every passing opinion, but righteousness stands firm and unchanging. The man who anchors his heart in what is right learns that approval from people is temporary, while integrity before God is eternal. He understands that doing what is right may cost him comfort, reputation, or acceptance, yet he chooses the path of righteousness because his loyalty is not to applause but to truth. When the crowd moves one way and truth moves another, conviction becomes the compass that keeps a man on course. It gives him the courage to walk the narrow road even when it feels lonely. Such a man knows that heaven honors those who refuse to compromise their principles. Though the harder road may be steep, it leads to strength of character, clarity of conscience, and the deep peace that comes from knowing he chose righteousness over popularity.

Scripture gives us a powerful picture of this kind of courage in the life of Daniel. Living in a foreign land under a pagan king, Daniel faced enormous pressure to abandon his convictions. The culture around him demanded compromise, and the cost of faithfulness could have meant ridicule, loss of position, or even death. Yet Daniel understood that true strength is not found in yielding to the pressure of the moment but in standing firm in devotion to God. His courage was quiet but immovable. Daniel remained anchored to the truth he had known since his youth. Daniel's example reminds us that courage is often revealed in daily decisions to honor God when it would be easier to conform. Because of that unwavering resolve, God honored Daniel's life and used him as a witness in the midst of a hostile culture. His story teaches us that when a man refuses to surrender his convictions, God can turn that steadfast faith into a powerful testimony that influences kings, nations, and generations to come.

Daniel's courage was the fruit of a life already rooted in devotion to God. When the decree came forbidding prayer, Daniel did not panic, compromise, or hide his faith. Instead, he did what he had always done - he opened his window and prayed to the Lord. His faith was not shaped by circumstances, public opinion, or political pressure. It was shaped by loyalty to God. Daniel understood that obedience to the Lord must never be negotiated, even when the cost could be great. True faith is revealed in moments like these. Daniel chose faithfulness over safety, obedience over approval, and reverence for God over fear of man. His quiet act of prayer was a powerful declaration that God's authority stands above every human command.

In a world that often pressures believers to dilute their convictions, Daniel's example reminds us that unwavering devotion honors God and strengthens the soul. When we stand firm in our obedience, we demonstrate that our allegiance belongs first and foremost to the Lord.

Daniel understood the approval of God is worth more than the approval of people. Even when it meant standing alone, even when it meant facing lions, he refused to compromise his devotion to God. He knew that the opinions of men are temporary, but the favor of God is eternal. A man who lives for God's approval develops a steady heart, a clear conscience, and a courage that cannot be shaken by criticism or rejection. Popularity fades, but faithfulness lasts forever. The cheers of the crowd grow quiet, and the praise of people eventually disappears, but the life that honors God leaves a lasting legacy. Daniel's faithfulness still speaks thousands of years later because it was rooted in obedience rather than recognition. When a man seeks God's approval above all else, he is freed from the exhausting need to impress others. Instead, he becomes steadfast, principled, and trustworthy - living each day with the quiet confidence that the only opinion that truly matters is the one that comes from heaven.

Standing alone can feel uncomfortable. It can even feel frightening. No one enjoys being misunderstood, criticized, or excluded. Yet throughout scripture, many of God's greatest servants discovered that the path of obedience sometimes requires standing apart from the crowd. Noah built while others mocked. Elijah stood against prophets who outnumbered him. Daniel prayed even when it placed his life in danger. In those moments, their courage was not rooted in popularity but in loyalty to God. When a man chooses truth over approval and righteousness over comfort, he may find himself standing alone for a season. But what feels like isolation is often the place where God strengthens conviction and deepens faith. The crowd may disappear, but God's presence does not. In fact, many times His guidance comes when the noise of public approval fades away. Standing alone for what is right is never truly standing alone, because the one who walks with God carries the strength of heaven with him.

Conviction is the quiet strength that holds a man steady when the winds of opinion begin to shift. When acceptance disappears and approval fades, conviction becomes the anchor of the soul. It reminds a man that his identity is not built on applause but on truth. A man who lives by conviction understands that the crowd is often unstable, but the Word of God is unchanging. When he knows what is right, he does not need the permission of others to stand for it. Truth does not bend simply because it becomes unpopular. Right remains right even when only a few are willing to defend it. The man of conviction may stand alone at times, but he never stands unsupported, for God honors those who refuse to compromise what is true. History and scripture testify that the greatest men were not those who followed the crowd, but those who followed truth. When conviction anchors a man's heart, he becomes immovable - faithful to God, steady in character, and courageous enough to stand when others fall away.

There will be moments in life when compromise looks easier than courage. The easier road will promise comfort, security, or acceptance. It will whisper that bending your convictions is harmless and that standing firm is unnecessary. Yet compromise quietly erodes the soul. When a man trades conviction for convenience, he may gain temporary peace, but he loses something far greater - his integrity. Courage, on the other hand, often demands that you stand alone, endure criticism, or walk through uncertainty. But every time you choose courage over compromise, you strengthen your character and align your life more closely with the truth God placed in your heart. The road of courage may feel difficult in the moment, but it leads to peace that compromise can never give. Regret rarely comes from doing what is right; it most often comes from knowing you surrendered when you should have stood firm. God honors the man who chooses righteousness over comfort and conviction over popularity.

Conviction demands a strength that does not depend on applause or agreement. It is the quiet resolve of a man who has settled the matter in his heart before God. When conviction grips a man's spirit, popularity no longer governs his choices and the approval of the crowd loses its power. He stands on truth because truth is right, not because it is easy or widely accepted. Even when his voice is the only one speaking, he refuses to retreat, knowing that integrity before God matters far more than acceptance among men. In those lonely moments, conviction becomes a shield for the soul. It steadies a man when the room grows quiet and the crowd turns away. While others bend with the pressure of opinion, the man of conviction holds the line with courage and humility. He understands that history and eternity are often shaped by those willing to stand alone for what is right. And when a man chooses faithfulness over comfort, God honors that courage and strengthens him to remain unshaken.

Truth without compromise is a rare quality in our time. Many people adjust their beliefs depending on who is watching. They shift their values to match the mood of the moment, bending their convictions to gain approval or avoid discomfort. Yet real integrity is not shaped by the crowd but anchored in something deeper. A man who walks in truth stands the same whether in public or in private. His character is not a costume he puts on for an audience; it is a foundation built on honesty before God. When a man refuses to compromise what is right, he becomes steady in a world of shifting opinions. God honors those who remain faithful to truth even when it costs them something. Truth may not always be popular, but it is always powerful. A life rooted in truth produces strength, clarity, and spiritual authority. It forms a man whose words carry weight because his life backs them up. The man who stands for what is right becomes a light in the darkness proving that integrity, courage, and faithfulness are still possible.

A man of God lives by a higher compass. While the crowd shifts with every new trend, his heart is anchored in the unchanging truth of God's Word. He does not measure his convictions by popularity or approval, but by obedience. When the world applauds compromise, he quietly chooses integrity. When others bend under pressure, he stands upright because his foundation is not public opinion but divine instruction. The Word of God becomes his standard, his guide, and his measuring rod for every decision he makes. Because of this, his character remains steady whether he is surrounded by supporters or standing completely alone. Applause does not inflate him, and criticism does not shake him. Even in solitude, he walks faithfully, knowing that true strength is revealed when no one is watching. Such a man understands that faithfulness to God matters far more than acceptance by people, and in that unwavering commitment he becomes a quiet but powerful witness to the world.

Integrity is most clearly revealed in the quiet places of life. When the crowd disappears, when the applause fades, and when no one is watching, a man stands face to face with his true self. In those moments of isolation, obedience to God becomes a matter of conviction rather than recognition. There is no reward from the world, no praise from others - only the choice to do what is right because it is right. True character is forged in the unseen hours where faithfulness is tested and integrity must stand on its own. The man who remains faithful in isolation develops a strength that applause could never produce. He learns that God's approval matters more than human attention. In those hidden places, integrity grows roots that run deep, anchoring a man's life in truth and honor. When the day finally comes for others to see the fruit, it will simply reveal what was already proven long before - in the quiet moments when he chose obedience without an audience.

A man who stands alone for what is right may feel the weight of isolation for a season. When others compromise, stay silent, or walk away from truth, the man who chooses integrity can appear to be standing on an empty battlefield. Yet what looks like loneliness is often the proving ground of courage. Throughout scripture and history, the men God used most powerfully were often those willing to stand when others would not. Their strength was not found in numbers but in conviction. When a man refuses to bow to pressure, corruption, or fear, he demonstrates a loyalty to God that cannot be shaken by the opinions of men. But the truth is this: a man who stands for God never truly stands alone. The Lord Himself stands beside those who honor Him. God strengthens the man who chooses righteousness over popularity and truth over comfort. In time, that lonely stand often becomes a beacon that inspires others to rise, proving that one faithful man can ignite courage in many.

History is filled with men who stood alone before they stood victorious. The prophets of old, the reformers of nations, and the leaders who shaped generations often walked through seasons of isolation long before their impact was recognized. Their convictions separated them from the comfort of compromise. While others blended in with the crowd, they chose to stand firm on truth. That kind of courage builds a foundation that time itself cannot erase. Loneliness becomes the proving ground where God refines a man's character and strengthens his resolve. When a man refuses to bow to pressure and remains faithful to what he knows is right, he joins the company of those who shaped history through unwavering conviction. God often prepares victory in the quiet places where a man must stand without applause or affirmation. But the steadfastness that separates him today will one day distinguish him tomorrow. The man who stands alone for truth today may soon stand as a pillar of strength for many.

When a man chooses to stand firmly in truth his life begins to shine like a light in a dark place. Others may be struggling silently with the same pressures, but when they witness someone who refuses to bend, refuses to abandon what is right, and refuses to walk away from

God's standards, something awakens within them. That steady example becomes a beacon, reminding them that faithfulness is possible and that integrity is still worth defending. Often the man who stands firm does not realize the influence he carries. Yet God frequently uses one courageous life to ignite courage in many others. Just as a single spark can start a fire that spreads across a field, one faithful believer can inspire a chain reaction of boldness, conviction, and renewed commitment. What began as one man's quiet obedience becomes a movement of strengthened hearts and lifted spirits. In this way, faithfulness is never wasted; it becomes a guiding light that encourages others to rise, stand, and walk boldly in the truth.

When the moment of decision arrives and the pressure of the crowd begins to rise, a man must remember where his true strength comes from. The voices around him may urge compromise, popularity, or comfort, but the voice of God calls him to conviction and courage. Standing alone with God may feel lonely for a season, yet it is never truly lonely. In that sacred place of faithfulness, God becomes your defender, your guide, and your reward. History and scripture both reveal that those who dared to stand with God - even when no one else would - became the very people through whom God accomplished His greatest purposes. Conviction may isolate you temporarily, but it also refines you and draws you nearer to the heart of God. The crowd may applaud compromise today and forget it tomorrow, but God honors the man who remains faithful to truth. When you choose righteousness over approval and obedience over popularity, you step into deeper fellowship with Him.

| 28 |

"GENERATIONAL IMPACT"

Every man eventually comes face to face with a sobering truth: life on earth is temporary. The days seem long when we are young, yet the years pass with surprising speed. One season flows into the next until we realize how brief our time really is. Scripture reminds us that our lives are like a vapor that appears for a moment and then fades away. Yet this reality is not meant to discourage us - it is meant to awaken us. God never intended for a man's life to drift by without purpose. Instead, He calls each of us to live with intention, to build something meaningful, and to invest our strength in things that will endure long after our footsteps fade from the earth. When a man anchors his life in faith, character, and obedience to God, he begins constructing a legacy that time cannot erase. His influence reaches beyond his own lifetime through the lives he touches, the wisdom he shares, and the example he leaves behind. Children, disciples, and those he encourages carry forward the spiritual seeds he planted.

A faithful man becomes a builder of eternal things. His life becomes a foundation upon which others can stand. A man may build great success and still leave nothing of lasting value behind. True legacy is not found in the spotlight of human praise, but in the quiet influence of a life that walks closely with God. When a person lives in obedience, humility, and devotion to the Lord, their life begins to shape others in ways that go far beyond what they can see. Real legacy is written in the lives that are strengthened, encouraged, and redirected because someone chose to follow God wholeheartedly. It is seen in the faith that is passed to the next generation, in the courage that is awakened in another soul, and in the wisdom that guides someone through a difficult season. When you walk faithfully with God, your life becomes a living testimony that continues speaking long after your voice is silent. The greatest inheritance you can leave behind is a trail of faith that leads others toward God.

The Bible repeatedly shows us that a single life surrendered to God can echo through generations. Abraham simply obeyed when God called him to step into the unknown, yet that obedience became the foundation of a nation and a promise that still blesses the world today. David, though imperfect, possessed a heart that continually turned toward God, and his faith stirred courage, worship, and devotion throughout Israel. Their stories remind us that God often works through ordinary individuals who choose to trust Him in extraordinary ways. One act of faith, one decision to follow God wholeheartedly, can begin a chain of influence far greater than we ever imagine. Our lives may seem small in the moment, but faithfulness today plants seeds for tomorrow. The words we speak, the integrity we live by, and the example we set can shape families and future generations. When a man walks in obedience, his influence stretches far beyond his years, leaving a spiritual legacy that continues long after he is gone.

Generational impact begins with the choices we make today because the example we set will echo through the lives of those who come after us. Every decision to walk in integrity and serve God faithfully plant seeds that will grow long after we are gone. A life devoted to God sends quiet ripples outward into our homes, our friendships, and our communities. What may feel like small acts of devotion today can become powerful testimonies tomorrow. When a person commits to living faithfully before God, their influence stretches far beyond their own lifetime. Values are passed down, courage is modeled, and faith becomes a legacy that shapes future generations. Churches grow stronger, families become steadier, and communities gain hope because one person chose to live intentionally for God. A devoted life does more than bless the present - it builds a foundation for those who will come after, proving that the greatest inheritance we can leave is a life that pointed others toward God.

Legacy is often imagined as something that begins in the later chapters of life, but in truth it begins today. The seeds of influence are planted in the quiet, ordinary moments of daily obedience. Every choice to honor God, every act of faithfulness when no one is watching, and every sacrifice made for what is right becomes a stone in the foundation of a life that will outlive the present moment. Legacy is not built in grand gestures alone; it is formed through consistent devotion, humble service, and the steady pursuit of God's will. When a person understands this, they begin to live with greater intention. They realize that today's faithfulness shapes tomorrow's testimony. The courage to obey God now creates ripples that reach far beyond what the eye can see - touching families, guiding future generations, and strengthening the faith of those who follow. A life surrendered to God becomes a living legacy, proving that the small acts of obedience today can echo with eternal impact tomorrow.

Mentorship is one of the most powerful ways a person can build something that outlives them. When you intentionally pour wisdom, faith, and encouragement into another person, you are planting seeds that will continue to grow long after your own season has passed. The truths you share, the example you set, and the confidence you help build in someone else become part of their character and direction. What God has placed in you becomes a living investment in the future through the lives of others. When you mentor someone, your influence multiplies far beyond what you can personally accomplish. The person you strengthen today will one day strengthen others, and the ripple effect continues from generation to generation. You are not merely shaping one life - you are helping shape the countless lives that person will impact through their words, choices, and leadership. When you invest in people, you are building something that time cannot erase.

Jesus Himself demonstrated the extraordinary power of mentorship. Rather than building a movement through crowds alone, He intentionally poured His life into twelve ordinary men. He walked with them, taught them, corrected them, encouraged them, and showed them what it meant to live in obedience to the Father. Day after day, through quiet moments and powerful miracles, Jesus shaped their hearts and minds. He knew that true transformation happens not only through words, but through relationship and example. His investment in those disciples shows that the most lasting influence often comes from intentionally developing others. The results of that mentorship changed the course of history. Those same twelve men, once fishermen and tax collectors, became bold messengers of the gospel who carried the message of Christ throughout the world. What began as a small circle of disciples grew into a global movement that still impacts lives today.

Mentorship is not about presenting a flawless life; it is about showing a faithful one. No person walks perfectly, and God has never required perfection from those He uses to guide others. What people truly need is someone who is present - someone willing to walk beside them, share wisdom, offer encouragement, and demonstrate what it looks like to pursue God sincerely. When a mentor shows humility, admits mistakes, and keeps moving forward with faith, it creates an honest and attainable example. Authenticity opens doors that perfection never could. When you live with humility and sincerity, your life becomes a visible path others can follow. They see how you pray, how you handle hardship, how you rise after failure, and how you remain committed to growth. In this way, mentorship becomes a living testimony of God's grace at work in an ordinary life. Faithful examples inspire courage in others, reminding them that they too can walk the path of faith, one sincere step at a time.

Living intentionally is one of the great secrets to building a legacy that truly lasts. A man who simply drifts through life - reacting to circumstances, chasing comfort, or living without direction - rarely leaves behind anything of lasting value. Days slip into years, and years slip into decades, with little eternal impact. But when a man chooses to live deliberately, aligning his decisions with God's truth and his actions with God's purpose, his life begins to carry weight. His choices are no longer random; they become meaningful steps in a larger story that God is writing through him. A man guided by purpose shapes the world around him in quiet but powerful ways. His words strengthen others, his character sets an example, and his faith leaves footprints for the next generation to follow. Intentional living turns ordinary moments into opportunities for influence and service. When a man wakes each day asking God how he can love, lead, and serve faithfully, his life begins to echo far beyond his own years.

Intentional living begins with the recognition that life is not meant to be drifted through but directed with purpose. A man who lives intentionally aligns his actions with the values he claims to believe. This often requires courage, because the right path is not always the easiest one. Choosing integrity when compromise would be simpler, choosing faith when fear whispers loudly, and choosing obedience when the cost feels high are all marks of a life that is intentionally surrendered to God's will. Every day provides a new opportunity to strengthen your influence for good. The small choices you make - how you speak, how you treat others, how you respond to pressure, and how faithfully you walk with God - quietly shape the legacy you are building. When we walk with purpose, humility, and faithfulness, our actions become a testimony that points others toward God. In this way, a life lived intentionally becomes a powerful instrument for good, leaving a lasting spiritual impact far beyond the present moment.

The world constantly urges people to chase what feels good in the moment - comfort, pleasure, recognition, and success. Yet these things, no matter how exciting they seem at first, quickly fade like mist in the morning sun. Instead of measuring life by temporary satisfaction, God invites us to measure it by eternal significance. When a person begins to see life through the lens of eternity, priorities shift and the heart becomes anchored in what truly matters. The love we show, the truth we stand for, and the people we influence for Christ all become part of an eternal legacy. While temporary pleasures disappear, the impact of a life surrendered to God continues to echo through generations and into eternity itself. Living with eternity in mind gives meaning to everyday choices and strength to endure temporary hardships. Those who walk faithfully with God discover that the greatest reward is not found in fleeting moments, but in a life that pleases Him and leaves behind fruit that will last forever.

A spiritual inheritance is one of the greatest gifts a person can leave behind. Money can be spent, possessions can be broken, and earthly success can fade with time, but a legacy of faith carries an eternal weight. When someone lives a life devoted to God, their example plants seeds in the hearts of others. Children, family members, and those who observe their life learn what it looks like to trust God, to walk in integrity, and to seek truth above comfort. Long after material things are forgotten, the testimony of a faithful life continues to speak. When a person teaches others to pray, to stand firm in difficult seasons, and to rely on God's promises, they are building something that will outlive them. A spiritual inheritance creates a chain of faith that stretches across time, strengthening families and guiding hearts toward God long after the original voice has grown silent. Such a legacy is not measured in dollars or possessions, but in transformed lives and enduring faith.

Parents, mentors, and leaders carry a sacred responsibility that reaches far beyond their own lifetime. Every word of truth they teach, every prayer they model, and every moment they demonstrate trust in God becomes a living lesson to those watching. Faith is rarely learned only through instruction; it is most powerfully absorbed through example. When a child sees a parent pray in difficult moments, when a student watches a mentor stand firm in conviction, or when a leader chooses integrity over convenience, those actions quietly build a spiritual foundation in the hearts of others. In this way, genuine faith becomes a lasting inheritance. Long after the teacher's voice grows silent, the seeds of truth continue to grow in the lives they influenced. The courage to trust God in uncertain times, the discipline to seek Him in prayer, and the commitment to live by His Word become part of the legacy they leave behind. A life lived with authentic faith shapes future generations who will carry that same trust in God forward.

The greatest legacy a person can leave behind is not carved in stone, written on plaques, or measured by earthly achievements. Buildings crumble, titles fade, and applause eventually grows silent. But the influence of a life lived for God continues to echo through the hearts of others. When a person walks faithfully, loves sincerely, and lives with integrity, their life becomes a living testimony. Those who witness that example are inspired to pursue a deeper relationship with God, and that influence quietly multiplies from one life to another. When people grow stronger in their faith because of your example, your legacy becomes something eternal. A word of encouragement, a moment of guidance, or a consistent display of godly character can shape someone's spiritual journey in ways you may never fully see. Long after your earthly journey ends, the seeds you planted will continue to grow in the lives of others. In this way, the impact of your devotion reaches far beyond your lifetime and into eternity.

God often accomplishes His greatest purposes through ordinary people who simply choose to live with extraordinary devotion. A person who quietly walks in obedience, prays faithfully, serves humbly, and trusts God daily may appear unnoticed by the world, yet heaven sees every act of faithfulness. What seems small in the eyes of people becomes significant in the hands of God, because devotion multiplies the impact of even the simplest acts of obedience. A quiet life surrendered to God can produce a legacy far greater than we ever realize. Seeds of faith planted through kindness, integrity, prayer, and example often grow in ways that reach generations beyond our own lifetime. When a person commits to walking with God day after day, their life becomes a testimony that inspires others, strengthens families, and shapes future believers. In God's kingdom, extraordinary impact is often born from ordinary people who refuse to live ordinary lives of faith.

When a man begins to live with legacy in mind, his perspective changes. The things that once seemed urgent - status, recognition, and temporary success - lose much of their power over his decisions. He begins to measure his life by a different standard. His time becomes more intentional, his words more thoughtful, and his actions more deliberate because he understands that every choice is planting seeds that will grow in the lives of others. A legacy-minded life is not driven by accumulation but by influence. Such a person becomes less concerned with personal advancement and more concerned with the people he is shaping along the way - his family, his friends, and those who are watching his example. He realizes that character, faith, and integrity are the true inheritance he will leave behind. Long after achievements fade and titles are forgotten, the impact of a life lived for God will continue to echo through generations. Living this way transforms everyday moments into eternal investments.

Every person has the opportunity to build something that outlives them. God did not design life to be lived only for the moment, but for impact that echoes far beyond our years. Through faith, a person plants seeds that continue to grow long after they are gone. When we mentor others, invest in their growth, and live with purpose, we are quietly shaping the future. Every encouraging word, every lesson shared, and every example of integrity becomes a brick in a foundation that others will one day stand upon. When a person chooses to pour wisdom, love, and spiritual truth into the lives of others, they are building something far greater than success or recognition. They are creating a spiritual inheritance. Generations are strengthened when someone chooses to live faithfully, teach faithfully, and lead faithfully. In this way, a single life surrendered to God becomes a strong foundation upon which countless others can build, grow, and continue the work of faith long after that life has passed.

When your journey on earth is finished, the true measure of your life will not be found in the things you accumulated, the titles you held, or the achievements you celebrated. Those things fade with time. What endures is the faith you lived and the strength you gave to others. Every prayer you prayed, every act of kindness you offered, every word of encouragement you spoke, and every example of integrity you demonstrated becomes a seed planted in the hearts of others. A man who walks with God leaves footprints of hope behind them, guiding others toward the same path of faith, courage, and devotion. Generations may rise who never knew your name personally, yet they will benefit from the spiritual inheritance you helped establish. This is the beauty of a life surrendered to God: its impact multiplies beyond your lifetime. When you live faithfully, you become part of a story far greater than your own - one where the seeds of faith you planted continue to bear fruit for years to come.

| 29 |

"EMOTIONAL ENDURANCE"

Life will inevitably bring storms. No man walks through this world without seasons of pressure, disappointment, or emotional fatigue. Trials are not signs that God has abandoned you; often they are the very places where He strengthens you. Storm-proofing your soul does not mean escaping hardship, but learning to stand firm in the middle of it. When your life is anchored in faith, disappointment does not destroy you, pressure does not define you, and fatigue does not defeat you. Instead, those moments become opportunities for deeper trust, stronger character, and a steadier heart. A storm-proof soul is built through daily surrender, disciplined thinking, and unwavering trust in God's promises. It learns to guard its thoughts, refuse discouragement, and remain anchored in purpose even when emotions are unsettled. Rest when you must but never retreat from who God has called you to be. The storms may shake the branches of your life, but they cannot uproot a soul that is firmly planted in faith.

The storms of life come in many forms - discouragement, rejection, uncertainty, and loss. They arrive unexpectedly and often with great force, shaking the foundations of a man's confidence and testing the strength of his faith. In those moments it is easy to question the path God has placed before you or to wonder whether the struggle is worth the cost. Yet storms have a purpose beyond the discomfort they bring. Just as fierce winds strengthen the roots of a tree, the trials of life deepen a man's character, refine his resolve, and draw him closer to the God who anchors his soul. When you remain steady, trusting God in the middle of the winds, the very pressures meant to break you begin to build you. Your faith grows stronger, your courage becomes steadier, and your perspective becomes clearer. The storm may rage for a season, but when it passes, the man who stands afterward is no longer the same - he is stronger, grounded, and more firmly rooted in the purpose God placed within him.

Discouragement is often the first wave that crashes against the soul, arriving quietly but carrying a heavy weight. When plans fall apart, prayers seem unanswered, or progress feels painfully slow, the heart can begin to question whether the effort is worth it. In those moments, discouragement urges him to lower his expectations, to abandon the vision God placed within him, and to settle for a smaller life than the one he was created to live. But faith calls a man to stand firm when the waves rise. Discouragement may knock at the door of the mind, but it does not have to take residence in the heart. God often works in seasons of waiting, shaping strength in the quiet places where perseverance is tested. What appears to be delay is often preparation, and what feels like silence is sometimes the soil where deeper faith takes root. When a man continues to trust God's promises, he discovers that the very storm meant to weaken him becomes the force that strengthens his soul.

Discouragement is a voice that whispers lies to the heart, attempting to convince a man that his efforts are pointless and his future uncertain. Yet discouragement only gains strength when it is welcomed and allowed to linger in the mind. A wise man learns to recognize this voice quickly. He understands that despair is not a counselor sent by God but a thief that steals courage, vision, and determination. Rather than entertaining these thoughts, he rejects them and guards his mind with the truth of God's promises. Instead of surrendering to discouragement, the wise man confronts it with faith and perseverance. He reminds himself that setbacks do not define his destiny and that God often builds strength through adversity. With steady resolve, he replaces doubt with truth, fear with faith, and weariness with hope. By refusing to let discouragement take root, he keeps his heart anchored in God's purpose and continues moving forward with quiet confidence and enduring strength.

When circumstances appear to stall your progress or when obstacles rise unexpectedly, it is easy for the heart to grow weary. Yet God's work in a person's life is rarely instant or effortless. Scripture repeatedly shows that seasons of delay and struggle are not signs of abandonment but instruments of preparation. In those difficult moments, faith learns to trust that God is shaping something deeper within the soul. God often uses delay, resistance, and hardship to form qualities that comfort and ease could never produce. Strength is forged when a person refuses to quit. Patience grows when waiting stretches longer than expected. Character develops when faith chooses to stand firm despite disappointment. What feels like a setback today may actually be a step in God's greater design for your life. If you remain anchored in Him, discouragement loses its power, and the very struggle that once weighed you down becomes the training ground for the strength God intends to build within you.

The enemy of your soul understands that a weakened mind leads to a weakened life. If he can fill your thoughts with doubt, fear, discouragement, and defeat, he can slowly erode your resolve to stand firm. Long before a man quits outwardly, he first surrenders inwardly. That is why the battle for endurance begins in the mind. The thoughts you allow to take root will either strengthen your spirit or slowly drain your courage. When you guard your mind with truth, faith, and disciplined thinking, you build an inner fortress that the storms of life cannot easily penetrate. Your thoughts are the battlefield where endurance is either built or destroyed. Every day you must choose which voices will shape your thinking - the voice of fear or the voice of faith, the voice of defeat or the voice of determination. When you deliberately focus on God's promises, rehearse truth, and refuse to entertain lies, your resolve grows stronger. A guarded mind becomes a steady mind, and a steady mind produces an unbreakable spirit.

Guarding your mind means being intentional about what thoughts you allow to take root and grow within you. The mind is like a gate to the soul, and whatever consistently passes through that gate begins to shape your emotions, your outlook, and ultimately your strength. When negativity, fear, and self-doubt dominate your thinking, they slowly chip away at emotional resilience, weakening your ability to stand firm in difficult seasons. Discouraging thoughts left unchecked can distort reality and magnify problems until they seem overwhelming. Faith, truth, and gratitude are powerful reinforcements for a strong and steady mind. Faith reminds you that God is still working even when circumstances seem uncertain. Truth anchors you in reality rather than fear. Gratitude shifts your perspective from scarcity to abundance. Together, these attitudes fortify the mind and help you remain steady, hopeful, and resilient no matter what storms arise.

A storm-proof soul understands that the greatest battles are often fought in the mind. Fear, doubt, and discouragement attempt to take root in our thoughts long before they ever appear in our circumstances. But a disciplined spirit refuses to allow anxiety to dominate the inner conversation. Instead of endlessly replaying fears and imagining worst-case scenarios, a wise believer intentionally rehearses the promises of God. When the mind begins to wander toward worry, faith redirects it toward the assurance that God is present, God is powerful, and God is faithful to fulfill what He has spoken. Rather than focusing on obstacles, a storm-proof soul remembers the victories of the past. It recalls the moments when God provided, protected, and carried it through seasons that once seemed impossible. A disciplined mind anchored in God's promises becomes steady even in turbulent times, because it knows that the same God who delivered before will deliver again.

Emotional endurance also comes from staying anchored. Ships survive violent seas not because the water is calm, but because their anchor holds them steady beneath the surface. In the same way, a man of faith learns that stability does not come from perfect circumstances but from a steady connection to God. Storms will rise, winds will howl, and waves of discouragement will crash against the soul, but the heart that is anchored in truth does not drift. Your anchor must be deeper than circumstances. If your peace depends on everything going right, it will disappear the moment life turns rough. But when your confidence is rooted in God's character - His faithfulness, His presence, and His unchanging Word - you gain a stability the world cannot shake. The storms may still rage around you, but they will not rule within you. Anchored in faith, you learn to endure the pressure, steady your heart, and remain firmly planted until the waves pass and the skies clear again.

For the man of God, the anchor that steadies the soul is faith in God's unchanging character. Circumstances shift, emotions rise and fall, and the winds of life can suddenly turn without warning. Yet God remains faithful, steady, and trustworthy in every season. His promises do not weaken with time, and His nature is not altered by the chaos around us. When a man fixes his heart on the reliability of God, he finds a stability the world cannot provide. His confidence is no longer tied to the unpredictability of life, but to the unwavering character of the One who holds all things together. When a man anchors his heart to God, the storm may rage, but it cannot carry him away. Waves may crash and winds may howl, yet the anchor holds firm beneath the surface. Faith does not deny the storm; it simply refuses to be ruled by it. Instead of drifting into fear or despair, the anchored soul remains steady, trusting that God is present, powerful, and purposeful even in the midst of turmoil.

Staying anchored in a turbulent world requires spiritual habits that continually reconnect the heart to God. Prayer quiets the noise of fear and invites divine strength into the soul. Reflection allows a person to examine their thoughts, motives, and direction with honesty before God. Time spent in His Word renews the mind and replaces confusion with truth. These practices are not empty rituals; they are lifelines that keep the spirit grounded when circumstances become overwhelming. Just as deep roots stabilize a tree during a hurricane, these spiritual disciplines hold a believer steady when storms of discouragement, uncertainty, or pressure arise. The winds may howl and the rain may fall, but a tree with deep roots does not collapse easily. In the same way, a life rooted in prayer, reflection, and Scripture develops a quiet resilience. The soul becomes anchored in something greater than shifting emotions or temporary struggles - it becomes anchored in the unchanging strength and faithfulness of God.

Without an anchor, a man becomes vulnerable to every storm that rises against him. One moment he is confident, the next he is discouraged. One day he stands firm, the next he is swept away by doubt. A life without a spiritual anchor drifts with circumstances instead of standing on conviction. But God never intended for a man to live tossed back and forth by every wave of adversity. He calls men to be steady, rooted, and grounded in truth. When a man is anchored in faith, his life gains stability that the storms cannot steal. The winds may howl and the waves may crash, but his soul remains steady because his foundation is secure. His anchor is not his emotions, his circumstances, or the approval of others - it is his trust in God and the strength of His Word. Anchored men do not drift; they endure. They remain grounded when pressure rises, and they stand firm when adversity tries to shake them. The stronger the anchor, the stronger the man becomes in the storm.

Storm-proofing your soul also requires understanding the difference between rest and retreat. Rest is an act of wisdom; retreat is an act of surrender. God never designed a man to carry every burden alone without pause. Even Jesus stepped away from the crowds to pray, to breathe, and to restore His strength. Many men collapse emotionally not because they are weak, but because they refuse the discipline of rest. They shoulder every responsibility, silence every struggle, and push forward long after their strength has been depleted. Eventually exhaustion clouds judgment, discouragement seeps in, and the soul begins to fracture under the weight it was never meant to carry by itself. Healthy rest is not quitting the mission - it is preparing for the next battle. A wise man steps back long enough to regain clarity, renew his spirit, and place his burdens before God. He understands that quiet moments with the Lord rebuild the inner fortress of his heart.

Rest is not weakness; it is wisdom. Even the strongest warriors understand that constant battle without pause leads to exhaustion, confusion, and defeat. A man who refuses to rest eventually dulls his strength and clouds his judgment, but a man who pauses to recover gains clarity and perspective. Just as a soldier cleans his armor and sharpens his sword between battles, a wise man steps back to renew his spirit, quiet his mind, and reconnect with the presence of God. Rest is not retreat from the fight - it is preparation for it. In moments of stillness, strength is restored, courage is rekindled, and vision becomes clear again. When a man allows himself time to recover, he returns to the battlefield stronger, steadier, and more focused than before. God often renews a man not in the noise of the struggle but in the quiet places of reflection and prayer. Through rest, the soul is refreshed, the heart is strengthened, and a man rises again ready to continue the fight with renewed power and unwavering resolve.

Rest and retreat may look similar on the surface, but they come from two very different spirits. Rest is a wise and necessary pause that God designed to renew strength, sharpen perspective, and restore the soul. Even the strongest warriors must step away from the battlefield for a moment so they can return with clarity and endurance. Rest does not weaken a man's resolve; it deepens it. When a man rests, he is not surrendering the mission - he is preparing himself to continue it with greater faith, wisdom, and strength. Retreat, however, is different. Retreat is when a man abandons his calling because the pressure becomes uncomfortable. It is the quiet surrender that happens when fear, fatigue, or discouragement convince him that the fight is no longer worth it. Rest strengthens resolve, but retreat abandons it. A man of faith learns to discern the difference. He may step back to breathe, pray, and regain his footing, but he never walks away from the purpose God has placed on his life.

The man who chooses rest over retreat will rise again with renewed courage, ready to stand firm and finish the work he was called to do. When the winds of life grow fierce and the waves of discouragement crash against the heart, wisdom teaches a man not to quit, but to steady himself. He steps back, quiets the noise, and allows God to restore clarity to his spirit. Even the strongest warriors must catch their breath, gather their focus, and remember why they began the journey in the first place. In those moments of stillness, the soul breathes again. Strength returns, faith steadies the heart, and purpose rises to the surface once more. A storm-proof soul refuses to surrender the mission simply because the battle has grown difficult. Instead, it regains its footing, lifts its eyes toward heaven, and presses forward with renewed resolve. Rest may come, but retreat does not. The storm may rage, but the mission remains, and a soul anchored in God will rise again with greater courage to continue the path.

When discouragement rises, when the winds howl, and when the waves of pressure crash against your life, remember that storms do not last forever. Every storm has an expiration date, even when the sky seems permanently dark. God never promised that life would be free of tempests, but He did promise His presence in the middle of them. The same God who commands the winds and calms the sea is also strengthening your heart in the midst of the struggle. What feels overwhelming today is often the very process through which your faith is being fortified, your character refined, and your endurance deepened. What ultimately matters is whether your soul is anchored firmly enough to endure until the storm passes. A soul rooted in faith does not collapse under pressure; it learns to bend without breaking. When the winds blow hardest, lean deeper into prayer, truth, and the quiet confidence that God is still at work. The storm may shake you, but it does not have the authority to destroy you.

Build a life that is firmly rooted in faith, not merely in feelings or circumstances. Faith provides the deep foundation that keeps a person steady when the winds of hardship begin to blow. Discipline your thoughts so they are not ruled by fear, doubt, or discouragement, but guided by truth, hope, and the promises of God. Guard your emotional strength carefully, refusing to allow bitterness, anxiety, or despair to take control of your heart. A life that is anchored in God learns to draw strength from His presence, wisdom from His Word, and peace from His unchanging character. When your heart is anchored in God, the storms of life lose their power to destroy you. Trials may come, and seasons of shaking will certainly arrive, but your foundation will hold firm. Like a tree whose roots run deep beneath the soil, you will bend without breaking and endure without collapsing. The winds may howl and the rain may fall, but the soul that trusts in God stands secure.

| 30 |

"THROW AWAY THE UMBRELLA"

There comes a defining moment in every man's life when he must choose between the shelter of comfort and the storm of purpose. Comfort offers safety, familiarity, and the illusion of peace, but purpose demands courage, conviction, and faith. God did not design a man to live timidly beneath the umbrella of convenience, avoiding the winds of challenge and the rains of responsibility. True faith calls a man to step forward even when the skies grow dark, trusting that God walks with him through every storm. It is in those moments of bold obedience that character is forged, strength is revealed, and a man begins to live the life he was created to live. Faith was never intended to be quiet, hidden, or passive. It was meant to be lived openly, courageously, and without apology. When a man lays down the umbrella of comfort, he discovers the power of a life surrendered to God's purpose. The storms that once seemed threatening become the very environment where faith grows strong and resilient.

Too many men have grown comfortable with a version of Christianity that demands little and risks nothing. It is a faith that stays safely inside church walls and avoids the discomfort of true surrender. This kind of belief prefers convenience over conviction and safety over sacrifice. Yet the call of Christ has never been a call to comfort. Jesus did not invite men into a life of spiritual passivity; He called them to deny themselves, take up their cross, and follow Him with courage. Real faith stretches a man beyond what is easy and pushes him toward obedience even when the cost is high. When a man truly encounters Christ, his priorities shift, his courage grows, and his life begins to reflect the character of the One he follows. Comfortable religion leaves a man unchanged, but authentic faith reshapes his heart, his habits, and his purpose. God calls men not merely to believe, but to become men who live boldly, serve sacrificially, and stand faithfully in a world that desperately needs genuine discipleship.

Jesus never called men to a life built on safety, convenience, or comfort. When He walked along the shores of Galilee, He did not offer the fishermen a safer boat or a more predictable catch - He asked them to leave their nets behind. When He approached the tax collector at his table, He did not promise security or status - He invited him to abandon the familiar and follow a higher calling. Again and again, Christ called ordinary men out of ordinary lives and into extraordinary obedience. His voice disrupted routines, challenged comfort zones, and summoned men to trust God more than their own stability. The call of Jesus still echoes the same way today. It is not an invitation to play it safe, but a summons to step into courage, faith, and surrender. Following Christ means walking paths that require trust, sacrifice, and bold obedience. It means leaving behind whatever keeps a man chained to comfort and stepping into the adventure of God's purpose.

Comfort Christianity whispers to a man to remain where life is predictable, painless, and safe. It encourages him to avoid difficulty, sidestep sacrifice, and stay sheltered from the winds of challenge. Yet the call of God has never been a call to comfort. Throughout scripture, the men God used most powerfully stepped beyond convenience and into obedience. True faith refuses to remain in the shallow waters of ease; it listens for the voice of God and moves forward even when the path is uncertain. Faith understands that growth, courage, and spiritual authority are born in places where comfort is left behind. When a man chooses obedience over ease, something powerful begins to change within him. Trials sharpen his character, challenges deepen his trust in God, and hardship forges conviction in his soul. Comfort may protect a man from struggle, but it will never transform him. It is the man who follows God into the unknown who becomes strong in spirit, steady in purpose, and bold in faith.

The umbrella of comfort may shield a man from the rain, but it also keeps him from experiencing the very storm that God often uses to shape his character. When a man constantly seeks ease, he may avoid pain, but he also avoids the deep work of transformation. Scripture and life both testify that strength is rarely formed in calm weather. It is the wind that strengthens the tree's roots, the fire that refines the gold, and the storm that teaches the soul endurance. A life spent hiding from difficulty may feel safe, but it produces a fragile faith that collapses when real trials come. The hardships a man faces are the training ground where perseverance is born. Each challenge strengthens his spirit and deepens his reliance on God. Without resistance there is no growth, and without endurance there is no maturity. The man who steps out from under the umbrella of comfort and faces life's storms with faith will discover that the winds he feared are the ones that forge his strength and prepare him for greater purpose.

Throughout history, the men God used most powerfully were those who refused to retreat when life became difficult. They stood firm when the winds of adversity howled and the rain of hardship poured down. In the storm, their faith was tested, their character was forged, and their resolve was strengthened. God raises men who trust Him when the path is hard and the outcome uncertain. These are the men who shape history, lead their families with courage, and build legacies that honor God. They do not wait for perfect conditions; they rise when the challenge appears. Their strength comes not from comfort, but from conviction. While others shrink back, they step forward.

While others complain, they persevere. Such men become pillars in their homes, anchors in their communities, and examples for the next generation. When a man stands firm in faith through the storms of life, he becomes the kind of man God uses to change lives and leave a lasting mark for His glory.

Courage is not a possession that a man acquires once and carries effortlessly for the rest of his life. It is a choice he makes again and again, often in quiet moments when no one else is watching. Each new day brings its own pressures and temptations to compromise. Yet a man of faith understands that courage is renewed through his commitment to God. When he chooses truth over convenience, integrity over popularity, and obedience over comfort, he strengthens the spiritual backbone that defines real courage. Every morning becomes a sacred opportunity to rise with purpose and resolve. A courageous man asks himself not what is easiest, but what is right. He stands for truth even when it costs him something, leads with integrity even when others take shortcuts, and walks faithfully with God even when the path feels lonely. Day by day, decision by decision, courage is forged in the heart of a man who refuses to drift with the world and instead chooses to live boldly for the One who called him.

The courageous man does not wait for perfect conditions before he moves forward. He understands that life rarely offers certainty, and faith was never meant to operate only in comfortable moments. Instead of waiting for every answer, he takes the next step with confidence, trusting that obedience matters more than convenience. Courage is not the absence of fear; it is the decision to act despite it. A man who walks by faith knows that progress often begins with a single step into the unknown. Such a man trusts that the God who called him will also guide him. The same voice that stirred his heart to move will not abandon him halfway down the road. Even when the path is unclear and the future is hidden, he moves forward with quiet confidence, believing that God orders the steps of those who trust Him.

With every step, his faith grows stronger, and his courage becomes a testimony that God does not call men to stand still - He calls them to move forward with bold trust.

Real manhood is not measured by physical strength, wealth, popularity, or influence. True manhood is revealed in the quiet moments when a man must decide whether he will follow convenience or conviction. Spiritual courage is the strength to speak truth when others remain silent, to defend what is just when compromise would be easier, and to live with integrity when no one else is watching. The mark of a real man is the courage to live by God's truth in a world that often rejects it. It takes strength to resist pressure, humility to admit wrong, and boldness to pursue righteousness when the path is unpopular. Spiritual courage means choosing character over comfort, obedience over approval, and faithfulness over fear. When a man stands firmly on what is right, he becomes a light to others and a testimony of God's transforming power. This is the measure of authentic manhood - not dominance, but devotion; not power, but the unwavering courage to do what is right before God.

A real man does not allow the ease of the moment to dictate the direction of his life. Instead, he anchors his decisions in truth, character, and the principles that God has written upon his heart. This kind of man understands that strength is not measured by comfort, but by the courage to do what is right even when it is difficult. His convictions become the compass that guides his steps, keeping him steady when the world around him drifts with every passing trend. He also chooses discipline over indulgence and purpose over passivity. Rather than surrendering to every fleeting desire, he trains his mind, his habits, and his character to pursue what is lasting and meaningful. Discipline builds the structure of a life that honors God, while purpose gives direction to every step he takes. Such a man refuses to sit idle while life passes him by. He rises with intention, lives with clarity, and acts with determination, knowing that God created him not for comfort, but for calling, not for passivity, but for purpose.

The world desperately needs men who will throw away the umbrella and step into the storm of responsibility. Too many hide beneath the shelter of excuses, blaming circumstances, other people, or the difficulty of the moment. But true strength is revealed when a man chooses courage over comfort. A man of faith understands that storms are not meant to be avoided - they are opportunities to stand firm, grow stronger, and demonstrate the character God placed within him. When a man refuses to retreat from responsibility, he becomes a pillar of stability for his family, a source of wisdom for his community, and a living testimony that faith produces courage. God is calling men to rise above fear, complacency, and passivity. The easy path is to stay dry beneath the umbrella of convenience, but greatness is forged in the wind and rain of challenge. The storms of life do not break such a man; they reveal him. And when enough men choose courage over comfort, the world begins to change.

These men lead their families with humility and strength, not by demanding control, but by carrying responsibility with grace. They understand that true leadership is not loud, harsh, or self-centered. It is steady, sacrificial, and rooted in love. A godly man does not rule his home with pride; he serves his family with patience, wisdom, and a heart that reflects Christ. His strength is seen in his consistency, his humility is revealed in his willingness to listen, and his character is proven in the way he protects, provides, and prays. He knows that greatness in the kingdom of God is found not in being served, but in serving others. These men also live with open hands and surrendered hearts. They serve others with generosity because they understand that everything they have comes from God. They pursue God with relentless devotion because they know that apart from Him they can do nothing. Their passion is not for applause, status, or personal comfort, but for the presence and purpose of God.

Such men understand that comfort is temporary, but character is eternal. Comfort so often whispers the lie that ease is the goal of life, yet the soul of a man was never designed to live in the shallow waters of convenience. True growth is forged in moments when a man chooses discipline over desire, conviction over convenience, and obedience to God over the applause of the world. The trials he faces, the sacrifices he makes, and the battles he endures shape something far more valuable than comfort ever could - they shape his character. They also understand that the path that builds strength, wisdom, and integrity is often steep, narrow, and demanding. Yet it is along that road that God forms men of who stand firm when others quit, who lead when others retreat, and who remain faithful when circumstances grow difficult. A man who embraces this truth no longer fears the hard road. Instead, he walks it with courage, knowing that every step of faith is shaping him into the man God created him to be.

Throwing away the umbrella means refusing to hide from the challenges God has placed before you. Too many men spend their lives trying to stay comfortable, protected from hardship, and sheltered from risk. But when you throw away the umbrella, you step fully into the rain of life with confidence that God walks with you. You stop shrinking back from difficulty and begin embracing the assignments that require courage, perseverance, and trust. The call of God is to live boldly, love sacrificially, and lead courageously even when the road is uncertain. A man who throws away the umbrella understands that real strength is forged in the storm. He chooses conviction over comfort, obedience over ease, and purpose over fear. This is the life of courageous faith that trusts God enough to step into the wind and rain without hesitation. When you throw away the umbrella, you declare that you will not live a sheltered life of small faith, but a bold life that honors God and inspires others to rise.

It means refusing to settle for mediocrity when God has called you to greatness of character and purpose. Refusing to settle for mediocrity means recognizing that God never designed your life to drift aimlessly or exist in quiet compromise. When a man understands that he is created in the image of God and called to live with intention, mediocrity loses its appeal. He begins to reject laziness, excuses, and small thinking. Instead, he pursues integrity, discipline, and growth, knowing that greatness in God's kingdom is measured by the strength of one's character and the depth of one's obedience. God calls His people to live with purpose - to develop the gifts He placed within them and to influence the world for good. When a person embraces that calling, their life begins to reflect excellence, humility, and courage. When a man refuses to settle for mediocrity and instead pursues the fullness of his God-given potential, his life becomes a living act of worship that honors the One who created him.

Today is the moment of decision. Every man eventually reaches a crossroads where comfortable faith is no longer enough. It is easy to remain sheltered in routines that require little courage, believing quietly while avoiding the deeper call of obedience. But God did not design faith to be a safe hiding place. He designed it to be a launching point. Real faith moves. Real faith risks. Real faith steps beyond the familiar and trusts God in the unknown. The question is not whether the path ahead will be easy; the question is whether you will answer the call. The life God designed for you waits on the other side of that decision. It is a life of purpose, courage, and growth - a life where character is forged and destiny unfolds. When a man chooses faith over comfort, he steps into the strength God placed within him from the beginning. Today is your moment. Do not shrink back into what feels safe. Step forward with conviction, trust the One who called you, and walk boldly into the man God created you to become.

Storms are a part of every man's journey. The rain may fall without warning, and the winds of adversity may rise with fierce intensity. Trials come in many forms yet the man who anchors his life in faith does not collapse when the storm arrives. He stands firm not because he is stronger than the storm, but because he is rooted in something stronger than himself. His confidence is in the unshakable power of God who holds him steady. When a man trusts God, the storm becomes a proving ground rather than a place of defeat. The winds may howl and the rain may beat against him, but his foundation remains secure. Faith reminds him that God is present in every trial, shaping his character, deepening his trust, and strengthening his resolve. A man whose strength comes from the Lord does not crumble under pressure - he rises with quiet courage and unwavering conviction. And when the storm finally passes, he stands taller, stronger, and more certain than ever that the God who sustained him will never fail.

Throw away the umbrella. Step out from the shelter of comfort and into the storm where real faith is proven. Faith was never meant to be safe, quiet, or hidden beneath layers of convenience. It was meant to be lived boldly in the wind and rain of real life. When a man chooses courage over comfort, he steps into the arena where character is forged and convictions become visible. Storms expose whether a man merely talks about faith or truly trusts God when the skies grow dark. The world is waiting for men who refuse the easy path and choose the courageous one. Families need it. Communities need it. The next generation desperately needs it. A man who lives his faith openly becomes a beacon in a confused and weary world. So stand up, step forward, and embrace the calling God has placed on your life. Throw away the umbrella and walk straight into the storm, because the strength, purpose, and courage you seek are often found on the other side of obedience - and that man can be you.

SUMMARY

By now you understand something most men never grasp: The storm was never your enemy. It was your training ground. Every chapter in this book has pointed to one central truth - toughness is not about noise. It is not about ego. It is not about dominance or intimidation. It is about endurance. It is about discipline. It is about a man who stands when it would be easier to sit down. Who speaks when it would be easier to stay silent. Who leads when it would be easier to disappear. Who loves when it would be easier to withdraw.

Storms don't weaken real men. They reveal them. Pressure exposes foundation. Resistance uncovers depth. Adversity measures backbone. And if you've been honest with yourself through these pages, you've seen where you've been strong and where you've been soft. That awareness is not condemnation. It's ignition. Because spiritual toughness is not something you either have or don't have. It is something you build. It is trained through obedience. Strengthened through discipline. Refined through humility. Anchored through prayer.

You don't become stormproof by avoiding storms. You become stormproof by standing in them long enough to stop being afraid of them. The world is not growing easier. Responsibility will not grow lighter. Temptation will not disappear. Pressure will not fade. So the solution is not escape. It is growth. This book was never about proving how tough you are. It was about discovering how strong you can become when you surrender fully to God and accept responsibility for your life.

Real toughness looks like a man who keeps his word. A father who models discipline. A husband who loves sacrificially. A leader who accepts accountability. A believer who prays even when heaven feels silent. A man who repents quickly and rises stronger. Toughness is quiet consistency. It's waking up early to pray when no one sees. It's controlling your temper when you could explode. It's refusing to compromise when everyone else bends. It's finishing what you started when quitting would be easy. It's strength under control.

The storm will still come. There will be days when your resolve feels thin. Moments when doubt whispers. Seasons when exhaustion tempts you to fold. But now you know something different. You were built for resistance. God did not design you for fragility. He designed you for responsibility. He did not call you to comfort. He called you to courage. The rain is not punishment. It is preparation. The weight is not cruelty. It is conditioning. The pressure is not proof you are failing. It is proof you are being formed.

And here is the final challenge: Stop reaching for umbrellas. No more excuses. No more blame. No more hiding behind past wounds. No more spiritual laziness disguised as "waiting on God." Stand. Stand in your home. Stand in your faith. Stand in your calling. Stand in your convictions. Stand in prayer. Stand when others shrink back. Because someday your children will watch how you handled the storm. Your wife will feel the stability you carry. Your friends will lean on the backbone you built. And your legacy will be measured not by how comfortable you lived but by how faithfully you endured.

Throw away the umbrella. Let the rain fall. Lift your head, square your shoulders, and feel every drop that heaven allows. Stop running from what was sent to refine you. The storm is not your enemy - it is your training ground. Rain washes away pride, strips off fear, and reveals the steel God placed inside you before you ever faced this moment. You were not wired for comfort; you were forged for courage. So stand in it. Let the wind push against you and the thunder roll around you. Refuse to bow. Refuse to retreat. Become the man God already designed you to be - steady, unshaken, and unashamed. The storm is here. Stand in it.

www.ingramcontent.com/pod-product-compliance
Lightning Source LLC
Chambersburg PA
CBHW051814150726

47998CB00001B/146